CHICANO SOUL

Recordings & History
of an American Culture

Tenth Anniversary Edition

THE AUTHOR WISHES TO THANK

Albuquerque, NM: Beenie Sanchez [Hurricane Records] Freddie Chavez [Chekkers], Mick Sanchez, Mike Sanchez [Rudy and the Soulsetters], Dick Stewart [Lance Records]

Corpus Christi, TX: Roy Tipton [Houserockers], Oscar Martinez, Bobby Galvan

Dallas/ Fort Worth, TX: Joe & Leticia Silva, Paula Estrada [Latinaires], Johnny Gonzales [El Zarape Records], Paul Martinez [Fats and the All Stars], Paul Rios [Rivieras], James "Geno" Reza, Chemo Martinez, Paul Ayala, Tommie Hernandez, Joe Palma [Heartbreakers], Jesse Palma [Heartbreakers], Cookie Teviño

El Paso, TX: Alex Martinez, George Reynoso, Bobby Rosales [Premiers], Tony Gomez [Jives]

Houston, TX: Jesse Casas [Crystals]

Laredo, TX: Carlos Landín [Rondels]

Las Lunas, NM: Rosie Hamlin [Rosie and the Originals]

Los Angeles, CA: Art Brambila, Dick Blackman, Steven Caudillo, Jerry Castellanos, Raul Cevallos, Frankie Firme, Mario "Cosmico" Flores [Aliez, Royal Checkmates], Fred Gallegos [Royal Jesters], Albert Garcia [Los Perros], Mark Guerrero [Escorts], Art Hernandez [In-Crowd], Jorge "Mr. Blue" Hernandez, Johnny Jay Jimenez, Manuel Jimenez, Ray Jimenez, Ron Lemos [Thee Runabouts], Bobby Loya [Blue Satins], Eddie Maciel, Jimmy Meza [Atlantics], Chris Montez, Sal Murillo [Blendells], Sal Padilla [Leggeriors], Dino Pataglia, Antonio Perez, Ray Reyes, Gil Rocha [Shilouettes], RudySalas [Tierra], Steve Salas [Tierra], Alvin Sanchez [Story Tellers], Eddie Torres, Eddie Torres, Jr., Pablo "Tripp" Treviño, Max Uballez [Romancers, Macondo], Joe Ursua [Royal Jesters, Rhythm Playboys, Pagents] Johnny Valenzuela [Veleveteens]

McAllen, TX: Noé Pro

Phoenix, AZ: Sandy Flores [Soulsations], John Dixon

Saginaw, MI: Larry J. Rodarte

Seguin, TX: Ramon Salazar

San Antonio, TX: Charlie Alvarado [Charlie & the Jives], Manuel "Bones" Aragon [Laveers, Harlems, Royal Jesters] Roy Cantú [Mike & the Hi-Fi's], Floyd Coleman [Playboys] Alfred "Guero" Cortinas, Mario Cortinas, Eloy Esparza, Sr. Esparza, Bobby Galvan [Danny & the Dreamers], Jesse Garcia, Dimas Garza [Lyrics, Royal Jesters, Dino & the Dell-Tones], Fidel Gil, Robert Gonzales, Rudy T. Gonzales, Roger Gonzales, Henry Hernandez [Royal Jesters], Oscar Lawson [Royal Jesters], Juan Mendoza, Joe Martinez [Satin Souls, Monsanto], Chente Montes [Sunliners], Vic Montes [Dell-Tones], Sunny Ozuna, Rudy Palacios [Sunliners], Frank Parilla, Henry Parilla [Laveers, Sunliners], Jesse "Chucho" Perales [Mando and the Chili Peppers], Joe "Jama" Perales [Eptones, Royal Jesters, Casino Royale], Domingo "Sonny Ace" Solis, Chris Varelas

San Jose, CA: Nick Aguirre, Tommy Siquiero, Lou Holscher

Temple, TX: Little Joe Hernandez, Cruz Garcia

Waxahachie, TX: Crazy Chuy Hernandez

CHICANO SOUL

Recordings & History
of an American Culture

Tenth Anniversary Edition

Ruben Molina
Forewords by Louie Pérez and Alex La Rotta

Second Edition Copyright © 2017 by Texas Tech University Press

First Edition Copyright © 2007 by Mictlan Publishing

Unless otherwise credited, all photographs courtesy of author.

All rights reserved. No portion of this book may be reproduced in any form or by any means, including electronic storage and retrieval systems, except by explicit prior written permission of the publisher. Brief passages excerpted for review and critical purposes are excepted.

This book is typeset in Monotype Amasis. The paper used in this book meets the minimum requirements of ANSI/NISO Z39.48-1992 (R1997). ∞

Designed by Kasey McBeath

Cover design by Dirk Fowler

Library of Congress Control Number: 2017945187

17 18 19 20 21 22 23 24 25 / 9 8 7 6 5 4 3 2 1

Texas Tech University Press
Box 41037 | Lubbock, Texas 79409-1037 USA
800.832.4042 | ttup@ttu.edu | www.ttupress.org

CONTENTS

Rollin' with the Beat: Early Influences & Pioneers 3
Para Los Pachucos, Honkin' Horns, Gil Bernal, The Jaguars, Little Julian Herrera, Chuck Rio, Ritchie Valens, The Lyrics, The Royal Jesters, Freddy Fender, The Sunglows

Something's Got a Hold on Me: San Antonio 21
The Westside Sound, The Sunglows, Sunny & the Sunliners, The Royal Jesters, Danny & the Dreamers

Shake, Shout & Soul: Southern California 45
Southern California, Rosie, The Perez Brothers, The Sevilles, Chris Montez, East Los Angeles, The Romancer, The Blendells, Cannibal & the Headhunters, Thee Midniters, Little Ray & the Progressions, The San Gabriel Valley, The Velveteens, The Story Tellers, The Premiers, The VIPs-El Chicano

Crazy, Crazy Baby: Texas Soul 83
Central Texas: Dallas/Fort Worth, Junior & the Starlites-Latinglows, Little Joe & the Latinaires, Hey, Paula, The Broken Hearts, South Texas, The Tex-Mex Influence: ? and the Mysterians, Sam the Sham & the Pharaohs, The El Paso Sound, The El Paso Premiers, The Jives, Houston

Soul Side of the Street: Phoenix & Albuquerque 106
Phoenix, Albuquerque, Freddie Chavez, Thee Chekkers, Lance Records, The Sheltons, Al Hurricane

Yo Soy Chicano: Brown Pride 117
Political Awakening, Texas: Returning to the Past, Los Angeles: Latin Rock-Latin Jazz, El Chicano, Little Joe Y La Familia, Macondo, Tierra

Conclusion 129

Discography 131

The Fabulous Flippers led by Floyd Coleman. Soon after, Coleman joined the Playboys, who recorded for Satin Records. Courtesy of Floyd Coleman.

PREFACE

The history of Chicano soul music is a vital but often overlooked chapter of the greater contemporary American musical experience. Chicano soul music of the 1950s and 1960s is a cultural treasure that still reverberates in Chicano communities today. This book tells the story of the roots of Chicano soul, the musicians who breathed life into it, and the enduring influence of that cultural phenomenon.

This rich form of music flourished in the Mexican American *barrios* of Albuquerque, Phoenix, San Antonio, and the greater Los Angeles region as well as in other cities in the American Southwest. This music had its roots in the Chicano infatuation with American urban black music. However, the Chicano bands that sprouted throughout the Southwest during the early and midsixties drew on a variety of influences. The birth and growth of Chicano soul came about because young Chicano musicians were exposed to several musical genres and because of the Chicano's hybrid cultural status—a status that was marked by dual social and cultural identities, which gave their musical expression its own unique identity.

Young aspiring musicians and music lovers were seduced by the allure of 1950s-era jazz, blues, jump blues, rock 'n roll and Latin jazz. What became Chicano soul music, in a sense, set Chicanos free from what could be called a cultural norm. That norm was represented by traditional Mexican music such as *ranchera* and *norteño* or *conjunto* music. It was an emancipation that led to a unique musical form, distilled from a variety of traditional and contemporary musical experiences.

The magnetism of a certain African American musical form of expression was so strong that, like the mythical Pied Piper of medieval times, it mesmerized kids from all walks of life—creating America's rock 'n roll generation. But at the same time one cannot ignore the influence of the traditional music of the Mexican homeland and the resonance it had for Chicano musicians as they started to reinterpret the rhythm and blues that greatly affected their creative process. It was a great cultural cauldron of varied musical ingredients. The *huapango*, *son jarocho*, *son huasteco*, the *mariachi*, the three-part harmonies of *los trios románticos* and other musical styles of Mexico and the Southwest are beautifully woven into the brown-eyed soul that developed during this period throughout *Aztlán*.

FOREWORD

"I am visible—see this Indian face—yet I am invisible. I both blind them with my beak nose and am their blind spot. But I exist, we exist. They'd like to think I have melted in the pot. But I haven't, we haven't."

- Gloria Anzaldúa, *Borderlands / La Frontera: The New Mestiza* (1987)

Oldies are forever. It's a mantra. A credo. A maxim for diehard sweet soul enthusiasts from Los Angeles to London, Toronto to Tokyo, and beyond. Ruben Molina's *The Old Barrio Guide to Low Rider Music* (2002) and *Chicano Soul: Recordings & History of an American Culture* (2007)—its sacred texts. Not since Paul Oliver's *The Story of the Blues* (1969) has a book and author so distinctively revived a vintage and marginal American music culture from obscurity to widespread and cult-like revelry. What was once a niche collector's category in the aughts and prior is a recognized subgenre in the twenty-tens: Chicano Soul. In the decade since its publication, *Chicano Soul*—like the long-lost recordings it so lovingly documents and historicizes—has itself become a collector's item. Original copies are highly-prized and sought after by record collectors, music aficionados, DJs, musicians, fans, and others. And, too, like much of the music in question: finally receiving its due reissuance. (Only this: a legitimate, not bootleg, reissuance.)

Its long-awaited return is timely. A brief review of the past ten years in popular music culture must surely include the massive reemergence of the vinyl music format (and its swift cooptation by the music industry); roots and vintage pop music revival (film/television soundtracks, documentaries, compilations, cultural histories, etc.); and the (ongoing) digital music revolution. Most notably, as it concerns the latter, one might also note the ascension of streaming media and video-sharing websites in democratizing and disseminating "rare groove" music of the analog past for broader audiences of the digital present. Further still, YouTube- and social media-based *soulero* (sweet soul) DJs and record collector cliques build notoriety as prized possessors of rare Chicano Soul records to wide acclaim—much of which builds on Molina's foundation. While the diffusion of music and cultural history in the past decade has broadened, the appreciation of this specific brand of soul music has expanded in tandem. You know it as the West Side Sound, the East Side Sound, Brown-Eyed Soul, Latin Soul, Lowrider Oldies, even *rock en español*—all components of the vast domain of midcentury Chicano Soul music culture principally documented in Molina's work. And a book that remains today the only single monograph devoted to the subject.

More importantly, *Chicano Soul* challenges the assumptions and stereotypes of what "Latin music" could or should be in both popular culture and preceding musical-historical analyses: tropical, exotic, and almost always distinctly foreign. Unequivocally, this music is none of those. It is, as the subtitle denotes, "an American culture." Molina's meticulous documentation of over 400 Mexican-American musicians/rock-and-roll combos spanning the American Southwest (née *Aztlán*)—and their collective thousands of independent recordings—deserves recognition if just for its impressive magnitude. But it's the paradigm shift that *Chicano Soul*, and other recent works from such scholars as Deborah Vargas, Roberto Avant-Mier, Anthony Macias, Josh Kun, and Deborah Pacini Hernández, among others, provides for the current discourse on racial identity, hybridity, and the origins of American popular music that warrants as much praise. In part, a response to the tired narrative surrounding America's supposed black/white racial binary and the forging of a national culture. Yes: Chicanos made soul music. Lots of it. And it's damn good, too.

It is no coincidence then that the *New York Times* and NPR have recently (finally) devoted ink and airtime to Chicano Soul music and history—to say nothing of the countless smaller media outlets that are discussing this vibrant music culture in varying degree. Or the recent and celebrated (and ongoing) compilations of San Antonio's West Side Sound by Grammy-nominated reissue imprint, Numero Group. Or the current and fast-growing Chicano Soul music revival occurring throughout shared spaces in Latinx arts communities, Mexican-American studies programs, and Chicana feminist organizations in the United States and Latin America. With its exclusive interviews, gorgeous photos, hard-to-find record scans, and original concert bills, *Chicano Soul* brings to life an integral and vibrant American culture once relegated to the forgotten recordings from the mid-twentieth century. But, then again, it's truly no coincidence when the mantra remains the same: *oldies are forever*.

Turn the pages. Absorb the culture. Get lost in the history. And tune in to the stunning sounds—from Whittier Boulevard to West Commerce Street—so lovingly captured herein.

Alex La Rotta, PhD candidate
University of Houston, December 2016

FOREWORD

The Chicano band Los Lobos stands on the shoulders of a legion of pioneering, innovative and fearless musicians whose cultural roots include the music of Mexico, rhythm and blues, jazz and early rock n roll. That distillation of music from the 1940s and 1950s and up into the dynamic 1960s is at the heart of what came to be called "Chicano Soul." And this remarkable collection of songs, stories, and artwork compiled by Ruben Molina represents a treasure trove of materials that tell the wonderful story of the evolution of an important realm of American music—Chicano music. Categorizing Chicano music, particularly what has come to be regarded as Chicano soul music, is no easy task. And that's as it should be, since it reflects such an abundance of traditions, influences and styles of music.

Pigeonholing the music of Los Lobos over these forty-some years has been impossible, and that's something those of us in Los Lobos are proud of. Critics and audiences can't easily categorize our music and that's just fine with us. We draw on a great variety of ideas, influences and experiences in creating our music. And so, too, did the early pioneers of Chicano music—in the neighborhoods of big cities and small towns throughout the American Southwest.

Listen to those early records by the likes of Ritchie Valens, Sunny and the Sunliners, Little Julian Herrerra, the Armenta Brothers, or Little Willie G and Thee Midniters and you hear strains of blues, R and B, jazz and all manner of American musical genres. And they tell stories about love, about hopes and dreams, and about just having a good time. But those early Chicano artists didn't cobble a clunky pastiche of sounds. No, they effortlessly and knowingly absorbed a variety of influences and styles and distilled them into distinct and astonishingly creative art. And that art is showcased in this remarkable exploration of a vibrant musical culture.

Those early musicians and their recordings represent an important chapter in our history as a *gente*. They are part of our mutual memories.

Like all of the founding members of Los Lobos, I grew up in East L.A. listening to every imaginable type of music. The radio belted out *corridos*, *rancheras* and *boleros* on the Spanish-language stations. The jazz and rock 'n roll stations brought amazing sounds to my ears. And records from the record stores on Atlantic Boulevard and Whittier Boulevard gave us a taste of artists from the 1950s. (And we all listened to our parents' records of *mexicano* singers Miguel Aceves Mejía and Pedro Infante.) We absorbed all of that—and more. It all swirled around in my head and was part of the foundation for the music that Los Lobos eventually created. We owe a debt of gratitude to those early recording artists—their creativity, their resourcefulness, and their perseverance.

And readers owe a debt of gratitude to Ruben Molina for his tireless work in researching the achievements of those early musicians who created a significant and enduring chapter of the overall American musical and cultural experience—something that can touch everyone. That passionate research and storytelling is captured here within the pages of this book. You certainly don't have to be Chicano to appreciate *Chicano Soul: Recordings and History of an American Culture*. You just have to be a music lover. I invite you to turn the pages of this book and immerse yourself in this very vital chapter of contemporary American music and history.

So I invite you to dust off an old vinyl record, put it on the turntable (if you can find one), and listen to the music as you thumb through this very cool *libro*.

Louie Pérez
A founding member of Los Lobos

CHICANO SOUL

Recordings & History
of an American Culture

Tenth Anniversary Edition

ROLLIN' WITH THE BEAT

Early Influences & Pioneers

"We were getting tired of the same music, you know, the big band stuff. There was this deejay named Hunter Hancock that was playing this new music and the word spread around town among a small minority of us and we were diggin' it. The new sound had that back beat, vocalist up front, guitar and wailing sax, gone was that big brassy sound."

Gil Rocha- vibes player: San Fernando, CA *[Shilouettes, Gents, Imperials]*

Rhythm and blues was at least ten years old when it finally jumped across into the pop market. Prior to 1949 the acceptable term given to black music by *Billboard* (the top music industry magazine of the day) was "race music." That term, as negative as it was, covered jazz, blues, gospel and a new sound that blended all three into a style known as *jump blues*. As this new form of music demanded its own identity *Billboard* changed the title of its "Race Records" charts to "Top Selling Rhythm and Blues" it still meant *black music* primarily for black audiences but the description now focused on the music rather than one's skin color. By 1951 songs like **Sixty-Minute Man** (Dominoes), **Chains of Love** (Joe Turner), **Bad, Bad Whisky** (Amos Milburn), **I Got Loaded**" (Peppermint Harris), and **Harlem Nocturne** (Johnny Otis) were laying down the beat that would inspire a whole new generation of artists and music fans. During 1952 and 1953 black artists in the R&B field continued to release exceptional recordings and as the demand for more of the same continued America was introduced to a parade of new stars. Johnny Ace, Lloyd Price, and Chuck Willis made their debut in 1952 while Shirley & Lee, the Spaniels, Marvin and Johnny, The Flamingos, and Jesse and Marvin ushered in the group harmony sound. American black music had a breakthrough year in 1954. That year Joe Turner released his all-time classic **Shake, Rattle and Roll,** the Spaniels waxed **Goodnight, Sweetheart, Goodnight,** and Hank Ballard and the Midnighters were on top with their erotic novelty single **Work with Me Annie,** a record that spun-off a whole line of risqué discs. Rhythm and blues was a spontaneous response to the world around the artists, whether it was the erotically delightful **It Ain't the Meat** (Swallows), the Jesse Belvin-penned **Earth Angel,** a melancholy love ballad that was recorded by the Penguins, or the string of singles released by the

Robins that spoke about the social environment on Los Angeles's Southside.

Para Los Pachucos

From the beginning of the rhythm and blues years Chicano musicians incorporated the hard rockin' beat of jump blues into the *danzónes, guarachas* and *rumbas* that they were performing. As early as 1946 Lalo Guerrero was recording *rancheras* with the lyrics sung in *caló* (a mix of English, Spanish and an urban dialect brought to Mexico via Spain that is neither). It was the slang vernacular of the *pachuco* and by 1948 he introduced the boogie-woogie style of Lionel Hampton, Louis Jordan, Roy Milton and other black swing combos into his music. Similarly, Edmundo "Don Tosti" Tostado and his group the Pachuco Boogie Boys, who were trained jazz musicians were, tuning into the music scene on Los Angeles's Central Avenue. The big band era was slowly being replaced by smaller more compact combos that played jump blues with a kind of controlled hysteria that caused quite a sensation among teenagers, the groups were led by the likes of Jake Porter, Chuck Higgins, Johnny Otis and Big Jay McNeely.

Don Tosti's 1948 recording of **Pachuco Boogie** was an accumulation of all the internal and external forces that created the Mexican American subculture of the *pachuco*. The recording, which sold over one million records, was a statement saying to America that five years after the Zoot Suit Riots the *pachuco* was still here and they were not going to hide their pride. It was also a clash between traditional Mexican culture and the newly emerging Chicano culture. Musically it was a fusion of what the Chicano youth were embracing: Afro-American beats mixed with

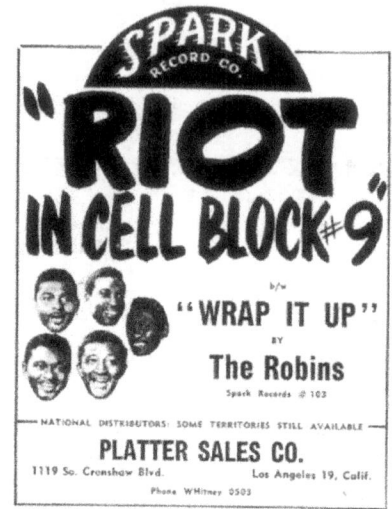

Spark Records advert for "Riot in Cell Block #9" one of Gil Bernal's signature tunes.

traditional Mexican rhythms, and a rebellious attitude in dance and clothing styles. Inevitably all music styles have a social responsibility or at least deliver a social expression, and the boogie beat of Tosti and Guerrero were no different. The adaptation of *caló* to deliver the stories of Tosti's folkloric characters in **Wine-O-Boogie, Pachuco Boogie,** and **Guisa Gacha** or Lalo Guerrero's **Marijuana Boogie,** and **Los Chucos Suaves** signified a cultural break with both Mexico and America and morphed into a hybrid of both.

Honkin' Horns

As the fifties rolled around the *pachuco* and *pachuca* slowly faded from the landscape of East Los Angeles. Chuck Higgins's 1952 recording of **Pachuko Hop** (with its curious misspelling of the word *pachuco*) came at a time when the mystique of the *pachuco* lived on in the less colorful, less hip *cholo* subculture. Gone were the flashy clothing and the ducktail

Big Jay McNeely blowing his horn on the streets of Los Angeles. Author's archives.

hairstyle, replaced by the Sir Guy shirt, khaki pants and slicked back hair. However, DJ Hunter Hancock knew that the record would be a hit with his audience and the Chicano kids who attended the shows at the Angelus Theater where Johnny Otis promoted tenor sax greats like Big Jay McNeely, and Chuck Higgins. The popularity of **Pachuko Hop** led to a string of saxophone-led instrumentals that targeted the Mexican American community: **Chicano Hop** (Joe Houston), **Tequila Hop** (Jack McVea), **Chicano Hop** (Jake Porter), **Boyle Heights** (Chuck Higgins) and **Wet Back Hop,** a single that was not well received by Higgins's core audience. In Jim Dawson's liner notes for Ace Records *Honk! Honk! Honk!* Higgins (a resident of Boyle Heights) recalls, "Things got real warm in the neighborhood for me after that record came out." The title was not Higgins' idea. Rather it was Dootone Records owner Dootsie Williams who gave the record its name, not realizing the term "wetback" was viewed as an insult by those of Mexican ancestry.

Gil Bernal

By 1954 Jerry Leiber and Mike Stoller were established R&B songwriters. They had written songs for Jimmy Witherspoon, Ray Charles, Amos Milburn and of course Willie Mae "Big Mama" Thornton who recorded the original version of **Hound Dog** in 1953 for Don Robey's Peacock Records. Three years later Elvis Presley made **Hound Dog** a national hit after his live performance on the *Ed Sullivan Show*, a performance that had him singing to a bassett hound. It was the success of **Hound Dog** and the lack of money they got from Robey that inspired Leiber and Stoller to form Spark Records. Although both Leiber and Stoller were Jewish Americans who were raised primarily on the East Coast, their lives were heavily influenced by both African American music and the dance culture that it created. While attending Los Angeles City College Mike Stoller met twenty-one-year-old saxophonist Gil Bernal. Bernal a native of Watts (a predominantly black community in the southern part of Los Angeles) had been working professionally since 1950, spending time in the big bands of Lionel Hampton and Spike Jones. At the time Bernal, whose father was Italian but performed under his mother's Mexican surname, was working with his own trio so Mike Stoller invited the veteran tenor man to record for his fledgling record company.

Although Bernal's total output for Spark Records consisted of only two singles, it is his sax work with the Robins and subsequently the early Coasters recordings that most rock 'n roll enthusiasts remember. **Framed, Riot in Cell Block #9** and **Smokey Joe's**

Café by the Robins and **Turtle Dovin'**, **Young Blood**, **Searchin'** and **Down in Mexico** by the Coasters all featured the saxophone of Gil Bernal. Author Robert Palmer wrote in the liner notes for the *Coasters: Youngblood* Atlantic LP: "There was super-hard blues saxophone (provided) by Gil Bernal, who didn't just solo but functioned as a voice in the group. Answering vocal phrases, commenting on the action with honks and shrieks. . . ." Bernal's contribution to rock 'n roll did not end with the Robins/Coasters sessions. Besides sitting in with other West Coast R&B acts his horn can be heard on Duane Eddy's 1958 hit record **Rebel Rouser.**

> May 17, 1954 the United States Supreme Courts announces their unanimous decision: ". . . in the field of public education the doctrine of 'separate but equal' has no place." The Court ruled that segregation in public schools deprives children of "the equal protection of the laws guaranteed by the Fourteenth Amendment."

The Jaguars

Several years before the U.S. Supreme Court made that historic announcement, Fremont High School located at 76th Street and San Pedro Boulevard on Los Angeles' Southside had already integrated. The school also produced one of the first integrated rock 'n roll groups. Herman "Sonny" Chaney (black), Charles Middleton (black), Val Puliuto (Italian), and Manny Chavez (Mexican) were all members of the school choir known as the Choraliers. Much like Jefferson High School down on 41st Street, Fremont High was bustling with vocal group activity. Don Julian and the Meadowlarks were there, as were the Flames, Medallions, Younghearts and the Calvanes to name a few.

After recording several unreleased sides for John Dolphin's Cash Records the Miracles teamed up with Bruce Morgan. Morgan's parents, Hite and Dorinda Morgan, owned a song publishing company and Bruce was a sound engineer and an aspiring songwriter who in 1956 wrote **Jailbird,** the "B" side to Sonny Knight's sleepy ballad **Confidential**. During the winter of 1955 Morgan took the Miracles to see Bob Ross for whom the group cut their first local hit **I Wanted You** a song written by Manny Chavez. Hunter Hancock was instrumental in making **I Wanted You** a success by inviting the newly named Jaguars to appear on his Friday night television show *Rhythm and Bluesville*. Next the Jaguars covered a song that Fred Astaire recorded for the 1936 film *Showtime* titled **The Way You Look Tonight.** Released in the spring of 1956 **The Way You Look Tonight** never made the national top 40 charts, but it quickly became another local hit for the Jaguars and is considered a West Coast classic. The group stayed busy throughout the fifties, recording for several record labels even through times when one or more members of the quartet were serving out their military obligations.

Little Julian Herrera

> I don't care what people say he was all Chicano. He knew Spanish, he ate our food, and he loved our culture.
>
> I always felt that he never got the recognition that

The **Jaguars** L-R Charles Middleton, Manny Chavez, Val Poliuto, and Sonny Chaney with Hunter Hancock *Rhythm & Bluesville* circa 1955. *Author's archives.*

he deserves. I still say that Little Julian Herrera was the first [Chicano rock 'n roll star] and I'm talking about 1954-1955 with Johnny Otis.
Johnny Valenzuela—guitar & sax player:
Pomona, CA [Velveteens]

With all of the musical activity going on around Los Angeles's Mexican American community during the late fifties, the Chicano community still did not have someone it could embrace as their own—a Chicano teen idol. Innovative band leader Johnny Otis knew that with all of the musical genres targeting the Eastside community it was still R&B and rock 'n roll that the kids wanted to listen to and dance to. Otis himself had been a favorite among Chicano teens since he started promoting dances at the Angelus Hall in 1948. By the midfifties Otis was joined by Hunter Hancock, Huggy Boy and Art Laboe who were also promoting shows that were heavily attended by Chicano teens.

Little Julian Herrera first "Chicano" rock 'n roll hero. Author's archives.

This was a perfect opportunity for a young Chicano singer to make his move. Well not exactly.

Ron Gregory, the teenage son of Hungarian parents living on the East Coast, managed to find his way to the East Los Angeles community of Boyle Heights where he befriended a Mexican family named Herrera, a name which he later took as his own. From that point on Herrera lived his life as a Chicano and has been considered the first Chicano rock 'n roll-star by fans and music historians alike. In his book *Upside Your Head* George Lipsitz relates a story he got from an interview with Johnny Otis. He writes "Johnny Otis had long enjoyed a substantial Mexican American following, largely because of shows he performed at Angelus Hall in E.L.A. and during his years at El Monte he discovered, produced and promoted the first Chicano R&B sensation, L'il Julian Herrera, who scored an enormous local hit with his black-style ballad **Lonely, Lonely Nights** in 1956. One day a probation officer showed up at Otis' door asking about a 'Ron Gregory.' Otis didn't know anyone by that name, but when the officer showed him a picture, he recognized L'il Julian."

Herrera became the first voice of what would become known as the Eastside sound, his subtle delivery on **Lonely, Lonely Nights, Symbol of Heaven** and **I Remember Linda** became the typical approach that many of the early Southern California Chicano groups followed. Groups such as the Heartbreakers, Rene and Ray, Rosie and Ron, the Perez Brothers, Terri and the Velveteen's and even Rosie and the Originals unconsciously followed the Julian Herrera blueprint. This may have been due to the lack of vocal training easily accessible to black artists through their church and community choirs that helped to develop a strong aggressive singing voice. It wasn't until '63-'64 that singers like Little Ray Jimenez, Max Uballez, Frankie "Cannibal" Garcia and Willie "Little Willie G" Garcia

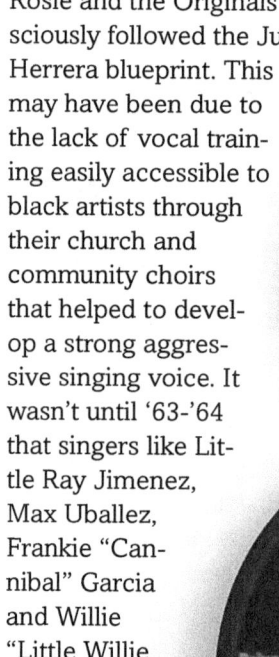

Herrera's 1956 hit singles Lonely Lonely Nights and I Remember Linda released on Art Laboe's Starla Records in 1958.

had each developed their own singing styles that we begin to see a stronger, more confident approach to the soul songs they were performing.

Chuck Rio

Rock 'n Roll was still in its infancy in 1958 and the boundaries had not yet been fully determined, giving musicians plenty of room for experimentation and creativity. Take the story of sax man Danny Flores who, along with an unlikely group of studio musicians, had a national hit in 1958 with a Flores composition titled **Tequila**. Film cowboy, country singer, entrepreneur and record company executive Gene Autry had signed a group of rockabilly musicians from Texas to his fledgling Challenge record label. The group led by Dave Burgess arranged for studio time at Gold Star studios in Hollywood so that they could record several instrumental records. Flores and his trio who were under contract with RPM records, were signed for the session as Chuck Rio and group. Their collaboration led to the 1958 release of **Train to Nowhere** backed with **Tequila** by the Champs. As was the case with many recordings in the early years of rock 'n roll **Tequila** was recorded as an afterthought and it is unlikely that the musicians involved knew that what they had created would become a number one hit and an enduring classic.

As deejays started to flip the record and play **Tequila,** its popularity grew and by the end of March it had reached number one. This was the type of experimentation that was possible in early rock 'n roll. Putting together two groups of individuals from two different perspectives, each contributing from their experiences. In this case Flores contributed a riff

Chuck Rio's sheet music for "Tequila" rated #9 best record of 1958 by *Cash Box* magazine.

that he had been performing as part of his stage act, which revealed the Latin rhythms of his roots.

Ritchie Valens

As **Tequila** was making its way up the charts seventeen-year-old Richard Steve Valenzuela was creating some excitement in Pacoima, a semi-rural *barrio* on

"Ritchie Valens was my inspiration for getting into music. I was just a kid when I saw him perform at the Rainbow Gardens in Pomona. I knew then what I wanted to do."

Johnny Valenzuela—guitar & sax player: Pomona, CA [Velveteens]

Richard Valenzuela seated, Walter Takaki sax, and Walter Prendez. Performing at Mary Immaculate Church in Pacoima, CA. Feb. 7, 1958. *Courtesy of Gil Rocha.*

the north end of the San Fernando Valley outside Los Angeles. Valenzuela, who was attending San Fernando High, was making a name for himself performing at neighborhood house parties and local talent contests. In October of 1957 Gil Rocha of the Silhouettes was looking for a saxophone player to round out his group. "I wanted to get a saxophone player because at that time there was Joe Houston, Chuck Higgins and Big Jay McNeely leading the parade," remembers Rocha. On the suggestion of the Silhouettes drummer Conrad Jones, Rocha decided to listen to this kid from San Fernando High who could play guitar and sing. "One day the door bell rings and there's this young angel faced looking kid standing at the doorway with a guitar in one hand and a little amplifier in the other hand. I automatically thought, 'what is this he doesn't

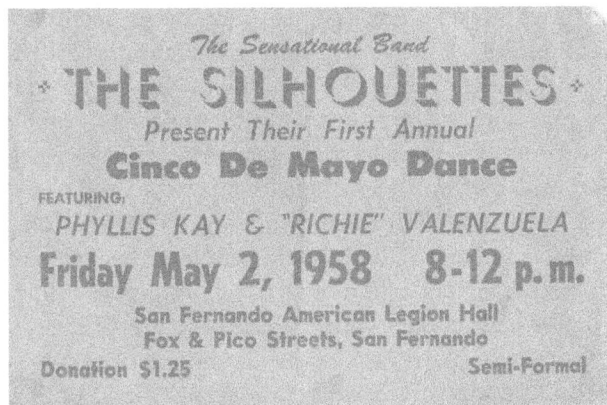

Handbill for dance featuring the Silhouettes early in Ritchie's career. *Courtesy of Gil Rocha.*

even have a guitar case or nothing, he looked awfully young' but I just said 'well come on in.'" He recalls, "Now remember I was looking for a sax player. I said 'Ritchie can you play this, can you play that' and he was saying yes to all of the songs I wanted to hear. I said 'play a couple [of songs]' and he did plus some Little Richard stuff, the real fast-up-tempo stuff with that new back beat sound. I said you're in."

At that time the bands around San Fernando were still playing the big band sound, some *boleros*, and then there was the cha cha cha craze, which was in vogue. So live rhythm and blues required a trip to East Los Angeles to see Johnny Alonzo and the Playboys or the Armenta Brothers band. "Now we would drive all the way to Los Angeles to the Eastside just to hear the Armenta Brothers 'cause they were playing some of that boogie stuff. Their music the rhythm and blues was intermixed with the *boleros* and the up-tempo Latin stuff including the *rumba* which we younger people weren't dancing to, it was more for the older folks like our uncles and aunts." Johnny Gamboa remembers the Eastside music scene like this: "The only groups that were around were totally from a period before the rhythm and blues thing started. There was the Armenta Brothers, they played stock charts, jazz standards **Tenderly** stuff like that. There were other bands but they wouldn't play what was happening they just played what had happened, they played the big band thing."

In May of 1958 Ritchie Valens with Sears Harmony Stratotone in hand stepped into Bob Keane's basement studio for his first audition. It had only been seven months since he had joined the Silhouettes. However, through his guitar playing, his showmanship and his determination he was quickly becoming a local star. Except for a gig in the Highland Park neighborhood of Los Angeles and one in

Ritchie Valens. Now using a Fender Stratocaster. *Courtesy of Gil Rocha.*

Ritchie Valens first hit record "Come On Let's Go."

Hollywood the Silhouettes did not wander far from home. The group did shows at the Carpenters Hall in Van Nuys, the American Legion halls in San Fernando and Pacoima and dances at local recreation centers. It was at one of the dances held at the American Legion Hall in Pacoima that 20-year-old Doug Macchia caught Ritchie's act.

Macchia worked for a printer that was doing some work for Del-Fi. On one of his deliveries he passed the word on to Bob Keane about the kid making some noise down in the valley. In his book *The Oracle of Del-Fi*, Keane recalls Macchia's tip: "Hey, Bob," he said "There's a sixteen-year-old Chicano kid out in the Valley named Richard Valenzuela. They call him the 'Little Richard of San Fernando' maybe you'd like to check him out." Keane followed Macchia's advice. The neighborhood theater held a talent show just before the morning matinee for kids. Keane sat in the back row of the theater and witnessed the energy that this kid was generating among the kids in the audience. After introducing himself to Valenzuela, Keane handed him a business card and suggested that they do some recording.

For the next several months Keane and Ritchie started meeting regularly for informal recording and song writing sessions. Ritchie's first formal recording sessions began in earnest during the summer of '58. Bob Keane surrounded Ritchie with top studio musicians from the rock 'n roll and jazz fields. Leading the group was the legendary guitarist/arranger Rene Hall who had worked with many of rhythm and blues' top artists including Larry Williams and Sam Cooke. On drums he had Earl Palmer, a New Orleans studio musician who had moved to Los Angeles in 1957. Palmer had worked with the Crescent City's rock 'n roll legends Lloyd Price, Fats Domino, Smiley Lewis and Little Richard. Keane also recruited two of Los Angeles's top guitarists, Carol Kaye and Irving Ashby, and award-winning bass player Buddy Clark.

This group of veteran session players gave Ritchie a strong foundation and worked to smooth out his lack of experience. Like several of the musicians who would create the Eastside sound of the sixties Ritchie's only experience was through what he heard on the radio and on record so it was important for these veteran musicians to show patience and understanding with the young rocker. According to Bob Keane in his book *The Oracle of Del-Fi*, it took 30 or so takes to record **Come On Let's Go**. One can only imagine the thoughts going through the seventeen year olds mind as he was trying to absorb what was going on around him, learn from the veteran musicians without being overwhelmed by them and trying to create a song from what was up to this point only music in his head. Ritchie's guitar playing was still developing so he played rhythm guitar while Rene Hall handled the solos. The flipside of the record was a remake of the Robins' **Framed** a classic story as familiar a scenario to young Chicano men as it was and continues to be in Los Angeles's African American community.

RITCHIE VALENS WITH BOB KEANE, PRESIDENT OF DEL-FI RECORDS

Valens and Bob Keane.
Courtesy of Del-Fi Records.

Immediately after getting a reference disc pressed, Keane went straight over to see KFWB disc jockey Chuck Blore. So impressed was Blore that he asked Keane to get Valens to the Los Angeles County Fairgrounds in Pomona. Just before the release of the record Keane convinced Ritchie that he should change his stage name to Valens. At the time there were no Latin rock 'n roll artists and any artists with Latin surnames sang in Spanish. Keane felt that Ritchie would have a better chance with DJs who might assume that a record by Valenzuela would be a Latin song. For the whole week Ritchie appeared at the KFWB booth live with the station's DJs, within two weeks the record went to number one in Los Angeles. By September **Come On Let's Go** had reached number 46 nationally and Ritchie Valens became the first Chicano rock 'n roll singer to cross over into the pop charts. Besides performing at Pacific Ocean Park, Long Beach's Civic Auditorium and Disneyland, Valens toured up and down the West Coast followed by his first U.S. tour. The national tour included stops in Detroit, Baltimore, D.C., Chicago, Buffalo and Cleveland and on October 6th he appeared on Dick Clark's *American Bandstand* in Philadelphia to perform **Come On Let's Go.**

In November of 1958 Valens was back in the recording studio. He had already recorded a song he had written titled **Donna** and needed a song for the "B" side of the single. Keane suggested that he record a song, which Valens would play around with, "I had heard **La Bamba** before while living down in Mexico," recalled Keane. "But it was the original ethnic version . . . . I had never thought about how it would sound the way Ritchie was playing it." Keane had to convince Valens that it was worth recording. Finally after guitarist René Hall and drummer Earl Palmer worked the song out Ritchie agreed to record it. Once again Keane took the demo to DJ Chuck Blore and once again Valens had a hit. This time it went national going to number one in several cities including Los Angeles and Chicago. With **Donna** and **La Bamba** Valens had a teen ballad backed with an ethnic folk song sung in Spanish taking America by storm; only through the open mind of early rock 'n roll was this possible.

The *son jarocho* is a Mexican music and dance style that developed around the coastal plains along the Gulf of Mexico, especially in the state of Veracruz. The style also known as the *veracruzano* was a fusion of Spanish, African and possibly Caribbean influences and the music of the indigenous people of the region. The most popular example of the *son jarocho* is the folk song **La Bamba**. In *Ritchie Valens: The First Chicano Rocker*, Beverly Mendheim explains the origin of **La Bamba**. The origin of the name bamba is African, meaning wood (language is not known, though there is a people and even several towns throughout Africa called Bamba). The wood referred to what dancers originally danced upon, emphasizing footwork that showed a heavy Spanish influence. Popularized in American by the *mariachi* groups that performed throughout the Southwest. **La Bamba** was never recorded with any success in the United States until Ritchie Valens's version.

As 1958 was coming to an end Ritchie was busy. He had a number one song with **Donna**, which was quietly being followed by **La Bamba** and he was in demand on the national spotlight. Valens was booked to appear on *American Bandstand* in December. In early January of '59 he was at MGM Studios for the filming of *Go, Johnny, Go!* a rock 'n roll film hosted by Alan Freed and staring Chuck Berry. Three days before leaving for the "Winter Dance Party" tour Ritchie had two appearances in Southern California, both of them on January 17th. TV host "Jolly" Joe Yokum staged his show, The Teen Canteen Dance, at West Covina High School. Valens was the headliner and was joined by Sam Cooke, the Vogues, the Accents and the Hollywood Flames. Later that evening he appeared at a show held at the Long Beach Civic Auditorium.

The "Winter Dance Party" tour began its fateful journey on January 23, 1959 in Milwaukee, Wisconsin where it was 25° below zero. Besides Ritchie Valens, the show included Buddy Holly and the Crickets, J. P. Richardson, Dion and the Belmonts and Frankie Sardo. The show moved by bus caravan with the stars sleeping in freezing and uncomfortable accommodations as the buses slowly moved through blizzard-like conditions. The troupe did shows in Kenosha, Kanato and Eau Claire, Wisconsin before moving into Montevideo and St. Paul, Minnesota, then it was onto Davenport and Dodge Iowa. The caravan rolled into Green Bay, Wisconsin on February 1st. By now the artists were worn and tattered, the heaters in the buses were not adequate enough to keep the winter cold out and several members were coming down with colds.

From Green Bay the troupe moved to Clear Lake, Iowa after their performance Buddy Holly, fed up with the buses and in need of a warm bed and shower, decided to charter a plane to Fargo, North Dakota. Their next appearance was scheduled for Moorhead, Minnesota and Fargo was the closest airport available. Initially only Buddy Holly and several of his group were scheduled to board the plane. However Waylon Jennings and Tommy Allsup gave their seats up to Ritchie and J.P. Richardson. On February 3rd, shortly after 1:00am the single engine Beechcraft Bonanza lifted off from the Mason City airport into the clear, cold night before vanishing from sight. Shortly after dawn the wreckage of the small plane was spotted eight miles from the airport. There were no survivors.

The tragic death of Valenzuela created a void in Los Angeles's rock 'n roll music scene. Keane had proven that a Mexican American kid from the barrio could make it on the national scene and there were several young Chicano artists with the potential to fill the void caused by his death. Southern California's underground music scene that Valenzuela came out of had spawned a variety of groups who were polishing their sound performing for car clubs, neighborhood parties and high school dances hoping to get into the recording studio, which could land them a gig at one of El Monte Legion Stadium's rock 'n roll shows. Similar efforts were under way in Mexican communities beyond California.

The Lyrics

The working class community in San Antonio, Texas was divided into three cultural and musical genres: country, *conjunto* and rhythm and blues. Around 1955 the young people of this blue-collar community fused the three styles together with rhythm and blues coming out on top as the dominant style. By 1959 Lanier High School and Burbank Vocational High were competing for the honor of being the center of San Antonio's teenage music scene. Rudy Tee Gonzales came out of Lanier, as did the Royal Jesters and Dimas Garza of the Lyrics. At Burbank there was Sunny Ozuna, Randy Garibay and the Rudy Guerra. What was developing at these high schools and the neighborhood street corners on the West Side of town was a unique sound that would become known as the West Side Sound. It was at Lanier that Henry Hernandez and Dimas Garza developed their friendship. "I was an only child so I spent a lot of time writing. When I started going to high school it was at Burbank High, which was all white at the time so I felt like I didn't belong."

Garza continues, "One day my mom caught me playing hooky, she said '*mijo* if you don't want to go to school that's fine but tomorrow I'm gonna fix you a lunch and you're gonna go out and get a job'. Well after two weeks I'd had enough and I told her I want to go back to school." Garza enrolled at Lanier High School, which was ninety-nine percent Mexican American. It was at Lanier that Mrs. Eichman, Garza's English teacher noticed that he was always writing poetry. She suggested that he write songs. When he replied that he couldn't sing she suggested that he join the school choir.

Henry Hernandez remembers those days just before the Royal Jesters were formed: "Oscar (Lawson) and I went to elementary school together it was a Catholic school and there was a lot of singing, I enjoyed singing in the choir and the harmonizing we did. Eventually I picked up the trumpet and when I started at Lanier I joined the band. The band room was across from the choir room and that's where I met

The **Lyrics** L-R: Abel Martinez, Alex Pato, Dimas Garza and seated Carl Henderson. *Courtesy of Dimas Garza.*

Far left: **The Royal Jesters** L-R: Oscar Lawson, Louie Escalante, Henry Hernandez, Dimas Garza, unidentified musicians. *Courtesy of Dimas Garza.*

left: Royal Jesters first show. *Author's archives.*

Dimas." In the summer of 1959 Dimas Garza's group the Lyrics released **The Girl I Love** backed with **Oh, Please Love Me,** a regional hit that made them local stars. National distributors Coral Records and Wildcat Records picked the single up and by November 16 of 1959 **Oh, Please Love Me** was listed in *Cash Box* magazine as a new release. Singing lead on the up-tempo **The Girl I Love** was the same Carl Henderson who would move to Los Angeles and record several soul classics including **Sharing You** for Anthony Renfro's Renfro label in the mid-sixties. The sweet teen ballad **Oh, Please Love Me** featuring Garza on lead vocals is reminiscent of doo-wop crooner Jesse Belvin's early ballads. With **Oh, Please Love Me,** the Lyrics' follow-up release **The Beating of My Heart,** and a song he recorded with the Kool Dips back in 1958 titled **I'm Trying to Forget** Garza was quickly emerging as one of San Antonio's top balladeers.

The Royal Jesters

Inspired by the success of Dimas Garza and the Lyrics, Oscar Lawson and Henry Hernandez decided to form their own group. "In the summer of 1959 Dimas Garza and the Lyrics had a record out so we went to their manager Joe Anthony for help," recalls Hernandez. The group consisted of Oscar, Henry, Mike Pedraza (lead singer, guitar), Charles Walker and Bobby Cantú. After performing at local record hops for the local top-forty stations KONO and KGSA Hernandez recalls the Royal Jesters testing the waters of San Antonio's black community on the Eastside. "We got to do some shows with black bands from the Eastside so we got to know them and eventually went to their clubs on the Eastside, which was all black." He said, "But we'd sing a couple of songs and every time we had a chance we would go back." In the spring of 1960 Joe Anthony was ready to record the Royal Jesters so they were teamed up with one of the hottest groups on the Westside at the time Charlie and the Jives. Recorded at Texas Sound Studios on Hildebrand **My Angel of Love** became an instant hit. "Joe Anthony had the biggest late night Rhythm and blues show in San Antonio and it seems like **My Angel of Love** was playing every five minutes." Remembers Hernandez. From this moment on the Royal Jesters would become one of the most important singing groups in San Antonio's great musical history.

Baldemar Huerta, aka **Freddy Fender**. *author's archives*

Freddy Fender

Rock 'n roll was sweeping the nation and the tiny South Texas city of San Benito was no exception. Located on the southern tip of the Rio Grande Valley, San Benito was established in 1904 by Anglo ranchers. With a population that was 87% Mexican-American the city was culturally closer to Mexico in those days than it was to the United States with the nearest big city being Matamoros, Mexico. However, the back beat of rock 'n roll and rhythm and blues reached across

"I was always different. I'm still different from what you call *La Onda Chicana* or *Tejano* music. I'm from the same era, but I was never involved with it. I was always trying to do something in English. That was my thing since 1957, when I started recording with Falcon Records I wasn't doing the *conjunto* stuff. I was doing rock 'n roll and ballads, just like I'm doing now, and rhythm and blues. *Conjunto* music didn't move me then, and the *orquestas* thought they were too hot shit for me."
Freddy Fender- singer/guitarist/songwriter: San Benito, TX

the barren desert landscape and captured the imagination of one Baldemar Huerta. Huerta formed a rock 'n roll garage band in the mid-fifties performing for anyone that would listen. In 1950's San Benito an audience probably wasn't that hard to find because there wasn't much else in the way of entertainment.

By the age of sixteen Huerta's restlessness found him signing up for a three-year tour of duty with the Marine Corps. After his discharge in 1957 Rafael Ramirez signed Huerta to his Falcon record label, billing him as "The Bebop Kid." Their first collaboration was **Hay Amor** with a Spanish cover of Elvis Presley's **Don't Be Cruel** as the flip side. Next Huerta teamed up with Wayne Duncan who was running a small jukebox route in South Texas. Duncan put up the money for the 1959 recording session that produced the English version of **Hay Amor**. Using a one-track recorder at a radio station in Brownsville, Texas Huerta recorded **Holy One** backed with **Mean Woman**. This combination sold 280,000 discs and went to number one in San Antonio, Dallas, Fort Worth, Baton Rouge, and New Orleans. Huerta, who had taken

In 1959 Freddy Fender recorded "Holy One" for Wayne Duncan's, Duncan label. The title was later changed to "Only One" because some people believed it had religious overtones. Many Chicano groups from throughout the Southwest have included "Only One" on their play list through the years.

The Sunglows

Manny Guerra was drumming for *conjunto* pioneer Isidro Lopez who had combined the big band sound of the *orquesta Tejana* with the accordion-dominated *conjunto* music to develop what is now considered the modern Tex-Mex sound. At the time Manny's brother Rudy had formed a band with some friends from Burbank High School, located on the Southside of San Antonio. The band's lead singer was fifteen year-old Ildefonso Fraga Ozuna or Sunny as he was known around friends and family. Sunny had formed a little garage band called the Galaxies back in 1957 but he had bigger plans and in the summer of 1958 he and Rudy Guerra formed the Sunglows. The Sunglows started playing at house parties, sock-hops and church functions in and around the *barrio*. During 1958-'59 Joe Anthony was the man a young Chicano group trying to put out an R&B record would go to.

Anthony co-owned Jukebox Records, the only record store in San Antonio that was devoted exclusively to the selling of R&B records. As a DJ Anthony had his late night R&B show *Harlem Serenade* on radio station KMAC where he would play the top national R&B acts as well as records by the young local talent, especially those that were on his labels. Harlem Records was a collaboration between Joe Anthony and E.J. Henke who tapped into the growing Chicano R&B scene. The Sunglows went to Harlem Records for their first recordings **So Long Darling** backed with **Bobby Socks and Stockings** and **From Now On** backed with **When I Think of You** joining the growing ranks of San Antonio's R&B groups. Like the Lyrics, the Royal Jesters, and Charlie and the Jives before them the Sunglows became local favorites and at least locally their records sold well. The following year Ozuna wrote **Just a Moment,** a song that

L-R: Gilbert Rodriguez of **Gilbert and the Blue Notes**, unidentified, and **Sunny Ozuna**. *Courtesy of Gilbert Rodriguez.*

the stage name of Freddie Fender, recorded several versions of **Holy One** for an array of record labels including Imperial, Paco Bentancourt's Ideal Records and Talent Scout for whom he recorded as Scotty Wayne. "We had a problem with the title **Holy One** as being religious or something. Instead of being understood as a tribute to a woman. [Wayne] Duncan worried so much that DJs would not play it that I had to change **Holy One** to **Only One**," Fender told David Nelson in an interview for the Arhoolie Records liner notes.

was released on the Houston based Kool label. What might be considered the definitive Westside sound ballad **Just a Moment** has been covered by several of San Antonio's artist through the years including Doug Sahm and Dimas Garza. During this period Manny Guerra left Isidro Lopez's group and joined the Sunglows as their drummer/manager. Shortly after joining the Sunglows Manny Guerra formed Sunglow Records.

The First record released on Manny Guerra's Sunglow label was **Pa Todo El Año** (Sunglow 101) in 1959, which was followed by a string of singles both in Spanish and English, covers of classic *rancheras*, top-forty R&B tunes and ballads. In the summer of 1963 the big break came for the Sunglows with a cover of Little Willie John's 1958 recording of **Talk to Me, Talk to Me** a song that singer Randy Garibay suggested that the Sunglows add to their play list. That song propelled the Sunny and the Sunglows from the *barrios* of San Antonio to the national spotlight and on to Dick Clark's American Bandstand. Sunny credits that recording to what he grew up listening to on the radio. The song climbed up the national charts peaking at the number 11 position and opening the way for a string of minor hits that made the Billboard 100 national charts. "In San Antonio we were brought up with a little R&B," recalls Ozuna. "The radio stations that played Spanish music had what they called 'English Oldies.' The DJ would play the Spanish songs but then he would pick some English oldies to add to that so we all grew up listening to our stuff but also listening to oldies. For example **Talk to Me** happens to be an oldie that by the time I went through my transition and was able to get into the recording studio I liked that song so much that I wanted that to be one of the first songs that I would record. Not knowing that it would be number one in the country," he recalls.

Through the guidance of Manny Guerra the Sunglows managed to bring together all aspects of the Mexican American musical landscape. The music of the *conjuntos* of which Guerra had been a part of, the *ranchera* which had been part of San Antonio's culture for generations, and the soul of Afro-American rhythm and blues which had made its way into Chicano culture and had become a strong influence on the Chicano sound.

What Freddy Fender, Ritchie Valens, the Lyrics, Gil Bernal, the Story Tellers, the Royal Jesters the Sunglows and a several other innovative Chicano artists did in 1958 and 1959 set the stage for the emergence of the Chicano Soul movement of the sixties.

El Monte Legion Stadium first Ritchie Valens memorial dance 1960. *Courtesy of Gil Rocha.*

SOMETHING'S GOT A HOLD ON ME

San Antonio

We started with a conjunto when we were thirteen and fourteen years old, my brother "Red" Manuel Gonzales and myself. We were inspired by groups like: Mando and the Chili Peppers. Then when I was in the 9th grade I started listening to rock 'n roll, things like "Lonely Nights" by Johnny "Guitar" Watson, and the Jacks' "Why Don't You Write Me." I just went ape. I thought man what kind of music is this, I may be Chicano but I love this stuff. I started going to the black clubs like the Bel-Air Club on Commerce Street just to learn what they were doing so I did rock 'n roll from the time I was sixteen until I was twenty-one. I got away from the conjunto stuff.

Rudy T. Gonzales- vocalist: San Antonio, TX *[Rudy and the Reno Bops]*

The Westside Sound

For ten years Sunny and the Sunglows toured the country from Florida to California. From Corpus Christi, Texas to Chicago, Illinois the band spread the Chicano soul of San Antonio, known within the Alamo city's limits as the "Westside Sound." Sunglows band leader Manny Guerra has been credited with the development of that sound but before he walked away from his job as drummer for Isidro Lopez's *conjunto* band to help develop the Sunglows' "new" groove, the musical gears of change were turning in the bars and beer joints on the Westside. In San Antonio and South Texas many of the young musicians, which had developed an ear for the combo based R&B that was popular in the local beer joints, were getting the opportunity to put their work on wax. Thanks to individuals like Joe Anthony (Harlem), Manuel Rangel (Rival), Jesse Schneider (Renner), Abe Epstein (Jox, Cobra), and Emil J. Henke (Satin) the early R&B sounds of San Antonio have been documented.

Things were also jumping at clubs and lounges like the Tiffany Lounge located downtown where several of the local bands went to learn their trade and pay their dues. Many of these young groups were integrated rhythm and blues bands like Rick Aguary (Aguirre) and the Keys, Mando and the Chili Peppers, Johnny Olenn and the Jokers, and Little Sammy Jay and the Tiffanaires it was white, black and Chicano musicians pounding out the new beat. "After I got out of Marine Corps in 1956," recalls Charlie Alvarado of Charlie and the Jives, "we started playing at the Key Hole backing Big Joe Turner then there was the Tiffany, the Celebrity, the North Side Lounge the Town Lounge and a jazz club called the Fiesta. The Cadillac Club didn't start until the sixties." Johnny Phillips's

Tito & the Silhouettes with Bobby Shannon. Circa 1959.

Al & the Exclusives L-R: unidentified, Vic Montes (guitar), Big Al (sax), unidentified, Tito Nieves (piano).

Eastwood Country Club was San Antonio's premier spot to catch the top black acts of the day. James Brown, Hank Ballard, B.B. King, T-Bone Walker, Lowell Fulsom and Junior Parker were just a few of the acts who performed there. These clubs also attracted guys in their early teens that were drawn to the mesmerizing rhythms and shady characters that spilled out into the night. Kids like fourteen-year-old Doug Sahm, brothers Chente and Vic Montes who would help form the rhythm section of the Sunliners, and singer/guitarist Randy Garibay would sneak into the Tiffany Lounge just to listen to the music.

Although there were laws that prohibited minors from entering these establishments, those not crafty enough to sneak in hung out outside where they could still listen to the music. "The Tiffany was far out in those days" recalled Doug Sahm, "Nothing but characters man. Hustlers, the whole bit, with their $300 sharkskin suits. I used to hang around outside and watch 'em going in with three or four chicks on each arm . . . . then the door would open and I could hear the music comin' through." In an interview with Andrew Brown the late Randy Garibay also recalled those days at the Tiffany Lounge. " . . . . It was a great place for people who loved the nightlife. Owner Johnny Jowdy was very particular about the bands he brought in there. This was in the days when you played like six nights a week at eight bucks a night." Garibay also remembered that the club was regularly patrolled by the cops—not because of the gangsters who hung there, but rather to intimidate the integrated bands. One thing that distinguished San Antonio from other cities in the south and maybe in the country during the fifties, was that in a time when everything was racially segregated, the clubs and musical groups were integrated. "As Hispanics I know that we were welcomed in the black community. There was

Unidentified group at the Cadillac Club.

two clubs that I would go to and that was the Ebony Club and the Eastwood Country Club, they were part of a circuit that national black acts would perform on," recalls guitarist Joe Martinez. "Little Jack's Inferno next to the Texas Theater was another place we used to go to," remembers bass player Chente Montes, "I was there playing for about a year at like fourteen or fifteen years old. The group I was playing with was called Bobby Shannon and the T-Birds—all black except for me."

Besides the Chicano soul singers there were several African American vocalists that honed their skills with the Chicano groups before moving on. Carl Henderson of the Lyrics moved to Los Angeles where he waxed several sides for Anthony Renfro, namely **Sharing You** a song that Sunny Ozuna covered in the late sixties. Bobby Taylor was the front man for Charlie and the Jives before leaving town for Motown where he recorded **Does Your Mama Know about Me** as Bobby Taylor and the Vancouvers. Another Jives alum was Benny Easley, who was stranded in San Antonio while touring with the Ink Spots and who went on to record with Chess Records. The Satin Souls had Madison Mitchell and the Playboys stole Floyd Coleman from the Fabulous Flippers. "I was practicing with the Fabulous Flippers and the Playboys were down the street listening," recalls Coleman, "they waited around until we finished, then they came up to me asking if I would sing with them, man they were persistent."

Life on the stage was so intoxicating that it cap-

Tito & the Silhouettes L-R: Hector "Tito" Nieves, Rocky Morales, two unidentified musicians.

tured the imagination of several of San Antonio's young musicians like the Montes brothers to the point that they quit school to make money performing in the clubs. "When I was young my dad had a problem with his back so we had to do something. We were making good money with music and when my dad saw the money coming in he said 'Well.'" Montes continues, "I was at Cooper Elementary, I quit in the ninth grade." A move Montes now looks back on with some regrets. "But now I don't know, I never really learned anything as far as school goes." Rudy T. Gonzales who had a *conjunto* group and worked at Joe Anthony's record shop discovered rhythm and blues while delivering posters for a show that Joe Anthony was promoting featuring Lowell Fulsom and Junior Parker. Rudy T. recalls those days in the late fifties: "When I first heard James Brown in 1957 or 1958; *no hombre!* I used to imitate him to the tee." He said, "Then I saw him at the [San Antonio] municipal auditorium and I saw his footwork, so I started imitating his footwork and his moves and in a way I made him popular with the *Mexicanos* all over the Valley and West Texas because they didn't know who the hell James Brown was and then they would ask

Guitarist Victor Montes.

ties the Royal Jesters, the Sunglows, Danny and the Dreamers, the Lovells, the Playboys and Dino and the Dell-Tones had lifted the "Westside Sound" to a new level. "In the early sixties the vocal groups started to come in and then horn sections got big," recalls Satin Souls' guitarist Joe Martinez. "So there was two types of groups the ones that carried one R&B singer like us and the Playboys. We played more in clubs like the Key Hole and the Cadillac Club and not the teen dances. Then there was the ones that had three-part harmony like the Royal Jesters and Sunny [and the Sunliners] and they played the teen dances." "Rhythm and blues was it," Manuel "Bones" Aragon says of the teen dances. "If we played one or two *polkas* a night that was enough, what people wanted was rhythm and blues."

Within this movement you find influences from an array of musical genres but there are two distinct ingredients that stand out in the "Westside Sound" the Hammond organ and horns. Henry Parilla gives Manny Guerra credit for introducing the Hammond organ to San Antonio's soul music. "I think Manuel Guerra was the one that brainstormed that whole thing. You see he wanted to do music but without the accordion and he didn't just want to have a horn band like an orchestra and they couldn't carry around a piano. . . . Once Sunny and the Sunglows started to use the organ that was it- everyone wanted that sound." In order to be heard above the horns, drums, electric guitar and bass the Hammond organ required a Leslie for amplification. "Once everything got electric the Hammond needed the Leslie for amplification there were no jacks for amps or anything just a Leslie. At first no one wanted to use the B3 because it was so big," Parilla continues. "I used the M3 forever I mean that thing was beat to hell. Sauce [Arturo Gonzales] was

me where did you get all that from and I would tell them and they started liking that stuff, it was just pure excitement." These and the dozens of other young singers and musicians that were waiting their turn to represent their school and their community were the characters that gave San Antonio its soul.

Before Guerra replaced the accordion with the twin sax sound of the Sunglows, the Dell-Kings horn section of Frank Rodarte, Rocky Morales and Cleto Escobedo added such a unique sound to the group's rhythm and blues tunes that they were dubbed the "Westside Horns." By the late fifties the heroes of the new sound were Sonny Ace and his Twisters, Charlie and the Jives, Randy Garibay and the Pharaohs, Tito and the Silhouettes, the Dell-Kings, Rudy T. Gonzales and the Reno-Bops and Doug Sahm. The Lyrics ushered in the vocal group sound and by the midsix-

The **Dell-Kings** L-R: Jimmy Casas, Frank Rodarte, Cleto Escobedo, Randy Garibay, Richard Garza. *Author's archives*.

the one that made it famous because he would emulate the accordion and that was the Tex-Mex sound." Guitarist Bobby Galvan of Danny and the Dreamers credits Booker T and the Memphis sound as an early influence on San Antonio's Chicano groups. "I would have to say that it was Lavine Elias and Little Henry Lee [Henry Parilla] that started to use the Hammond B3. Otis Redding, James Brown and of course the Stax Records sound coming from Memphis had a big influence on these guys. So that Eddie Floyd, Sam and Dave, and Rufus Thomas sound was incorporated into the San Antonio Sound," recalls Galvan.

The Sunliners were ahead of everyone when it came to the horns. With the Sunglows, Guerra used the two sax sound that several of the other local combos were using and again we have the influence of the accordion being replaced by the two saxes, but the Sunliners created the brassy soul that many groups would try to emulate. The horns or the *pitos* as they are affectionately known developed into a large section with trumpets and a trombone under the direction of Rudy Guerra. However their popularity among the groups came through the influence of the Dell-Kings and their predecessor Spot Barnett who had *the* rhythm and blues band in San Antonio during the late fifties. Although the Dell-Kings rarely recorded, they were extremely popular with the locals especially at the Eastwood Country Club where the audience capacity was one thousand. Hired by a promoter to perform several gigs in Hawaii, Los Angeles, San Diego then finally to Las Vegas the Dell-Kings left San Antonio and never returned. Performing as

The **Satin Souls** L-R : Joe Flores (bass), Roger Sanchez (sax), Madison Mitchell (vocals), Emilio Moran (sax), Joe Martinez (guitar), kneeling Henry Garcia (drums). Circa 1963. *Courtesy of Joe Martinez.*

the Dell-Kings then as Los Blues the group had a long twelve-year run at the Sahara Hotel in Las Vegas.

By 1965 the Sunliners had a full horn section complete with two trumpets and a trombone, which they used to emphasize their Latin rhythms. Sunny felt the horns gave their music some class. "With the brass all we were trying to do was to give the music a little more class. You know, get it out of the *cantinitas* and beer joints, so we were doing a lot of the same songs but with a little more class." This was the sound that set the bar for groups trying to emulate the Sunliner sound first in San Antonio with Henry and His Kasuals, the Lovells, the Playboys, the Satin Souls and the Royal Jesters. Then as Sunny and the Sunliners toured up and down the country and especially in the Southwest, groups started to pop up all over. Sunny recalls the influences that the Sunliners and Little Joe and the Latinaires had on their audiences: "As the bigger groups were getting calls to go and do shows in the smaller towns and cities, they would go and plant a seed. The local teens would get enthused and they would go out and start a group and it spread. Then maybe the next time we'd go back to Albuquerque, or El Paso, or even in Wisconsin they would say 'Yea we have some groups like you guys, we have so and so and so and so.' Then you say to yourself, 'Wow! Look at this.'"

If Sunny Ozuna's assertion that what he Manny Guerra and Little Joe were doing in the early sixties was planting seeds, then by the mid-sixties the fruits of their labor were ready to be picked. Vocal groups, R&B combos and Latin soul *orquestas* flour-

Charlie & the Jives L-R: Bobby Taylor, Jimmy Casas, Richard Garza (kneeling), Randy Garibay, Charlie Alvarado on drums. Circa 1959.

Sonny Ace & Charlie Alvarado.

ished throughout the Lone Star State. What Nashville was to country music, San Antonio became its equal in Chicano music. Unlike Los Angeles, San Antonio did not have a network of ballrooms and dance halls nor the population that could sustain such a vibrant music scene. There was the military base circuit, a few teen canteens, and the high school dances that were available for the teen groups like Danny and the Dreamers and the Royal Jesters. The R&B groups like Sonny Ace and the Twisters, Charlie and the Jives, the Playboys and the Latin Souls were more conducive to San Antonio's night club and bar scene. Places like the Cadillac Club and the Eastwood Country Club where audiences were adult and racially mixed provided them with a livelier atmosphere. However, if a group was looking for a wider audience they were going to have to pack their bags and hit the road.

Throughout the sixties and well into the seventies R&B groups leaving Laredo, Corpus Christi, San Antonio, Austin and Dallas followed the routes that their *conjunto* counterparts had been taking since the late fifties. They would be entertaining a new group of factory workers and farm laborers who were migrating north and establishing small communities. Buses, cars pulling U-Haul trailers, and motor homes carrying musicians moved along highway 40 to Tennessee, then north on highway 65 to Kentucky, Indiana, Michigan, and Ohio. Chicago was a must for all of the groups where the Zuniga Brothers ran the show, then on to Wisconsin before heading back through Iowa, Kansas and Oklahoma. Then there was the route west that started on highway 20 in Dallas and headed right through Abilene, Big Springs, Odessa, Pecos and El Paso. From El Paso these troubadours headed north through Albuquerque to Denver then into Los Angeles and up the West Coast to Bakersfield, Fresno, San Jose and Sacramento performing their brand of soul for farm workers, blue collar laborers and college students as well a new generation of adoring fans. This was all going on during the same time that the great Motown Revues were traveling the country with acts like Marvin Gaye, the Miracles, the Supremes and the Temptations. However, very little is known about the Chicano musicians, the music they created and the joy they brought to American workers.

The Sunglows

In 1963 Sunny left the Sunglows and Sunglow Records for Chester Foy Lee and Huey P. Meaux's Tear Drop Records. It's actually through Meaux's distribution contacts that **Talk to Me** managed to become a national hit. Guerra's fledgling Sunglow label did not have the muscle to push the record beyond South Texas. Meaux then teamed up Ozuna with a group of musicians from Houston known as Little Jesse and the Rockin' Vee's and renamed the group Sunny and the Sunliners. The line-up of Sunny Ozuna (vocals), Jesse Villanueva (drums), Oscar Villanueva (guitar), Ray Villanueva (sax), Tony Tostado (bass), Gilbert Fernandez (sax), Alfred Luna (organ) was only together for a short time before Sunny pulled together another group of musicians from various San Antonio groups including some of his ex-band mates from the Sunglows.

The departure of Sunny left the Sunglows without a frontman so for the next couple of years the group went through a variety of lead singers including Bobby Mack, Freddy Sal, Rudy Guerra and probably the most eccentric of them all Joe Bravo. Jose Jasso Bravo started his recording career in 1963 with a group called Little Joe and the Harlems while still attending Harlandale High School on San Antonio's Southside. Long time Royal Jesters drummer Manuel "Bones" Aragon was twelve years old when the Harlems went into the recording studio. "In our neighborhood, and I mean about a five block area, there was at least three garage bands," remembers Aragon. "When I was about twelve years old I started practicing with a group called Roger A and the Ethics. They had a drummer, James who was about fifteen years old. He had a drum set because his parents could afford it. James was really into girls so he would ask me to show up at the dances then after about three or four songs he would let me take over so he could mingle with the girls. Eventually I became the full time drummer for about three or four shows with the Ethics."

Aragon continues, "Meanwhile James was dating this girl Linda who lived three blocks down from me, and Linda's sister was dating Joe Bravo. Joe was trying to put together his first band so he asked James to play drums. James knew he didn't play so he told Joe 'Bones is a good drummer why don't you talk to him.' Joe was about seventeen or eighteen years old at the time and he lived in a little house on the southside of town. We had a seven-piece band with two horns, drums, bass, guitar, organ and Joe, Well at practice with a seven-piece band we filled up the house. We recorded **Crying in the Chapel,** which got a lot of play locally. There were a couple of stations here in town that would play all of the local stuff KUKA and KEDA. So on those stations **Crying in the Chapel** went to the top five might have even gone to number one on their charts. These stations were great for

Sunglows album circa 1965
L-R: Manny Guerra, Joe Bravo.
Courtesy of Joe Silva.
The **Fabulous Sunglows**. *Author's archives.*

local bands, that's how Mike & the Del-Rays, Royal Jesters, Rudy & the Reno-Bops and Henry Peña got their music played. Then maybe KONO would pick them up."

The Harlems recorded three singles for the Tina label and were quickly becoming a popular group on San Antonio's teen circuit. Another group on the circuit was the Satin Kings, a group from Edgewood High School who Aragon remembers as being "a real professional band." The Satin Kings also had a record out, having recorded a cover of Cookie and the Cupcakes' **Matilda**. Bravo eventually fired his whole group and hired the Satin Kings to become the new Harlems but after their drummer dropped out Aragon was back in. "So now we're playing at Edgewood canteen, and those were really fun and they always had good bands," recalls Aragon, "This Wednesday night it was us [Harlems] and the Sunglows. Sunny had just left to form the Sunliner Band. That night Manny (Guerra) talked to Joe and he took Joe away from the band. Joe came over to us and said 'Well guys this is a real good opportunity for me so I'm going with the Sunglows' and here we go again without a singer."

With Bravo now as their lead singer the Sunglows recorded one of their most popular tunes of all time. Written by Manny Guerra **It's Okay** is a song about a guy that's just lost his girl. However, the song gets its strange personality from Joe Bravo who even with his previous recordings seems to be living life on the edge. Whether or not Guerra intended the song to be a song about revenge and anger Bravo's, performance is one of a kind.

What was happening in San Antonio was a movement that began from the bare roots with kids who were learning as they went along. The musicians in many of these groups were extremely young, who upon given the choice to play it safe and stay in school or join the Sunglows, the Sunliners, or the Royal Jesters chose the later. Twelve-year-old drummer Manuel "Bones" Aragon recalls playing stickball on the street with the neighborhood kids when the band [Harlems]

Before joining Sunny and the Sunliners Henry Parilla had a big local hit with "What To Do" in the summer of '63. **Little Henry and the Laveers** (above) Henry Parilla is at the Hammond M3 organ and Vic Montes (far left) is on guitar. *Author's archives.*

would roll up to pick him up for a gig. "I would have to go in the house and my sisters would clean me up," he recalls. Chente and Vic Montes grew up on the streets of Westside San Antonio and began by performing rhythm and blues tunes for the *pachucos* in the neighborhood bars when they were in their early teens and walked away from school by the ninth grade because they were to busy with music. Henry Parilla recorded his first record with his group Little Henry and the Laveers when he was thirteen, guitarist Rudy Palacios ran away from home with the Sunliners when he was fifteen years old because he knew music was his calling. Palacios fondly remembers being called up by the Sunliners, "Arturo 'Sauce' Gonzales was a good friend of mine we lived on the Westside together and I was playing at a place called the Cadillac Club and 'Sauce' would say 'hey, *carnál* one of these days I'm gonna get you into the Sunliners band.' So with that I was encouraged to learn more and to practice hard 'cause I wanted to be with the Sunliners band." Palacios continues, "One day 'Sauce' called me and said 'Hey, *carnál* are you ready' well I was in the eighth or ninth grade and I left school to go with the Sunliners. It broke my mom's heart because I was like fourteen or fifteen and back then they had truant officers and I remember sneaking out the back door while the truant officer was knocking on the front door because I hadn't been going to school so I broke my mom's heart. That day we left for Kentucky in an old Pontiac sedan pulling a trailer. We went to Kentucky, Wisconsin and Ohio."

Bassist Roy "Robo" Cantú started performing in the family group Mike and the Hi-Fi's before reaching his teens and has performed as a sessions man for Abe Epstein's Cobra Records as well as going on the road with many groups including the Sunliners and Joe Bravo. "All the bands from San Antonio would go to Chicago and we would stay in motels and I mean we were young," recalls Cantú. "Joe Bravo had just quit the Sunglows this was after he recorded **It's Okay** we went to Chicago with his new orchestra and he left us all in the room and came back to San Antonio with all of the money. Well when the lady said 'check out time is at eleven and you'd better have the money' all the little guys were there, all young and scared and I was the oldest one. We were going to go to jail but one of the guys Roy Perez had his parents who were a little better off than most so they sent the money for all of us through Western Union."

Sunny and the Sunliners

For the new Sunliners line-up Sunny recruited Arturo "Sauce" Gonzales (keyboards), Rudy Palacios (guitar), Chente Montes (bass) and Armando Alba (drums). The Sunliners horn section was heavier than what Ozuna had with the Sunglows and was a key element in what would become known as the "Westside Sound." The horn section was led by Rudy Guerra (alto sax) and included, Johnny Garcia (tenor sax), Charlie McBurney or George Morin (trumpet) and Jay Johnson (trombone). Like the Sunglows the Sunliners recorded a mix of Spanish and English records that made them the premier Chicano group in the country. **Talk to Me** propelled the group to an unimaginable level of popularity, which kept them on the road for ten years, rolling into San Antonio once in a while for a short rest and recuperation break before heading out again. Sunny recalls running the group like a business using time on the road for rehearsals and trying to stay ahead of pack. "Being on the road was such a fun time because we were get-

Sunny and the Sunliners left to right: (baritone) Rudy Guerra, (trumpet) RubenGutierrez, (keyboards) Arturo "Sauce" Gonzales, (tenor) Johnny Garcia, (guitar) Rudy Palacios, (drums) Toby Reyna, (vocals) Sunny Ozuna, and (bass) Chente Montes. *Courtesy of Geno Reza.*

The success of the **Sunliners** *Talk to Me* put the spot light on San Antonio and the many soul recording groups that emerged from the city's Westside throughout the sixties.

ting such a high off of **Talk to Me** and everything that followed." He adds. "Our way of life seemed to roll faster than anybody else's but it created a lot of jobs as we were moving from town to town. We were writing our songs and creating different ideas for the bandstand, knowing that other groups were copying and checking out what we were doing. What is that saying? 'Uneasy rests the head that wears the crown.' We just kept getting better, and better and better from everything we did. We worked out the harmony, the horn arrangements, the guitar and keyboard parts on the road. We were coming up with ideas from experience and the more we did it, we moved up to different levels and we would change and move up again."

When the Sunliners went on stage it was a total experience and everything from their flashy suits, tight horn arrangements, smooth vocal harmonies, and their ability to appeal to all aspects of Chicano culture was part of their charm. Whether the Sunliners were in Los Angeles's Hollywood Palladium performing in front of screaming teens wanting to hear **The One Who's Hurting Is You** or in Milwaukee performing **Cariño Nuevo** for an audience of migrant workers, they had no problem winning over the audience. "In the early sixties here in Texas we did pretty much everything in English," remembers guitarist Rudy Palacios. "We catered to the kids and I mean if you did Spanish *polkas* they wouldn't dance they wanted more of the 'in thing.' Later on if we went towards Chicago, Milwaukee, Utah we played a lot of English but if we were in Texas, Oklahoma, Colorado and Florida we played a little more Spanish." Palacios recalls the night Sunny and the Sunliners headlined at the Hollywood Palladium "Something, that I will never, never forget in my life was the night we played at the Hollywood Palladium for the first time. We were the headliners and on the bill was Sonora Santanera from Mexico and Thee Midniters." Palacios continues, "You know the stage was round and the curtain follows it, well as we start playing our intro number, which is an upbeat number and the MC is saying 'Ladies and gentlemen it's time for a little brown eyed soul. . . .' And the curtain starts to open and you start to see the place jam packed on three levels and the people are cheering. Right there I thought man here we are Chicanos from San Antonio in Hollywood, California and I thought who would ever believe this. And I'm thinking of my mom and that I had told her at age seven that I was gonna make it. All this while the curtain is opening and people are clapping and hollering."

The **Sunliners** band entertained Chicano audiences throughout America during the sixties. They were an extremely professional and creative group of musicians that inspired a whole generation of groups that emerged throughout the Southwest. *Courtesy of Geno Reza.*

In every small town or bustling city that Sunny and the Sunliners made a stop they left a musical foot print that was so impressive that by the time they came through that area again there would be a band imitating their sound. But Sunny knows he wasn't alone, Little Joe and the Latinaires were out there doing the same thing. "Little by little a lot of the groups started imitating what I was doing and what Little Joe [and the Latinaires] was doing." Ozuna continues, "Then along the way Augustine Ramirez, Freddie Martinez, Ruben Ramos, and these guys all came into the picture and kind of trying to imitate the basic concept of what we were doing. Then they started to branch out on their own and as each one found their way, it created like a little branch. Off the same tree just a little branch." Many of the groups that were imitating the Sunliners would not fully commit to the R&B sound but the appeal among the musicians was there. Laredo's Carlos Landin and his group the Rondels recorded several singles and a handful of albums for Carlos Guzman's Impacto label and Luther de la Garza's Capri label, but only two of their singles were R&B tunes with English lyrics. "We started our career back in 1959 we had a combo with a keyboard, two guitars, bass, and drums," recalls Landin. "We did local school gigs in Laredo then we started doing the

military base circuit; Laredo Air Force Base, Lackland in San Antonio and so on. As time went on we integrated the horns, we started with a tenor, alto and a trumpet. We were listening to Sunny and the Sunliners and to us they were our idols, it was like one day we're going to be like them." The Rondels situation was typical throughout Texas with many of the smaller towns and cities having their own soul scene.

One of the biggest supporters of the Sunliners was Houston DJ Skipper Lee Frasier who was at radio station KCOH, and who also owned Ovide Records. Frasier was aware of the Sunliners' popularity in Houston and they would regularly draw a large Hispanic audience. "We used to do this rhythm and blues thing in Houston for these radio stations and they liked the band a lot because we used to dress up real flashy," recalls keyboard player Little Henry Lee. "We had red suits, yellow suits, green suits, pinned striped suits and black sharkskin suits, we had suits up the yang. The black artists liked it a lot and we would open shows for the radio stations hoping they would play our records." He continues, "That's how we got to meet Skipper Lee." Little Henry Lee had replaced Arturo "Sauce" Gonzales as the group's keyboardist and was with the Sunliners from 1966 through 1969. In 1966 Frasier asked Sunny to work with a soul group called Archie Bell and the Drells that had been opening up for the Sunliners. "Skipper Lee was the main DJ at KCOH in Houston and he's the one who said 'Why don't you guys cut a song with these guys?' Rudy Guerra was another guy, he was like a visionary he always said like if these guys get the right song they're gonna be out there." At the time the Sunliners had upgraded to a Winnebego with generator power supply so that the group could rehearse en route. Sunny, Rudy, Henry and Chente Montes got together on the way up to Houston and wrote **She's My Woman, She's My Girl,** which was Archie Bell and the Drells' first single. It did not become the hit that everyone expected but it opened the doors for the Drells, whose follow-up single **Tighten Up** was a huge national seller for Atlantic Records.

Through the years Sunny has been affectionately known as *"El Orgullo de Tejas"* (The Pride of Texas), *"El Monito de Chocolate"* (The Chocolate Doll), and a host of other names. However, it is the nickname "Little Mr. Brown Eyed Soul" that Houston DJ, Skipper Lee Frazier gave him and that soul enthusiasts have labeled this whole genre of music "Brown Eyed Soul" had it's roots in Sunny's dream of creating music with soul and passion. Sunny has appeared on more than fifty different television programs through the last fifty years, he has performed in nearly every state in the union, and he has received countless awards and through it all he has brought recognition and respect to San Antonio's great musical culture.

The **Royal Jesters** performing with **Sunny and the Sunliners** at Patio Anda Luz in San Antonio. On the Hammond organ is Arturo "Sauce" Gonzales. *Courtesy of Dimas Garza.*

Handbill, Easter dance in San Antonio. *Courtesy of Dimas Garza.*

Dimas Garza circa 1965 during his time with the Dell-Tones. *Courtesy of Dimas Garza.*

The Royal Jesters

With their 1959 release of **My Angel of Love** the Royal Jesters propelled the teen group scene that existed in San Antonio to another level. Until then the only local groups creating excitement with the city's teens were the Lyrics and the Pharaohs. The formula that Henry Hernandez and Oscar Lawson used to create the Royal Jesters' sound was a simple one of smooth harmonies and a mix of old R&B favorites and current top forty soul. Lawson explains the Jesters concept: "The Royal Jesters came together specifically to perform English rhythm and blues mainly the Motown Sound. We based our harmonies on the Mexican *trios* like Los Tres Diamantes, Los Tres Aces, and Los Panchos which were very similar to the group harmony sound we were listening to on the radio."

The Royal Jesters signed on with San Antonio record producer Abe Epstein who was recording South Texas artists from all corners of the music spectrum. The line-up on his Jox and Cobra labels boasted artist from the country, rock, rhythm and blues, *ranchera* and *conjunto* fields. Like Johnny Gonzales in Dallas, Epstein was recording anyone that had a decent sound. He was looking for a breakout record, which did not come until 1964 with René and René's **Angelito**. Meanwhile the Royal Jesters kept the label busy with a steady stream of quality Spanish and English records, especially during the short period when Dimas Garza was fronting the group. In 1962 Henry Hernandez enlisted in the Army Reserves and had to take a short leave from the group. "When Henry left the Jesters for military duty Oscar called me to join the them," recalls Garza. "Things with the Lyrics were not going well, we couldn't get recorded so I

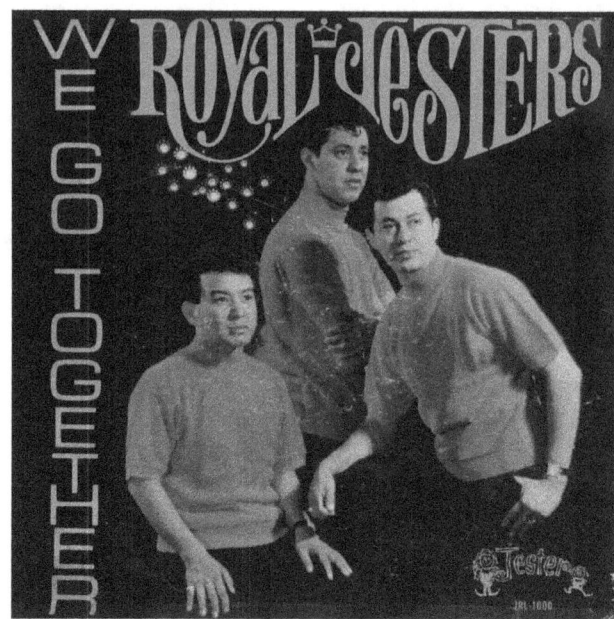

The **Royal Jesters**' 1965 album *We Go Together*.

```
JUST IN- NEWEST DESIGNS IN 15-YR. INVITATIONS
WEDDING INVITATIONS – DANCE & PARTY INVITATIONS
      SOCIAL AND COMMERCIAL PRINTING

              Pan-American Press
San Antonio's leading rish, cut rate printers   Since 1931
417 W. Hudson                                   CA 7-7932
```

JESSE & SAM
KUKA'S TOP TEEN TUNES
TOP 10
AUGUST 27th to SEPTEMBER 3rd

Song Title – Label	Artist
1. Together Again- AAA	Rudy & the Reno-Bops
2. Crying In The Chapel – Tina	Little Joe & the Harlems
3. Honeychild – Sunglow	The Sunglows
4. Whip It On Me – Georgia – Laveer	Little Henry & the Laveers
5. I'm In The Mood For Love – AAA	Ambrose & the Royal Bops
6. Lucille / Gotta See Baby Tonight – Cobra	Sonny Ace & Twisters
7. La Bolla Negra / Que Seas Felis – Cobra	The Royal Jesters
8. La Enorme Distancia– Cobra	Sonny Ace & the Twisters
9. Somethings Got A Hold / I Love You - Gunzo	The Markels
10. On My Knees – Tina	Little Joe & the Harlems

TOP TUNE OLDIES BUT GOODIES

1. I Know, I Know – Double L	Pookie Hudson
2. A Year Ago Today – Renner	Doug Sham
3. Guess Who – Sunglow	The Sunglows

TRIPLE T THREAT

1. Pretend – Jox	Skytones

FROM 5:15 TO 7:00 P.M.
MONDAY THRU SATURDAY

Radio station KUKA in San Antonio was instrumental in getting the city's local artists known by playing their records. Their *Top Teen Tunes* show aired every afternoon at 3pm, this survey is from 1963 and loaded with local talent.

joined the Jesters. After Henry returned we all stayed together."

Before being called upon by the Royal Jesters Dimas spent some time fronting another popular local group called Dino and the Dell-Tones, The Dell-Tones recorded two Spanish language records **La Media Vuelta** and **El Peor de los Caminos** before recording another of Garza's signature ballads **Don't Leave Me Baby** in 1961. The Royal Jesters quickly capitalized on Garza's writing and singing style, a style that Garza says he patterned after Etta James' melancholy approach to her songs. They recorded a pair of his doo-wop styled ballads **Love Me** and **I Want to Be Loved** before his departure in 1964. After a brief hiatus from the bandstand Garza was back behind the microphone in 1966 with what some consider his finest soul recordings. Once again both **You Succeeded** and **I Won't Love You Again** were beautiful ballads written by Garza. The two singles were released on Clown Records a label that Lawson and Hernandez formed in 1966 to record the Royal Jesters and related projects.

The Royal Jesters were busy in 1965 with the departure of Garza they were back to the three-part harmonies of Louie Escalante, Henry Hernandez and Oscar Lawson. They formed their own Jester record label and released their first album *We Go Together*. One of the bolder moves that they made was leasing Patio Anda Luz, a small dance hall on the Westside of town that Hernandez remembers as a popular place for community weddings and dances. "Sunny Ozuna started playing at a place called Patio Anda Luz, which had a outside patio downstairs and an indoor dance hall upstairs for the colder weather," he said. "Originally it was strictly for adults and then they started to have teen dances and it became popular. We started to do the same thing until the lady's husband died and she didn't want to run it. She eventually leased it too us for about three or four years. So then whenever we heard there was going to be a school holiday we would put together a dance for the night before, we'd be on the radio doing announcements and we'd pack the place. The band would have a dance once a week and then we would rent it for weddings and dances."

Until 1964 the Jesters were a vocal group relying on other groups like the Sunglows, Sunliners and the Reno-Bops to back them at dances and shows. Demand for them to appear at shows from Houston to the South Texas border towns had grown prompting Lawson and Hernandez to form a band that would allow them the opportunity to put on a complete show. "Once we had it together" recalls Lawson, "our competition was Abraham Quintanilla and Los Dinos from Corpus Christi. At least once a month the groups would get together in Corpus and battle it out." With a new band, their own label and Patio Anda Luz as their headquarters the Jesters set out to become San Antonio's top band. With the *We Go Together* album they established their sound. While many of San Antonio's groups were touring throughout the United States the Royal Jesters stayed home and that was just fine with Oscar Lawson. "Our success was strictly local. We heard later that we were popular in Pittsburgh but we never left Texas."

In 1967 sixteen-year-old bass player Joe Perales, guitarist Robert Gomez, and vocalist David Mares recorded two singles for Abe Epstein's Jox label. The two singles **Making Me Cry** and **A Love That's Real** backed with **No One Else but You** have become two of the most sought after records by Chicano R&B enthusiast because of their rarity and the quality of the recordings. **Making Me Cry** and **No One Else but You** are original ballads sung as a duo and **A Love That's Real** is a hard driving version of the Intruders hit from 1967. Shortly after their recording session the group fell apart and Joe Perales was invited to audition for the Royal Jesters. "Back then you get two calls and then you're big time, the Royal Jesters and the Sunliners. So when I got the call from the Royal Jesters there was no hesitation, I said 'shit yea!' We had a lot of good bands here in San Antonio but the heavies were the Royal Jesters and Sunny and the Sunliners." Becoming a member of San Antonio's most popular group had its pros and cons and Perales' first days with the group were difficult for someone who had been an outside admirer. "Oscar Lawson and Henry Hernandez had a place called Patio Anda Luz that they used for the Royal Jesters' dances as well as practice. I showed up for the audition and as I was carrying my gear up the steps the bass player they had just fired was coming down with his gear. As we met on the steps he stopped and said 'Watch these guys they'll do you wrong.' I went upstairs set up, the guys talked to me told me what we were going

Danny and the Dreamers with Gilbert Sanchez singing lead. *Author's archives.*

Jimmy Edward Treviño also known as **Jimmy Edward.** Before becoming the voice of the Chicano super group Latin Breed Treviño sang with Danny and the Dreamers, and the Lovells. *Courtesy of Geno Reza.*

to play and then counted off the first song. After a few songs they told me the job was mine. Rehearsal was the following day, I was handed my uniform and then just before we started Oscar Lawson had an announcement to make. 'I'm not singing with the group anymore' he said 'I'll stay on and manage but I'm not performing.' Okay! We still got Henry and Louie Escalante." Perales continues, "My first gig as a Royal Jester was on Saturday at Patio Anda Luz. The musicians count off the first song of the night and as we are getting into it I'm paying attention to everyone but the singers all of a sudden the music stops, I look to where Henry and Louie should be and they are rolling around on the floor fighting. I thought 'I've waited so long to be part of the Royal Jesters and within two days of me joining the group everything starts to fall apart.'"

Meanwhile the Royal Jesters had recorded **Private Number** and needed a song for the flip side Joe offered a song that he had written called **Girl I Can't Forget.** With Escalante out and Hernandez' role exclusively that of a harmony singer the group promoted Perales to the front man position and recruited former Eptone vocalist David Mares. Like many teens from all walks of life, Perales was first inspired into a life as a musician by the British invasion of '63-'64, specifically the Beatles. However, as a singer he considers himself a soul singer or as he puts it "I'm a black singer in a Chicano body." With **Girl I Can't Forget** and his two 1968 singles **I've Got Soul** and possibly the most sought after Chicano Soul recording ever **My Life,** Perales established himself as one of the better Chicano vocalist. By 1969 the Royal Jesters joined many of the groups that were leaving behind rhythm and blues and going "Chicano" a format that the Sunglows, Sunliners, and Little

Joe and the Latinaires had pioneered-Spanish lyrics Latin soul rhythms.

In 1967 guitarist Robert Gomez who had been with Joe Jama and David Mares in the Eptones helped to form one of the last of the popular R&B groups before the Tex-Mex movement pushed aside all remnants of San Antonio's soul era. Casino Royale was formed in 1967 built around vocalist Tommy Zumudia (**Don't Mistake Me for a Fool**) and Fernando Arragua (**To Be My Girl**). With the Royal Jesters 1970 decision to go "Chicano" Joe decided to join Casino Royale "In 1970 I quit the Royal Jesters to join another young group that was making some waves here in San Antonio. I heard them and I knew they were gonna be good. I liked their concept and I was looking for something else. I stayed with them from 1970-1973."

Danny & the Dreamers

The story of Danny and the Dreamers, the Lovells and the Royal Knights is tangled up in a series of name changes and personnel that started on San Antonio's Westside in the early sixties and continued well into the seventies. The Lovable Lovells as they were known in the early years came together while the group was attending Fox Tech High. The group consisted of Aaron Torres (guitar), Roy Cantú (bass), and Ernest Camarillo (vocals), with Tony Jimenez eventually coming over from Roger A and the Ethics. Meanwhile, at Horace Mann Junior High Danny Escobedo was putting together a group called Danny and the Dreamers with vocalist Gilbert Sanchez who was later joined by Jimmy Edward Treviño. "We started with three guitars and a drummer and I was lead vocals," remembers Gilbert Sanchez. "Then after a couple of years we got Jimmy who sang, played guitar, bass and saxophone. We started off doing the Beatles thing, then we started going more towards soul music, primarily I would do a James Brown act you know **Please, Please, Please** and **It's a Man's World** which was a stage act. Jimmy and I would also do some Righteous Brothers, Sam and Dave and Wilson Pickett stuff." Danny and the Dreamers' first recording came in 1964 with a guitar instrumental titled **Eternal Love** for Dreamer Records a label started by Escobedo's father who was the group's manager. **Eternal Love** was an instrumental ballad spotlighting the guitar work of Danny who was inspired by Santo and Johnny's **Sleepwalk** just as the Los Angeles based Jaguars were when they recorded **Where Lovers Go.**

By 1964 the band whose members were all fourteen years old or younger had been performing at all of the popular teen spots in San Antonio, but it was at the battle of the bands where many of the local groups would try to establish themselves as the best group around, at least until the next battle. Sometimes it was not just the group's sound that got them over the top as Gilbert Sanchez recalls a battle that Danny and the Dreamers won. "We were playing at a battle of the bands at a small upstairs hall called Villa Fontana. By the time the night was coming to an end it was us and Bobby Shannon and the T-Birds going against each other, we were doing a lot of soul music and people voted more towards our group. Thing is Bobby Shannon's group was all black I mean they 'were' soul. But we came out ahead I think the reason we won had to do more with the fact that we were young kids, we were all from thirteen years old and down so that got us votes. It was that night that some promoters asked Mr. Escobedo if we would like to go to Las Vegas, But we were too young and we had to go to school. But we beat out Bobby Shannon and the T-Birds." Another highlight for the group was San

Antonio's 1964 Teenage Fair held at the Joe Freeman Coliseum where they performed alongside the Rolling Stones.

The second Dreamers single was a beautiful melancholic ballad titled **Baby Something's Wrong,** which featured Treviño on lead vocals and helped to establish him as one of San Antonio's smoothest voices. According to Sanchez, whenever Danny and the Dreamers would perform with Sunny and the Sunliners the audience would request that Sunny and Treviño sing together because their voices and singing styles were so similar. "The measuring stick at the time was Sunny, [Ozuna] everybody wanted to be like or sound like Sunny. He was the leader, he was the pioneer."

After Treviño left the Dreamers to join the Lovells Danny and the Dreamers recorded a very soulful version of the Four Tops' **Ask the Lonely** backed with a cover of Gene Chandler's **Think Nothing about It** for Chester Foy Lee's Tear Drop label. These recordings, With Danny Escobedo singing lead are a good example of the ability of the musicians to insert their own Tex-Mex flavor into soul tunes.

Meanwhile Gilbert Sanchez left the Dreamers shortly after their first recording to join a group that was being put together by Johnny Esparza called the Royal Knights. A large group with a full horn section and two vocalists the Royal Knights were soon making the rounds at all of San Antonio's dance halls like Salon Tella, Pato Anda Luz, the Ashby House and Villa Fontana, as well as going out to Hondo and Seguin. Esparza also kept the group busy on the military base circuit, which included Laredo Air Force Base, Randolph Air Force Base. The Royal Knights recorded **I Can't Please You** b/w **I Need You** for Tear Drop Records in 1967 a record that sold 5,000 copies locally.

Not long after the release of **I Can't Please You** Sanchez joined the Air Force. The military draft had also been taking its toll on the groups since the mid-sixties and it was inevitable that some volunteers and draftees would not make it back. Unfortunately the Royal Knights drummer Martin Lechuga and trumpeter Daniel Medina lost their lives in Vietnam.

In 1969 the Lovells were without a lead singer so Tony Jimenez recruited Vic Love to front the group. Love grew up singing in the halls of Burbank High School alongside Sunny Ozuna and Randy Garibay who was singing with the Pharaohs. He eventually found himself singing with one of San Antonio's early doo-wop groups the Sequence. In 1959 they waxed a version of Tony Allen's classic **Night Owl** for Pegaso Records, which got a little airtime on local radio station KTSA. With the Lovells Vic Love recorded a number of Spanish and English singles and had a local hit with a ballad titled **Let's Make a Celebration** However, it was not their English tunes that people were coming out to see. "We traveled throughout Texas, Waco, Corpus, Houston and we performed with Johnny Canales, Rocky Gil and the Bishops, Los Dinos, and Augustine Ramirez," recalls Love. "The crowds that we played for wanted Spanish *polkas* and that stuff although we did play some English stuff I don't think that was the reason they came to see us." This was true for most of the bands from Texas, as the rhythm and blues era had slowly come to an end.

The rhythm and blues groups of San Antonio's Westside have left a rich cultural legacy that continues to this day.
Top left: The **Lovells** | Top right: **Little Jr. Jesse and the Tear Drops**
Middle left: The **Pharaohs** | Middle right: **Vic Love and the Lovells.** *Courtesy of Vic Love.* | Bottom left: **Royal Knights**
Bottom right: The **Playboys**. L-R: Ernie Saldana (keys), unidentified (sax), Robert Reyes (bass), Roger Sanchez (trumpet), Floyd Coleman (vocals), Henry Garcia (drums), others unidentified. *Courtesy of Floyd Coleman.*

SHAKE, SHOUT AND SOUL

Southern California

A lot of what we did in East L.A. that helped the music develop its uniqueness is the fact that we didn't have access to a lot of things. If you notice a lot of the Eastside sound recordings have no piano on them. In black music the piano came from the church and the gospel music but in our neighborhood no one could afford a piano and then move it around. Eventually there is some piano only because it was in the studio and we decided to use it.

Max Uballez- vocalist/guitarist: Los Angeles [*Romancers*]

Southern California

The decade of the sixties for Southern California's Chicano groups started with a number of artists and groups from the greater Los Angeles area that shared their common desire to create rock 'n roll linking together to create a network, which helped them to promote themselves outside of their respective communities. Once these community networks that popped up in Pomona, East Los Angeles, San Gabriel, El Monte and San Fernando linked together a vibrant Chicano music began to take form. This fledgling movement began to attract outside record producers, booking agents, promoters and DJs that created somewhat of a support system that gave the groups much needed exposure. Groups like the Perez Brothers, the Carlos Brothers and the Velveteens now had a way to produce, promote and distribute records creating a teen craze that took the Chicano community by storm. Most of the bands that emerged from this music scene were never heard outside of the ballrooms and neighborhood dance halls that dotted Los Angeles's landscape. However, they were an integral part of the Mexican American community. Early on several Los Angeles DJs like Dick Hugg "Huggy Boy," Johnny Otis, Hunter Hancock, and Art Laboe saw untapped potential in the Chicano community and besides catering to the musical needs of the Eastside, they also stepped in to help promote these up and coming groups.

In 1961 Huggy Boy promoted a two-day event at the Boulevard Theater on Whittier Blvd., the show featured many of the most popular rhythm 'n blues artists of the time especially those from nearby South Los Angeles like Tony Allen, Richard Berry, the Penguins and the Turks. On hand were several Chicano

Poster for 1965 concert hosted by KRLA DJ Dave Hull at the Shrine Auditorium on Los Angeles's Southside. Eighteen groups performed in alphabetical order during the most exciting musical renaissance in the history of East Los Angeles. According to Mark Guerrero of Mark and the Escorts, attendance was low. "Kids that were used to taking the bus or walking down the street to a dance just didn't show up." Another factor for the low turnout was the music scene in East Los Angeles was like the community's little secret that few Angeleno's knew existed. *Poster courtesy of Jimmy Meza.*

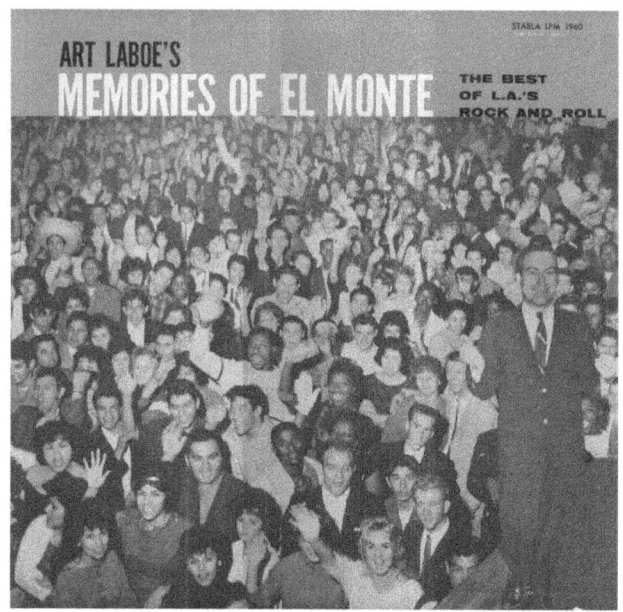

Since 1960 Art Laboe's "Oldies but Goodies" series of albums have been extremely popular with Chicano record buyers. For several musicians his early compilations were their introduction to rhythm and blues.

groups like the Velveteens, the Perez Brothers and the Carlos Brothers. In a way this event solidified the union between black rhythm and blues and the Eastside community's rock 'n roll generation. In the following years the British invasion groups played a key roll in music and style however, for the most part the sound stayed true to its roots. By 1963 several DJs from radio stations KFWB, KDAY and KRLA joined Huggy Boy and just like Chuck Blore had done with Ritchie Valens, Larry McCormick, Casey Kasem, Bob Eubanks, Wink Martindale and others started using Chicano bands at events they were promoting, and this in many ways helped to "professionalize" groups like the Blue Satins, the Ambertones, the Romancers

The late Dick Hugg "Huggy Boy" circa 1952. "Always imitated, never duplicated." As an eighteen year old assistant manger at the Boulevard Theater on Whittier Blvd. Hugg was introduced to rhythm and blues by his younger Chicano co-workers. For the following 30 years he was the DJ Chicano's identified with most. *Courtesy of the late Dick Hugg.*

and Thee Midniters. The period between 1960-1963 was a period of growth and recognition and by 1964 it would become Los Angeles' most vibrant music scene, one that brought kids of all ethnic backgrounds from all over Southern California to the Eastside for music and entertainment.

Rosie

The first huge hit of the sixties for a Chicano artist would come out of National City's Sweetwater High School located just outside of San Diego, California. Rosalie Hamlin and her group the Originals recorded a demo of a song she had written titled **Angel Baby**. After several failed attempts at getting the record heard by a record company they headed down to Kresge's Department Store in San Diego. Kresge's had an in house system where they played the latest record releases. The Originals talked the manager into letting them play their demo. The timing was perfect because a representative of Highland Records was in the store on business, and was willing to take the demo to his boss Syd Talmadge in Hollywood. The Originals turned their demo over to the stranger and the next time they heard their song was on Alan Freed's radio show on KDAY. The charm of **Angel Baby** comes from its childish simplicity and heartfelt lyrics, which Rosie Hamlin lends her angelic voice to. The demo was recorded in an old airplane hanger with amateur musicians. Had Highland Records chosen to re-record the song in studio with top musicians chances are they would have lost the innocence and charm of **Angel Baby**. It is one of those recordings that could never be duplicated.

Although Rosie and the Originals had a national hit with **Angel Baby** it was the Mexican American community that embraced her and showered her with

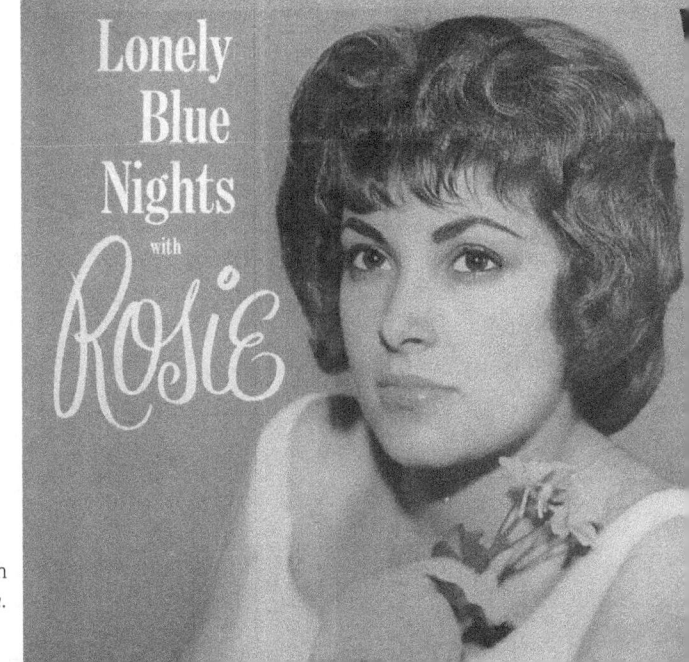

Rosie was the first Mexican American female singer to have a national hit with **Angel Baby** and the first to record an album. *Courtesy of Rosie Hamlin.*

love. Hamlin, whose grandparents on her father's side immigrated from Scotland, and whose grandparents on her mother's side trekked to California from the Mexican provinces of Chihuahua and Mazatlán, gave Chicano youth especially the girls their first anthem. In the following years the female voice would play only a small role in the Chicano soul scene and none could top the lasting success of **Angel Baby**. Nationally **Angel Baby** climbed up the charts to number five. Rosie followed the advice of Jackie Wilson in 1961 and signed with Brunswick Records for her follow-up single **Lonely Blue Night** and an album of the same title which, features several songs that Hamlin had written.

The Perez Brothers

After the departure of Ritchie Valens from the Silhouettes, Sal Barragan, Gil Rocha and Walter Takate continued on by adding Danny Rosales who was formerly with Rulie Garcia and the Imperials and had just been discharged from the Navy. Louie and Ralph Perez were still attending Canoga Park High School and had been performing at local parties as a duo. The brothers came from a family with some musical history. Their father was a guitarist who performed with local *trios* and their uncle Bob Perez was also a local musician. Encouraged by their family they followed in their father's footsteps. The Silhouettes recruited the brothers to front their group. According to Louie Perez, "It was Danny Rosales who suggested that they change their name to the Gents."

Ofie's Record Shop was located in neighboring San Fernando and was owned by Ofelia Martinez. Martinez arranged a recording session for the Gents with Wolfie Records a small Hollywood record company owned by a Jewish couple. The session resulted in the Perez Brothers only single **Truly, Truly Yours** backed with **(At Night) Dream a Little Dream**. Both sides were remakes of fifties doo-wop classics, **Truly, Truly Yours** was a Robert and Johnny original from 1958 and **Dream a Little Dream** was penned by Fred Parris for his group the New Yorkers in 1961.

Released in 1961 the single quickly caught on in Southern California. Before long the Perez Brothers were performing at the Montebello Ballroom, the Shrine Auditorium and the El Monte Legion Stadium. At the time Louie was seventeen and Ralph was sixteen but as they made their way through Los Angeles area dance halls they were befriended by other young Chicano stars like Rudy and Steve Salas, Max Uballez, Julian Herrera and Willie Garcia. Besides performing about five shows per weekend the group was featured on several television dance shows including Larry McCormick's *Kicksville* show on channel 5. During the same period Louie was also pursuing a career as a professional fighter, fighting as Louie "The Lion" Perez. According to Perez, "I was fighting all over California and scheduling was tough on the group." Wolfie Records filed for bankruptcy in 1964 so Ofie Martinez kept **Truly, Truly Yours** alive by re-releasing it on her own Ofie's label in 1964 and neither of the Perez Brothers knows how many records she sold through the years.

The Sevilles

In 1961 Manny Chavez and Sonny Chaney singing as Frankie and Johnny recorded a beautiful ballad written by Tommy Boyce titled **My First Love**. They had been members of the Jaguars of **The Way You Look Tonight** fame however, times were rough for the

Right: Al Perez started using some of the young local talent for shows that had been heavily dominated by the more established R&B acts. On this show in 1962 some of the early stars of the "Eastside Sound" start to emerge; the Gents band from San Fernando with the **Perez Brothers** Louie and Beto, from Hawthorne **Rene and Ray** with their big hit :"Queen Of My Heart." From Lincoln Heights the **Romancers** with Max Uballez and guitarist Andy Tesso were a new group with a lot of raw talent, which would inspire a new generation of musicians.

Handbill courtesy of Dino Pataglia.

Courtesy of Max Uballez.

groups as Uncle Sam kept taking their members. Also in 1961 Manny Chavez and a group of studio musicians recorded a song he had co-written with Sonny Chaney called **Charlena**. In an interview with music historian Jim Dawson for the liner notes to the Jaguars compilation album Chavez recalled the Charlena story, "Nobody wanted to record **Charlena** we sang that song for everybody for more than a year." Unfortunately the timing was bad for the Jaguars. "I was getting ready to go into the army, they'd just drafted me . . . . It was supposed to be a Jaguars record but because of the time frame we just weren't able to pull it off," said Chavez.

In **Charlena** you have all of the West Coast influences wrapped up into one fine, fine, fine record. Unlike many of the Jaguars previous hits this is a shoutin' rocker typical of the Don and Dewey school of R&B complete with Mexican style guitar intro by Manny Chavez and a wailing sax by a long forgotten horn man. The song was revived in a 1964 version by the Ambertones but it simply did not have the raw emotion that the Sevilles single had. Refusing to go away quietly **Charlena** made still another comeback. This time Los Lobos covered it for the 1997 film *La Bamba*.

Chris Montez

In 1958 Ritchie Valens was the headliner at a dance in Hawthorne, California. Seventeen-year-old Chris Montez waded through the crowd trying to get a glimpse of his idol. "It was a VFW type dance hall here in Hawthorne that held maybe 300 people and it was so crowded but I didn't care I just wanted to be in the same room with him," recalls Montez. "Well turns out he was standing next to me in the back of the hall, so I just shook his hand and said I want to be a singer too. He kinda laughed and said cool. Within like two months Ritchie was dead."

That moment and Ritchie Valens' music kept Montez focused on creating music. He had been playing with a small group, Chris on vocals and guitar, Mike Garcia on drums and Bill Boyd on guitar, no bass because they were hard to come by. In 1958 Chris Montez and the Invicibles went into a small recording studio in Long Beach and recorded their first demo **Forgive Me** backed with **She's My Rock-**

in' Baby. "We just wanted to hear what we sounded like." recalls Montez. What Chris sounded like was a very young version of his idol Ritchie Valens. Meanwhile, the group was busy performing at local parties and dance halls. "I would take my little group and we'd play in Pomona and East Los Angeles and they had these big nine piece bands. We were getting like $45.00 a dance and I'd split it with the guys so I kind of felt bad for the guys from the other bands."

Even with the success of Valens it was still hard for a Chicano kid to make it in the music industry so Montez figured out that he would have to make a change. I used to wear khakis, French toe shoes, and long sleeve shirts rolled up. But that was my dress and I always kept it clean, I wasn't trying to be bad or anything, it was just a style." He said, "It was my sophomore year I just decided screw this, I'm gonna play their [music industry] game and I'm gonna beat them at it. So what I did was take my khakis off and I started wearing regular shoes and Ivy League shirts, I cut my hair short and started to part it. I was coming from some hard times, my parents never spoke English, my brothers and sisters who were older than me took off and got married. So I was left to fend for myself."

Meanwhile the engineer from his recording session played the demo for Jim Lee who was starting up Monogram Records. Lee contacted Montez about signing with the fledgling label. In the summer of 1962 Montez released his second Monogram single a rockin' dance tune titled **Let's Dance**. Like **She's My Rockin' Baby** it is evident that he was still being inspired by Valens's legacy. "If it wouldn't have been for him I wouldn't have had any kind of aspirations to be a singer." Says Montez, "I had no direction. But he gave me direction."

Not only was **Let's Dance** a top ten hit in the U.S., it went to number one in England where Montez was in demand for live shows. "They sent me to England because **Let's Dance** was number one," he said. "The Beatles were just starting so they would open and do stuff like **Love Me Do** then Tommy Roe who had **Sheila** out, and I would close the show. We did that for four weeks." When he returned back to the states Montez toured with the Miracles, Jerry Butler, Clyde McPhater, Sam Cooke and the Drifters this meant performing on the old Chitlin' Circuit. "This was during the whole Freedom Rider period (of the year 1963)" recalls Montez. "I reflect on this sometimes because it was dangerous and scary, I mean what were we gonna do if they started throwing fire bombs. I never got used to the whole black only, whites only thing. I'd have to go and get bags of food from the burger joints because the black artists didn't want to go to the back door and get treated like shit."

After three years of touring Montez returned to Los Angeles and it wasn't until 1965 that he would return to the recording studio. A&M producer Herb Alpert contacted him with a proposal. He wanted Montez to record soft pop rather than rock 'n roll something that Montez was not too happy about. However, after some thought he agreed and in January of 1966 he released **Call Me** his first A&M single. Montez became an international star with a series of singles and albums making him one of the most successful Chicano artists.

> We had a chicken coop and my dad had
> some fighting roosters. Well one day one
> of his roosters got his eye knocked out
> and he was recuperating. It was late but
> my mom sent me out to check on the

rooster, but that night my dad and a six or seven piece band were rehearsing. I ended up staying there listening to all the music and before I knew it, it was midnight. My dad came to me the next day and said 'Looks like you like music, I'm not gonna teach you 'cause I don't have the patience for anything, I'm not paying for lessons 'cause I don't have the money, but there's a guitar in the closet that Candelas made, when ever you're ready it's yours, If you never use it that's fine too.

Johnny Gamboa- guitarist/vibes/singer: Los Angeles, CA [Johnny and the Crowns]

East Los Angeles

Sometime between 1960 and 1962 a handful of bands that started performing around the Boyle Heights area, Johnny Gamboa and the Crowns, the Royal Jesters, the Leggeriors, the Blue Satins, the Fabulous Gentiles and the Romancers were using their garages as laboratories to create their own distinct sound. As these groups continued to evolve there was a constant change in direction and personnel, however, with each change and realignment another group would come into the fold and by the end of 1962 the blue print for the "Eastside Sound" had been established. The actual foundation for "Eastside Sound' was laid by Johnny Gamboa and the Crowns and in 1962 they were still the group that other groups aspired to be like However, as each of the individual groups started to establish its own sound they started to contribute to a music scene that was growing and spilling over into other areas of Los Angeles. The Leggeriors came together in '62 the way most of the early groups formed, usually two guys sitting around a record player trying to mimic their favorite rock 'n roll tune. In this case it was vocalist Johnny Gonzales and guitarist Sal Padilla. "We'd sit around playing oldies I'd play guitar and Johnny would sing," remembers Padilla. "Then Frank Uballez started hanging around and he picked up the drums, Phil Ruiz joined us on sax. Now we're practicing at the recreation center on State Street, then fourteen-year-old Bobby Hernandez joined us so we moved practice to his basement." During this period Huggy Boy had his late night radio show and Padilla would listen for songs that would fit the band, then he'd go to Flash Records on Washington Blvd. to buy the records and finally the band would practice them until they had the songs perfected. This was the typical routine with many of the groups and it paid off when they got gigs as house bands playing behind local R&B groups like the Penguins, Blue Jays, Sonny Knight, the Righteous Bros, and the Rivingtons or popular artists from out of town passing through Los Angeles as they toured the country.

By the time Johnny Gamboa enrolled at Salesian High School in 1958 he already had music running through his veins. Both his grandfather and his father were musicians. Guitarist Pepe Gamboa had been featured in *Down Beat* magazine and had been working with the likes of Desi Arnaz, Hernan Valdez, Les Baxter, Lalo Schifrin and Pedro Armendariz. It was in this environment that Johnny developed his desire to make music his life.

Up until the time the Crowns came along the only groups that were doing R&B were combos like Rulie Garcia and the Imperials, Johnny Alonzo and the Playboys, and the Armenta Brothers who were performing *polkas*, jazz standards and some R&B covers. With the Crowns came a new generation of musi-

Royal Jesters
from R-L
Robert Martinez (tenor sax),
Lico Gallegos (lead guitar),
Jimmy Horvath (alto sax),
Johnny Diaz (rhythm guitar),
Joe Urzua (baritone sax),
Raul Ceballos (bass),
Freddy Ayala (drums),
Frankie Garcia. *Courtesy of Raul Ceballos.*

cians that did not want to look back at what had been popular, they wanted to play what was happening and ninety percent of what they played was what kids were hearing on the radio. Another source of inspiration and knowledge was Bill Taggert, Salesian High School's music director who introduced these young musicians to jazz, and the big band sound, and just as important he taught them how to read charts and the theory of music, all of this knowledge was incorporated into their rock 'n roll format. "In 1960 radio station KRLA sponsored a battle of the bands and the Crowns made it all the way to the finals, which were at the Los Angeles Theater," recalls Johnny Gamboa. "All of the TV and radio stations were there and Wink Martindale was the host. All of the groups there were white except Johnny and the Crowns and we came out on stage in tuxedos and we just wiped them out."

As band director at Our Lady of Lourdes Elementary School, Taggert actively recruited young musicians in Boyle Heights who showed some potential. Baritone saxophonist Joe Ursua recalls getting recruited by Taggert in the early sixties, "I learned to play the sax because of Mr. William Taggert, who was instrumental in teaching a lot of the kids from around the Boyle Heights *barrio* how to play instruments." He said, "I went to Salesian High but before that I learned in the Lourdes band, see I was at Assumption Elementary and Taggert was recruiting musicians from other Catholic schools in the area into the Lourdes band. So he came around to our school and recruited me from there. That's where it all started at Our Lady Of Lourdes." Brothers Tony

Garcia and Bobby Loya were also greatly influenced by his ambitious music program. "It was Bill Taggert who introduced us to Jazz." recalls Loya, "We would get to listen to his record on his hi-fi and he played stuff by Count Basie, Woody Herman and Stan Kenton, that's how we got introduced to jazz. That was just a starting point for many of us so playing with El Chicano, Tierra, Thee Midniters, the Progressions we were able to incorporate all of those influences and in the process we created our own style.

As a freshman at Salesian High school in 1958 Johnny Gamboa started performing solo and gradually developed the first of East Los Angeles's many rock 'n roll bands. Recalling his days at Salesian High Gamboa said, "I did the first rally at the school and that was by myself, little by little I had a group going, first a trio and then by the end of 1958 I had a six-piece band.

> "By 1962 I had a seventeen-piece band that backed up Little Richard at the Shrine Exposition Hall. A lot of those guys would become great musicians Bobby Rodriguez (trumpet), Tony Garcia (sax), Romeo Prado (trombone), Jimmy Espinosa (upright bass), Benny Lopes (bass), Ronnie Figueroa (guitar) and most of the members that would become Thee Midniters. The rhythm and blues craze started things **Over the Mountain** by Johnny and Joe, **Heaven and Paradise** by the Meadowlarks- with the Crowns we did all those tunes and it was terrific."

The Catholic Church had a strong spiritual, social and educational presence in the *barrio*. Many of the parishes provided elementary level education and some had facilities for social gatherings. For teenagers the Catholic high school system provided an education that far exceeded that of the public school system and many neighborhoods had a Catholic Youth Organization facility located nearby for social events. The CYO building located at 3802 Brooklyn Ave., (renamed Cesar Chavez Ave.) in Boyle Heights provided a safe environment where young Chicano musicians could compete against each other. This is where lifelong friends Raul Ceballos and Fred Gallegos entered their first battle of the bands. They were drawn together by rock 'n roll and their desire to be guitarists and in 1962 their makeshift group started to come together. They recruited drummer Fred Ayala, guitarist John Diaz and sax player Robert Martinez. Gallegos was the youngest and still attending Belvedere Jr. High and Martinez who was nineteen years old was the eldest and eventually became the Royal Jesters leader. Horn players Joe Ursua and Jimmy Horvath filled out the horn section and Bobby Montenegro became the group's singer. After perfecting a few songs the band entered its first battle of the bands. Ursua still remembers the Royal Jesters' first battle "We went up against a band that was playing on a regular basis at the CYO They were known as the Enchantments." He said, "They had music stands you know a real fancy band, kinda like a swing band set up. The Enchantments ruled around the CYO area and they played a lot of popular tunes. At the battle of the bands one of the judges was [promoter] Al Perez who used to throw the dances at the Shrine Exposition Hall. Well we won the battle of the bands and we took over at the CYO we became the regular band there."

When Montenegro abruptly left the group Diaz

stepped up to front the Jesters and they recruited Frankie "Cannibal" Garcia as a background singer. Gallegos remembers Garcia singing around the *barrio* with a vocal group, "Cannibal wanted to sing with us but he had some other singers and we were getting to be to big to take them all." He continues, "Anyway we only took Frankie on to be the background singer for Johnny Diaz."

Al Perez, who was the print shop teacher at Roosevelt High School, was also the top promoter in the area during that period. However he had his own artists like the Metalics, Ron Holden, Don Julian, Rulie Garcia, Don and Dewey and the Penguins so it was difficult for the younger groups that didn't have any recordings, or established track record to get a break until Johnny Jay started doing shows in Boyle Heights. Jay booked dances at places like Pontrellis, the CYO, Union Hall, the Alexandria Hotel and the Casa de los Mexicanos that was the circuit that the Royal Jesters worked on until they broke up in 1963.

"I was just a teenager, myself." recalls Johnny Jay, "When I starting having gigs at the CYO hall. The dances got so big there, that the priest from St. Alphonsus raised the rent on me, so I moved to the Casa Mexicano. After that I started having gigs at the Carpenters Hall then at the Paramount Ballroom."

Things started to change for East Los Angeles in 1963. Three individuals from opposite life experiences and each with a different vision of what they wanted to accomplish in the community stepped in to help pull these scattered bands into one cohesive music scene. Eddie Torres, Billy Cardenas and Eddie Davis can equally be credited for elevating the Eastside sound from a garage band scene to a vibrant teen movement that had not previously existed in Los Angeles prior to 1963 and has not been equaled since its demise in the late sixties and early seventies.

Texas born, ex-Marine Eddie Torres came upon East Los Angeles in the late fifties while stationed at the Marine Corps Air Base in El Toro. "After serving in Japan, Okinawa and Iwo Jima I was stationed in San Diego and then El Toro Air Base." Recalls Torres, "My girlfriend who became my first wife was living in East Los Angeles on Ford and Whittier Blvd. so I stayed there and drove everyday to El Toro." After his military discharge Torres made East Los Angeles his home and after graduating from East Los Angeles College he went to work for the Department of Social Services. In his capacity as a social worker, trying to keep kids out of gangs, he came across the bands that were performing at the CYO What Torres saw in these young Chicano musicians was an opportunity to create a positive social environment for neighborhood teens, and an opportunity to get involved in something that he loved. "I always loved music, and as a kid I grew up listening to a local DJ in Brownsville [Texas] named Squeezer Garcia," he said. "We used to hang around with him in the early fifties. He had a late night show called *The Border Bomb Show* so I grew up to stuff like Andy Russell."

Torres's first venture into the E.L.A. music scene was a show he promoted at the CYO He saw potential in a group that had been practicing there called Benny and the Midniters a group that included Raulie Ceballos, Benny Ceballos, Richard Ceballos, Richard Farfan, Benny Lopez, Larry Rendon, Danny Lamont, Bobby Cochran and Willie Garcia. In order for the show to be successful Torres went to Billy Cardenas and asked for the Romancers to be the featured attraction. "The first time I met Eddie Torres was through Billy Cardenas." recalls Max Uballez of the Romancers, "The Romancers were already a big thing

Eddie Torres moved into an apartment above the Golden Gate Theater located on the corner of Atlantic Ave. and Whittier Blvd. Torres used the theater for rehearsals and shows. In the seventies it was on this corner that all the artists going on the road with Torres Productions would meet to board their buses. "The building looked kind of like a palace, Eddie had a balcony right on the corner. So it was like he was looking over his kingdom." Ron Lemos- Thee Runabouts The 1987 Whittier earthquake compromised the building's structure. The Golden Gate Theater was condemned and demolished shortly after.
Photo courtesy of Eddie Maciel.

in East L.A and Billy came by and said 'we're going to do a gig at the CYO Hall, this guy Eddie Torres has this band Benny and the Midniters and he wants people to see them but the only way that people will come is if the Romancers band is there." For his next show Torres went to see Bobby Day of **Rockin Robin** fame who was performing at the Acorn Room on Beverly Blvd. He asked Day to headline a show at St. Alphonsus Church. That is the show that Torres credits with the beginning of his career as the top show promoter in East Los Angeles. For the shows featuring Bobby Day, the Righteous Brothers and other popular artists that Torres promoted he used Thee Midniters as the house band giving his young group much needed exposure and stage experience.

For the next 15 years Torres promoted shows that not only featured Thee Midniters and his brothers' group Thee Runabouts, but also included some of the top R&B and oldies acts of the time. Mary Wells, Don Julian and the Larks, the Intruders, the Young Hearts, Sly Slick and the Wicked, Rosie and the Originals, Tony Allen and Brenton Wood were all featured guests of Eddie Torres's productions. "Eddie was all business," remembers Rosie Hamlin. "He never had time to joke around or laugh, he was a very serious person. I never even saw him drink a beer even after the day was done and the show a success." During the British invasion period Torres would be a regular on Hollywood's club scene looking for the latest acts, and bringing them to East Los Angeles. Kids on the Eastside were able to attend live performances of the Animals, Them, Sonny and Cher, and the Turtles because of Eddie Torres.

Every couple of months Torres would put together a caravan that left from his home [above the Golden Gate Theater] and head up north through towns like

Hayward, Stockton, Fresno, San Jose and Sacramento. Ron Lemos of Thee Runabouts recalls how the audiences up north accepted these musicians from East Los Angeles: "I used to think the Big Union was big but this was bigger. The audience was all farmworkers." He said, "They thought we were different 'cause we came from Los Angeles. But Spanish music wasn't that big with them. On the Eddie Torres tours they [the audience] weren't looking for Spanish music, what they wanted was this East L.A. sound."

In East Los Angeles Eddie Torres was a respected businessman who brought to the community top quality entertainment for all to enjoy. Torres lived above the Golden Gate Theater complex on Atlantic Ave. and Whittier Blvd. "Eddie Torres's apartment was above the Golden Gate and the building looked kind of like a palace, Eddie had a balcony right on the corner. So it was like he was looking over his kingdom." Recalls Lemos, "He was the king of East L.A."

Billy Cardenas stepped onto the Boyle Heights scene in 1962. The stocky ex-paratrooper saw a need for Chicano entertainment, not only on the stage but in the recording studio as well. Cardenas grew up on rhythm and blues and early on aspired to be a musician but now his goal was to promote the musicians in the community. The first group that he approached was the Romancers band which, featured singer/songwriter Max Uballez whom Cardenas saw as the next Ritchie Valens and the future of Chicano rock 'n roll. Cardenas had made some in-roads into Hollywood's recording business as a freelancing A&R man for Crown Records giving him some insight into what it took to produce a record. As an A&R man for Crown Records Cardenas canvassed neighborhood *cantinas* looking for *mariachi* groups, that he could bring into the recording studio. When Cardenas started looking for rock 'n roll groups to manage he simply replaced the *cantinas* with the community CYO's, teen centers and recreation centers in and around Lincoln Heights and Boyle Heights this time signing up artist like Robert and Rey, Yolanda Lea, the Jaguars, the Heartbreakers, the Royal Jesters and the Romancers. In the nearby San Gabriel Valley he discovered the Premiers, the Blendells and the Atlantics.

In 1962 Billy Cardenas met record producer Eddie Davis. Davis had a small independent record company called Faro Records, which opened its doors in 1958. His foray into pop music had been somewhat of a failure. However, rather than giving up he decided to take his company in another direction. Faro Records started its second incarnation in 1961 when KRLA DJ Dick Moreland suggested to Davis that he record a duo from Oxnard, CA. Davis took Phil and Harv and their band the Mixtures into the recording studio and recorded **Darling**. He then proceeded to book the Mixtures at the Rainbow Gardens in Pomona exposing the group to an almost exclusively Chicano audience. Although Cardenas had been taking groups to Bob Keane at Del-Fi Records (the Romancers and the Heartbreakers) it was a struggle dealing with Keane. With Eddie Davis Cardenas found someone that embraced Chicano culture and strived to give the Eastside musicians a forum, which they could use to express their creativity.

For the next couple of years Cardenas and Davis were instrumental in promoting the future stars of East Los Angeles. Through their hard work and financial backing young artists were able to perfect their craft and create their unique brand of music that would eventually become world renowned through groups like Tierra, and El Chicano.

The Romancers

> "One of our first gigs as the Romancers was at a house party in Pacoima. At the time we were doing some Ritchie Valens tunes and my voice was very similar to his. So we are doing this gig and we go into "Donna" next thing we know there is some commotion in the back you know tables and chairs moving around. Then some guys come up to us and say hey you'd better pack up and leave that was Ritchie's brother and he's gonna go get his boys and come back. As we were driving away I was sitting in the back seat with my head back looking at the night stars and I thought to myself 'hey they think I sounded like Ritchie Valens.'"
> Max Uballez-guitar / vocalist:
> Los Angeles [*Romancers, Macando*]

The Romancers recording background vocals. L-R: Albert "Bobby" Hernandez, Manuel "Magoo" Rodriguez, Ralph Ventura and Johnny Diaz. *Courtesy of Max Uballez.*

The Romancers were possibly the most creative of East Los Angeles's first group of bands to come up in 1962. Creative in the way they developed their music and creative in the way that they promoted themselves and the groups that were part of their musical circle, which included the Heartbreakers, Sal and Marge, the Occasions, and Robert and Rey. Initially the Romancers started their ascent up the Eastside's music ladder like all of the other groups of the time covering obscure R&B tunes and popular rock 'n roll hits. However, as Uballez started writing and producing his own music the Romancer sound developed into music that was unique and in many ways ahead of the curve. The group was probably the first to step away from the orchestral set-up that their contemporaries like the Blue Satins, the Enchantments and Johnny and the Crowns had. The Romancers set-up was more of an early rock band with horns, possibly the first "true" garage band to come out of East Los Angeles. Without the knowledge of music's inner workings Uballez was determined to have music be his outlet and early on certain events in his life seemed to push him toward his goal. "I was going to Nightingale Jr. High and one of the classes I had was band. I wanted to learn the saxophone but they gave me the violin. That wasn't for me so they put me in choir. Because I was so disruptive they put me up front where the teacher could keep me under control. At the time I also started to write poems." Uballez also remembers his early inspiration being the

left: The **Romancers** top row-Ralph Ventura, Manuel "Magoo" Rodriguez bottom row- Cesar ?, Max Uballez, Manuel Mosqueda. *Courtesy of Max Uballez*.

away an old guitar from a pawnshop. Whenever the *mariachi* group from down the street practiced on the porch Max would sit on the bottom step and strum along. "Sitting on the rail of his front porch was KiKi, my neighbor, singing with an entire *mariachi* band playing along . . . guitars, violin, trumpets." recalls Uballez, "I ran home, returned with my guitar in hand and sat on the steps, discreetly out of view. I focused on the guitarist's fingers, trying to learn the chords, and play along. KiKi moved away a short time after this and I never saw him again. Several months later, I heard he had made a recording. I purchased KiKi's record, **La Noche y Tu** by Eliseo (KiKi) Gonzalez and the Mariachi Los Camperos . . . a magnificent recording. I remember the day, holding that 45 record in my hands and daydreaming of someday holding "my" record in "my hands." These were events that helped shape Uballez' concept of what the music in his head should sound like. "For a long time I didn't have a record player so if I heard something cool on the radio I'd go home and try to work it out on my guitar, somehow," he said. "So a lot of times the chords were wrong, the rhythms were wrong, the changes were wrong but they all cumulated to create a certain foundation of how I felt the music. I was interpreting music but I wasn't aware of how I was doing that because I was just expressing myself in my own way." Eventually Uballez's fingerprints would be all over many of the Rampart recordings the Blendells, David and Ruben, Cannibal and the Headhunters and the Atlantics were all co-produced by him.

In 1962 Max Uballez was tangled up in the legal red tape of the music business. He recalls: "I had recorded **Rock Little Darling** as Max Uballez for Bob Keane at Del-Fi. When we recorded for Magic Circle the record was going to be released as Max Uballez.

group harmony sound of the fifties doo-wop groups, a sound that played a key role in several of the Romancers' recordings. "We would hang out at a friend's house in Lincoln Heights." recalls Uballez, "He had a record player so we would buy a gallon of wine and go over to his house and listen to his brother's records. The one album that really caught my ear was *The Paragons Meet the Jesters*."

Using an old reel tape recorder Uballez rigged up a sound system that he could sing through, next he laid

Russ Reagan the record promoter for Magic Circle said my name was too ethnic and I would never get airplay so they changed my name to Maximilian. The record went on KFWB on the first day it was released. Bob Keane then claimed he planned to release **You'd Better** and had the rights to it. I was forced to go back to Del-Fi and released a single on Del-Fi and Magic Circle responded with a law suit and I was banned from recording as a vocalist for five years.

At this point the Romancers were probably the most influential group in East Los Angeles especially among the younger groups coming up, so this was a set back for the early Eastside music scene in general. Once again Max, Billy and the Romancers had to depend on their creativity to overcome their setback. In 1963 they recorded two instrumental dance albums for Bob Keane *Do The Slauson* and *Do The Swim*. "We had to take advantage of the opportunities that were before us," recalls Uballez, "We initially went in to record **Slauson Shuffle** but when Keane asked me 'what else do you have kid?' we just kept on playing, making stuff up as we went along." The LPs showcase the sax work of Armando Mora, the guitar work of Andy Tesso and in many ways, because all of the songs are instrumentals the Romancers bare their souls and you see their inspirations laid before you, honking R&B sax, Latin rhythms, chugging and sometimes bluesy guitar riffs. The album, which was written, and arranged in a span of four hours is the first album ever recorded by a Hispanic band from Southern California.

Understanding that their options were limited as far as being able to get gigs with promoters like Al Perez who was promoting shows at the Shrine Exposition Hall, Max Uballez and Billy Cardenas created their own solution. Uballez organized a girls' social club called the Romancerettes, which became the conduit through which the bands could get their music to the people. Through the Romancerettes, Uballez and Cardenas were able to rent locations like the Carpenters Hall, the GiGi Hall, Lincoln Heights Gym and other small dance halls in Lincoln Heights and Boyle Heights. This move created a new social movement by local teens for local teens one that would give young musicians an opportunity to express their musical creativity.

It is uncertain that Cardenas and Uballez knew at the time that what they were creating in 1962 would grow into a network of layers that supported each other including musicians, youth social clubs, and community business owners (tailors, photographers, record stores, etc.) each helping to create the area's music scene. "By the time I did move to Los Angeles groups like the Romancers were already there and they had already been doing their thing," recalls Little Ray Jimenez. "Thee Midniters were not even formed until I got together with Willie, the Ceballos guys and all of a sudden at the same time the Beatles were happening, Motown was happening, and then we came onto the scene. So we created this phenomenon of energy but it was just another slice. It took guys like the Romancers and groups like that to get there first so when we came on it was perfect timing."

Eventually the Romancers were performing three or four gigs a night, which was logistically possible because many of the halls in the area were relatively close to each other. The GiGi Hall in Lincoln Heights was approximately four miles from the Carpenters Hall in Boyle Heights, which was three miles from the Paramount and Casa Mexicano, which were about five miles from the Little Union Hall.

Between 1964 and 1966 Uballez and the Romancers, had gone through several personnel changes, and recorded a series of singles for Eddie Davis' Linda label. Unlike many of the bands during this period the Romancers were writing and arranging most of their own material, of the ten sides they recorded for Linda nine were Max Uballez compositions. The group was so musically progressive that their recordings seem a bit out of place next to some of the other Eastside groups, yet it was their eccentric creativity in the studio that gave groups like the Blendells, the Atlantics, the Majestics and Cannibal and the Headhunters that little added ingredient that gives a song its identity i.e; the muffled trumpet line on **La La La La La,** and the *mariachi* strings on **Girl of My Dreams.** Jimmy Meza of the Atlantics recalls working with Max Uballez on the recording of **Beaver Shot** a minor hit for the Atlantics in 1965. "I remember exactly where we recorded **Beaver Shot.** We went to a mansion up in Pomona and in one of the rooms they had all of this recording equipment. Well Max [Uballez] made it up right there on the spot. He voiced out the parts for the bass player, then he had me follow him on the guitar, then he told the horns what to do, I swear he created it right there on the spot."

Despite all of their musical talent and exceptional recordings the Romancers were unable to break out of East Los Angeles. Their remake of **My Heart Cries** a song previously recorded by Etta James and Harvey Fuqua, made an impact on the local charts. A tune about the universal power of love that the Romancers worked into what some could argue is the greatest two minutes and twenty-seven seconds to come out of East Los Angeles.

"Magoo the Romancers' bass player, came in one day and said there's this great song **My Heart Cries** that we should be doing," recalls Uballez. "Magoo who's a great musician played the piano line of the original recording on his bass and then he basically hummed out the melody and the words. We used the actual chord progressions because he knew them, to this day I don't know what they are I just know we go up a key, down a key, and back up a key."

It is the interaction between the vocal harmonies, Bobby Hernandez's melodic guitar lines and Max Uballez's passionate singing that give the song an almost a mystical feeling. "When we started working it out that day we didn't have the recording we just had Magoo showing us the parts." Uballez recalls, "Then Bobby Hernandez created that guitar line because he just couldn't get the rhythm it's different than on the original record and Magoo kept saying 'nah! You're playing it wrong' and Bobby would say 'that's the way I feel it.' The guitar line is the thing that sews the whole thing together it's close to the original but the original is more staccato." The recording session was done with David Brill (drums), Bobby Hernandez (guitar), Magoo (bass), Max Uballez (lead vocals, guitar). As the group worked out the song Uballez envisioned it having *mariachi* strings and trumpets, things that were unavailable to them, then Eddie Davis suggested that they do those parts with voices. "So what we did is we did the ooohs and aaahs using the lines I had in my head for strings. I saw this big grandiose thing as two counter melodies of two lovers coming together, different but they worked together. The song is enveloped by these two different layers descriptive of the two lovers. Bobby Hernandez and Eddie Davis are doing the top parts but Eddie is doing a falsetto thing similar to what the Beach Boys were doing." Uballez continues, "Personally what touched

Reprise Records leased the **Blendells** single La La La La La from Rampart Records for national distribution. As the record's popularity grew it crossed the Atlantic to European markets. This is the picture sleeve for the French pressing of the Blendells EP.

The Blendells

The first national hit to come out of the Eastside was the Blendells' 1964 version of Little Stevie Wonder's **La La La La La.** The Blendells' version peaked at 92 on the national charts but as Sal Murillo put it "It did well where it was supposed to." Besides being number one on KRLA in Los Angeles it was big in Dallas, Philadelphia, Chicago, Phoenix, Albuquerque and New York. The band began its evolution while Mike Rincon was attending Cathedral High School located just south of Lincoln Heights in the Chinatown area of Los Angeles. Rincon, who had grown up on his parents' jump and swing records, and was also heavily influenced by his brother's rock 'n roll records, was given his first guitar when he was eleven years old. Initially the group was made up of guys from the school band but eventually as the group progressed. The less dedicated were replaced by those willing to sacrifice their afternoons and weekends for rehearsals and non paying gigs. Rincon (bass) and Ron Chipres (drums) recruited Rudy Valona (guitar) from another local group called the Ambassadors eventually the group was joined by Tommy Esparza (rhythm guitar) and Don Cardenas (sax) and three singers.

Running on a parallel course that was about to intersect with Rincon was Sal Murillo who had been singing on the local teen circuit with Chicano duo Robert and Rey as the Occasions before teaming up with Marge Cabera. Sal and Marge, Robert and Rey, the Occasions as well as the Heartbreakers were part of the Romancers' circle something that might be considered the original "Eastside Revue." Sal Murillo credits the Romancers for his success: "Our idols were Max Uballez and the Romancer band because they were like two or three years older than us. We got a lot of tutoring from those guys." The Blendells

me about the song is that it's talking about a love that is all consuming and larger than the whole universe. I mean 'I was like a Shepherd boy. . . .' You think to yourself out in the wilderness standing on some hill with a bunch of sheep and you're seeing the wonder of the universe around you. For me it touched a chord because all *ranchera* music and *mariachi* music has that really expansive I love you 'til the death and blood, and the heart and my whole life and is so emotional. Even though there is a lot of affection in American music there is no way to translate what I feel when I listen to a Mexican love song they are always so immense that it's to big to express."

Faro recording group the Blendells

started playing at weddings, *quinceañeras* and like many of the local bands dances at the Paramount and Little Union halls. Around 1963 Mike Rincon turned over management duties to Billy Cardenas who kept the Blendells busy on the Eastside circuit, all the while the group started to gel and become one of the more popular groups. "Things started to move real fast and things just started to fall into place for the group. After the group had a blow-up with their three singers it was Cardenas's idea to bring Murillo onboard. "I was singing with Marge Cabera when the Blendells had some problem with their lead singer so Billy suggested that I sing with them."

Each member of the Blendells was responsible for introducing new material for the band to play. Mike Rincon described the selection process to Mike Dugo of the *Lance Monthly*. "We would each take turns selecting our material and when Ron introduced **La La La La La** to the band there was some resistance. But he insisted that's what he wanted to do and it was law; [so] we did it." The song was inserted into the group's playlist right at the time Cardenas was taking a harder look at the group he noticed the Blendells growing popularity and a need to get them on record so he invited Eddie Davis out to La Puente to catch the group's performance. Sal Murillo remembers that night "Eddie Davis heard us do **La La La La La** and said 'I think you guys have something there." Within a couple of weeks the band was in the recording studio.

The Blendells took a simple and obscure Stevie Wonder song that came from Wonder's first album and seemed to be a showcase for Little Stevie's drumming. The Blendells gave the song depth and appeal with elements of big band jazz inserted into it. **La La La La La** is one of those simple songs that you listen to once then you can't get it out of your head. From Chipres's tom-tom Indian beat intro backing Murillo who's telling you these cats you are about to listen to are bad, to the muffled trumpet solo, **La La La La La** is a strong example of how Chicano teen groups were fusing all of their influences; big band, blues, jazz and rock 'n roll. Like almost everything that came out of the Eastside during this period **La La La La La** happened by chance. It was a collaboration of the area's musical community that starts to build momentum before anyone involved knows what the final outcome will be. In the studio you had Billy Cardenas and Murillo improvising the opening lyrics,

Cannibal and the Headhunters on top of the "banana" a yellow and white Ford airport shuttle used during road trips. Ambulances, hearses, and postal vans were also popular among traveling bands because there was room for equipment and musicians. *Courtesy of Albert Garcia.*

Cardenas suggesting that Ralph Ventura who was on loan from the Romancers muffle his trumpet giving it a jazzy feel and the girls providing the background noise came compliments of the Chevelles car club- a community effort. "In fact I was in high school when **La La La La La** came out," recalls Murillo. "I took a demo to school and we played it during lunch period and everyone was saying 'who's that?' Six weeks later it was number one on KRLA it just happened real fast from coast to coast."

Eddie Davis leased **La La La La La** to Reprise Records for national distribution. However as the record was climbing up the charts things started to fall apart. The band had a national hit and naturally friends and family thought they should have been rolling in money, so the guys started to get bombarded with ideas, which eventually turned into discontent. Sal Murillo's father had been partners with Billy Cardenas in promoting dances, however when Cardenas hooked up with Eddie Davis the relationship changed and a three-way struggle over the Blendells eventually caused the break-up of the band.

Murillo was the first to go, followed by Valona and Tommy Esparza. The band had already recorded **Dance with Me** so the Romancers had to finish the single with **Get Your Baby** for the flip side. However Rincon had already packed up what was left of the Blendells and moved to another booking agency leaving Davis and Cardenas without a group to promote the single.

Cannibal and the Headhunters

One of the most popular groups associated with the Faro/Rampart record label was Cannibal and the Headhunters, The group's top selling single **Land of a Thousand Dances** transcended the boundaries of East Los Angeles and became a national hit in 1965. The group consisted of brothers Bobby and Jojo Jaramillo, Richard "Scar" Lopez and lead singer Frankie "Cannibal" Garcia. Lopez and the Jaramillo bothers grew up in and around the Ramona Gardens Housing projects and it was there that they picked up the art of singing harmony. "The projects were really a black neighborhood at the time so black music was a big influence on us," recalls Robert Jaramillo. "There was a group that lived in the projects called the Showcases Pops, U.C. Tommy, and Hubbert. As they walked home from school they would be singing accappella and there would be a crowd of people following them. Then we would follow them into the projects and watch them perform. I did this for a while then James Hubbert took me under his wing and taught me how to harmonize, he taught me all of the parts, bass, baritone, tenor and so on."

While attending Lincoln High School in 1961 Richard Lopez invited his friend Bobby Jaramillo to

Cannibal and the Headhunters on stage.

join the men's choir at the school shortly after they decided to form a singing group and along with Ernie Loana they became Bobby and the Classics. Before long Bobby's brother Joe joined the group, according to Jaramillo, "We were from Hazard [a gang base in the projects], I was a member of the Scorpions and "Jo Jo" was in the Diablos, which were the younger guys. We didn't hang around together much but he was the only one that could sing those high notes like on **Lovers Island** so we recruited him into our group. Because he was younger than us, he was really proud to be part of the group."

Cannibal and the Headhunters. *Courtesy of Albert Garcia.*

On a suggestion from Tommy Keyes of the Showcases the Classics tried out a friend of his who was living in the Aliso Village housing projects. Keyes's friend was a kid who was attending Jackson High School named Frankie "Lil' Cannibal" Garcia. He had been singing in the Boyle Heights area with the Royal Jesters, however they had just broken up and Garcia was without a group. Garcia had been given the street name "Lil' Cannibal" in honor of his older brother "Big Cannibal." As the story goes, Pelón, [Frankie's brother], was jumped by a rival gang while walking through the community park. Having taken away a knife that one of his assailants was brandishing Pelón turned it on them and when the dust settled he was the only one standing. As the story spread through the neighborhood he was given the name "Cannibal."

As is custom in the barrio Frankie then became "Little Cannibal."

With a hungry lead singer and three dedicated harmony singers Bobby and the Classics started to make the rounds performing wherever they could get a gig. Eventually they came under the management of Billy Cardenas who suggested that they change their name to Cannibal and the Headhunters. One of the songs that they were performing was Chris Kenner's **Land of a Thousand Dances,** a song, which had its roots in the gospel music of New Orleans. "We started doing **Land of a Thousand Dances** the way Chris Kenner did it, then while we were rehearsing at the Rhythm Room in Fullerton it all changed," recalls Jaramillo. "The band started playing and Frankie went blank, the band kept going over the intro and then he finally started going na, na, na, na, na . . . na, na, na, na, na, na. We had hand signs on stage so Frankie gave us the sign and we just started doing what he was doing in unison and Eddie Davis said 'Hey! That's a hit.' So now we had to learn it that way." Several groups were using the Chris Kenner tune in their repertoire however, Garcia's misstep created a mad rush to record their version of **Land of a Thousand Dances** first among groups in Southern California then by soul singer Wilson Pickett.

While Eddie Davis was busy making arrangements for his group to record a live version at the upcoming battle of the bands at East Los Angeles College, well-known disc jockey Casey Kasem heard Ronnie and the Pomona Casuals performing the song complete with the Headhunters new intro. An excited Kasem called his good friend Eddie Torres and suggested that Thee Midniters get into the recording studio and record **Land of a Thousand Dances.** According to Lopez and Jaramillo the Headhunters were sched-

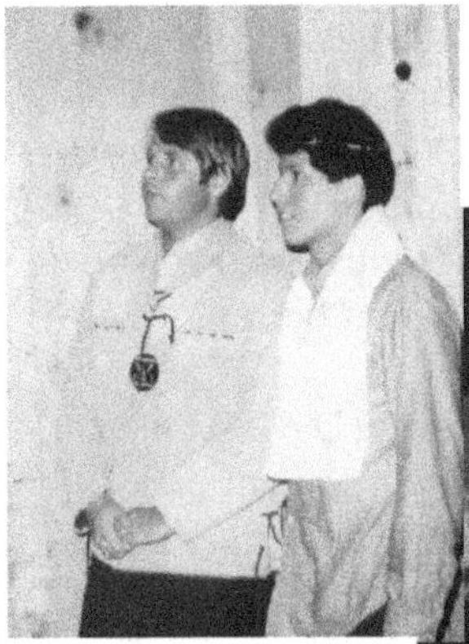

1. Carl Wilson [**Beach Boys**] & Cannibal
2. Bill Medley [**Righteous Bros**] & Cannibal 1967
3. Cannibal & Smokey [**Miracles**] 1967
4. Pal McCartney [**Beatles**] & Cannibal 1965
5. The Headhunters with Brian Epstein [Beatles manager] during the Beatles' 1965 tour.
6. Cindy Birdsong [**Supremes**], Cannibal & Mary Wilson [**Supremes**] 1967
7. Rabbit, JoJo, **Joan Baez** & Cannibal
8. above promotional photo from the *Record Rack* 1965 L-R Frankie "Cannibal" Garcia, Richard "Scar" Lopez, Robert "Rabbit" Jaramillo & JoJo Jaramillo
All photos courtesy of Albert Garcia.

uled to record **Land of a Thousand Dances** at the battle of the bands but they were locked out of the auditorium by Eddie Torres who was managing Thee Midniters. When Davis got wind of what was going on he rushed the Headhunters into Stereo Masters Studio in Hollywood and with help from the Blendells, friends and family who provided controlled shouting they recorded their own version. Session producer Max Uballez adds some notes on the session "Cardenas was going into the studio to record "Land of a Thousand Dances" with the Pomona Casuals, for Bob Keane . . . .The Rhythm Playboys [also under Cardenas' management] were the band scheduled to back Frankie (Garcia) on his version however, Billy Cardenas who had a falling out with Davis called the band and told them they would never work again if they did the session. Bass player Billy Watson was the only one that brushed aside Cardenas' threat and showed up for the session."

Although Thee Midniters and the Pomona Casuals released their versions first, it was the Headhunters' version that caught on across the country propelling them into the national spotlight. Bobby Jaramillo credits Rudy Benevides with saving the record from obscurity "When we first released the record it had an intro with Cannibal singing 'You know I feel alright children. . . .' But the record wasn't going anywhere. So Eddie went to see Rudy at Flash Record Store to see if he had any ideas. Rudy suggested that Eddie knock off eleven seconds from the intro. So now the record starts with a drum and bass dance beat and the record took off." Once the record broke, life for the Headhunters changed dramatically. First came the teen television programs like Dick Clark's *American Bandstand*, the *Hullabaloo* show in New York and the rock 'n roll shows that were crisscrossing the country. It was at one of these shows that Wilson Pickett heard their version of **Land of a Thousand Dances**. According to Lopez "Wilson Pickett was really impressed with our version He told Eddie Davis, 'I am going to cover that song and take it to number one.'" Pickett not only took it to number one it became his biggest all time seller.

Things between the Headhunters and Davis would eventually sour and by 1967 the group stopped performing together. However, for two years they showed the world that four kids from the projects could not only hold their own on stage with the Beatles [who at the time were taking the world by storm] but they could win over audiences whose fascination with the Beatles made it difficult for any opening act. They managed to cross cultural barriers and entertain black, white, and Chicano audiences and get the same enthusiastic response.

Thee Midniters

> "I've often thought through the years how much raw talent there was in East L.A. However, I thought that the East L.A. bands were too influenced by soul music. They started by imitating others, then they started imitating themselves. That's where I see the difference between Thee Midniters and the rest because Thee Midniters did do something unique. Willie didn't try to sound like anyone else. They created their own sound."
>
> Ron Lemos- guitarist:
> Los Angeles [Thee Runabouts]

Thee Midniters Willie Garcia and Benny Lopez.

Thursday, January 25, 2007 a crowd of about 250 people gathered inside of Amoeba Records in Hollywood for a promotional show. The crowd, a mix of "rockabilly" kids, punk rockers and silver-haired men and women in their late-fifties were there to see a group, which has been a fixture in East Los Angeles for the past forty-three years. The kids colorfully tattooed from their wrist to their neck with jet black hair forming the perfect pompadour politely mingled in with the fifty-something other half who clutched old albums, photos, and posters as if they were family heirlooms. They were all here to see Little Willie G and Thee Midniters who were promoting the release of their new Norton Records compilation album. Unlike shows normally performed for the *veteranos* on the Eastside circuit or at oldies dances this show was a hard driving show that included only one ballad **The Town I Live In** a song requested via a shout-out from the crowd by a *veterano* who made the trip to the westside of town to hear the group's popular sentimental ballads. However, the night's set was a high-powered mix, which included **Love Special Delivery, I Found a Peanut, Empty Heat** and **Never Knew I Had It So Bad** songs that spotlight the diversity and creativity of Thee Midniters during the sixties.

Those in the crowd who grew up with Thee Midniters music reminisced about the good old days when the group was performing at dance halls throughout Southern California, while those who were not even born yet listened with envy. Silvia, an energetic woman in her mid-fifties who grew up in Compton, remembered going to the Huntington Ballroom to see Willie G. "He was our Frank Sinatra," she said. "He was our star and he brought so much happiness to our lives."

Forty-three years ago Benny and Thee Midniters stepped onto the stage at the CYO hall on Brooklyn Ave. in Boyle Heights and introduced themselves to the world. This early version of the group consisted of Benny Ceballos (manager & congas), Larry Rendon (sax), George Salazar (drums), Raul Ceballos (guitar), and Willie Garcia (vocals). Bass player Benny Lopez who had studied under Bill Taggert at Salesian High and had been playing with Johnny Gamboa's Crowns came on board shortly after. Gamboa and Lopez had been friends long before their high school days however, Lopez thought that the Crowns were too jazz-oriented and wanted to move on. This was the group that Eddie Torres booked into the CYO in

1963. By the time Thee Midniters were performing their first teen dances at St. Alphonsus Auditorium Lopez had recruited Romeo Prado (valve trombone), another one of Bill Taggert's disciples.

In 1964 an ambitious sixteen-year-old singer from Delano, California moved to Los Angeles in order to boost his singing career. Ramon Jimenez was the son of farmworkers who had come to America during the *Bracero* Program of the forties. He had been singing with a Delano R&B group called the Rhythm Kings since he was eleven years old and the popularity of the Rhythm Kings in the San Joaquin Valley had made him somewhat of a star. "When I finally moved to L.A. I was in my sophomore year." Recalls Jimenez, "I was real ambitious and in Delano you're either going to work the fields or you're going to work at Carl's Shoe Stores selling shoes. I was making good money for a kid my age performing at the Rainbow Garden in Fresno, the Convention Center in Sacramento, and all of the little towns and cities like Visalia, and Stockton. Even though we [Rhythm Kings] were very popular throughout the San Joaquin Valley I needed to make the move if I was going to make it." Jimenez had been spending time in Los Angeles and had performed at shows that Johnny Otis and Art Laboe were sponsoring. His first recording came in 1961 for Dore Records. "I did my first recording with the help of Ed Cobb who was the bass singer of the Four Preps," recalls Jimenez. " He saw me singing in Sacramento at the Convention Center, I think he was the next act. After hearing me he got my name and then he picked me up in Delano and we went to Hollywood where I recorded **There Is Something on Your Mind**.

Once he arrived it did not take Ray long to get involved in East Los Angeles's young music scene. It was his sophomore year in high school and before his first week at Garfield High was over he would be a member of a car club and lead singer of a band. "When I moved to L.A., literally the first week I joined the Stockers Car Club and I didn't even have a car," recalls Jimenez. "They were just a bunch of guys with no cars and the main guy was Benny Ceballos who really wasn't a musician he just played the congas and he had a group called Benny and the Midniters. A guy who used to live in Delano and who saw me sing there, saw me walking through school. This guy is all excited and tells me 'Hey, man you've got to join this car club and they have this band' and so he brought me to one of their meetings. They asked me to sing which, I did and they said 'wow!" This was a big boost for the up and coming Midniters. They now had an experienced singer with the natural ability to sing soul music and to do it with the passion and energy of a veteran soul singer.

As the group evolved they attracted experienced, more professional musicians that were trained under Bill Taggert and Johnny Gamboa. Both Romeo Prado and Larry Rendon could re-arrange the horn lines to the songs they were covering to fit Thee Midniters sound. The group also practiced constantly with new material from the pop and soul fields. A big plus for them was having an experienced singer that was willing to work with the raw talent possessed by Willie Garcia. Jimenez knew how to use a professional band he knew the piano, and harmonies. During his short stay with the group Jimenez and Garcia developed a good working relationship so that by the time Jimenez moved on Garcia was a soulful, confident singer with a large fan base. "Willie was about two years older than me and he could drive so he would pick me up," recalls Jimenez. "I was still pretty

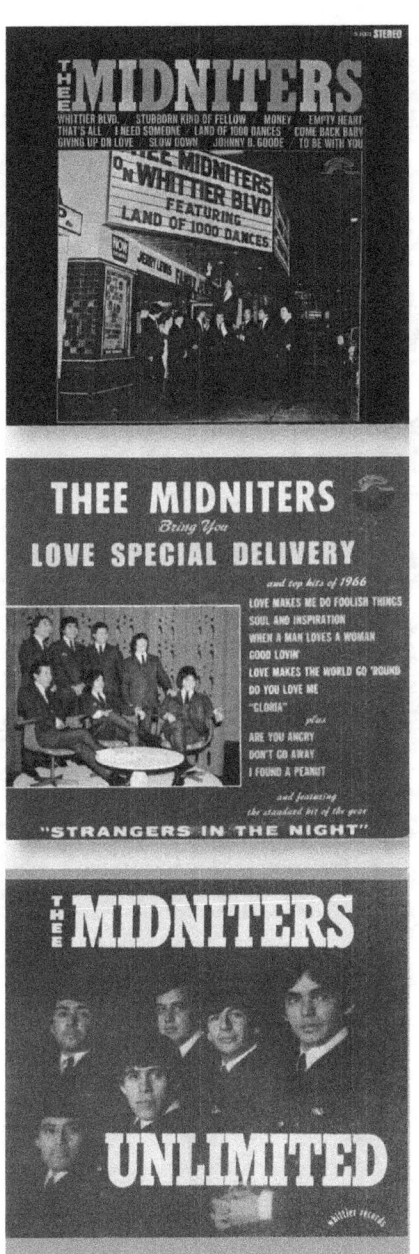

much country-fied but I had been around gigging for so long that I was a little more sophisticated in my performance, I knew piano, I knew about harmonies so I started working with Willie on his harmonies, we became like brothers. After I missed a show because I was stuck in Delano they realized that they could do it without me. I was ready to form my own group and they had Willie so everything worked out."

In Eddie Torres the group had a manager that put all of his efforts into promoting his group. Torres was not looking to build an empire but with Thee Midniters' talent, he did just that. From their first show in 1963 until 1969 Torres dedicated himself to promoting Thee Midniters. Booking them with some of the most popular R&B and pop groups of the time. From his apartment above the Golden Gate Theater on the corner of Whittier and Atlantic he directed his operations. After concerts and dances anyone involved with Torres's productions would rendezvous at Brandy's Coffee Shop for coffee, dinner and to discus the day's events. "Eddie held court at Brandy's," recalls Ron Lemos. "Everyone who was anyone would be there sometimes until 4:00 am." Rosie Hamlin [Rosie and the Originals] remembers Eddie Torres as a tireless promoter. "Promoting was his life." She said, "If we didn't have a show he was driving around with a trunk full of posters and flyers promoting the next show."

The excitement caused by the many groups that emerged from 1963 through 1966 created an atmosphere of musical activity only seen in sixties teen movies. "When we played behind Jonson's Market on a flatbed truck, that's when I knew we were hot." recalls drummer George Salazar, "After our show the girls started chasing us down Whittier Blvd. trying to

Thee Midniters. *Author's archives.*

tear our clothes off. I think Eddie Torres set all that up."

It was not uncommon for Thee Midniters to perform two or three shows a night. After each performance the group would walk away from their equipment and roadies would pack everything up and get it to the next location. According to Torres if the next location was halfway across the state they would fly. "Art Laboe called me one day to ask me how many Midniter groups there were." He said, "I told him 'one' and he asked 'How can you have them in San Diego and San Jose the same night?' I said to him, 'We fly." Torres had a lady friend at Tri-City Air Port in San Bernardino and she used to fly them sometimes to Salinas, San Jose and then Fresno.

One of the few Eastside groups that could rock the house with dance tunes like **Whittier Blvd, Gloria** and **Love Special Delivery** and then woo them with ballads like **Sad Girl**, **The Town I Live In** and **Giving Up on Love**. Each member had input into what the band recorded and as their musical taste varied from the Rolling Stones, to John Coltrane, to Nat King Cole there was quite a myriad of material to chose from. It was Willie G, however who brought in those obscure ballads: **Come Back Baby** (Roddie Joy), **Giving Up on Love** (Jerry Butler), **The Town I Live In** (Mckinley Mitchell) and of course **Sad Girl** (Jay Wiggins) were all little known ballads that the group popularized among Chicano teens. One of the group's most popular ballads was **That's All** a song which Dick Hugg "Huggy Boy" used to end his nightly shows on radio station KALI from 1965-1967.

Thee Midniters released the first of four albums in 1965, which featured eleven covers of hits and obscure R&B songs. It also featured a tribute to the L.A.'s hottest cruising spot **Whittier Blvd** a song written by Benny Lopez and Roy Marquez. Starting with Ronnie Figueroa's *grito* (yell) "aríba! aríba!" **Whittier Blvd** is two minutes of rock 'n roll madness with a taste of Latin soul. Shortly after the album release Lopez departed, making way for Jimmy Espinosa, a Salesian High alum and a veteran of several local groups including Johnny Gamboa's Crowns. In May of 1966 **Love Special Delivery** b/w **Don't Go Away** from the L.P. of the same name got its debut on L.A. radio station KRLA. **L.S.D.** stayed on the lower half of KRLA's most requested list for eight weeks.

Radio personality Casey Kasem befriended the group in the mid-sixties and helped to get the band on shows at the Hollywood Bowl, Anaheim Stadium and the Shrine Auditorium. Although, Thee Midniters were extremely popular in Chicano communities from San Diego to Fresno, Los Angeles to El Paso they were never able to attain national attention. In 1969 after several years of performing live shows throughout California and neighboring states Willie G left for a career as a solo artist.

Although an era had come to an end Thee Midniters were never lost in the memory of Los Angeles's Chicano community, after all they were considered the "Beatles" of East L.A. Kept alive through the efforts of Jimmy Espinosa the group continued to perform at oldies shows and have recently regained their status as one of East Los Angeles's most popular groups.

Little Ray & the Progressions

> "Little Ray was really into music. I don't know why he's not a giant in the music

business. He was like between James Brown and the Righteous Brothers he was so energetic with his up-tempo stuff and then he would do these emotional ballads. He was really into trying to make this thing work."

George Salazar- Drummer:
Los Angeles [Thee Midniters]

With Little Willie G and Thee Midniters on their way to becoming icons on the Eastside music scene Little Ray set out to build his own band. With Salesian alum and Bill Taggert protégé Tony Garcia as his bandleader they built one of the most dynamic bands to come out of East Los Angeles. The Progressions consisted of Tony Garcia (tenor sax), Joe Urzua (baritone sax), "Bones" Ramos (trumpet, French horn), John Pride (keyboards), Mike "Bozo" Rodriguez and Marshall Tavarez (bass). From Delano Jimenez brought in Clarence Playa (guitar, vocals), and Tony Escalante (guitar). "We were trying to emulate the Motown sound and the groups that we loved," recalls Jimenez. "We came from so many backgrounds my folks loved *ranchera* music and I was born into that and my brother loved rhythm and blues. One of the very first albums that I ever heard was Art Laboe's *Oldies but Goodies Vol. 1*, which had the Jaguars' **The Way You Look Tonight** and the Penguins' **Earth Angel** so it was my first subliminal thing that got captured in my psyche."

Unlike most of the vocalists at the time Jimenez had already learned how to use passion in his approach to the songs he was singing. "I always like the middle of the road R&B music like Motown." He said, "But I also dug the hard thing coming out of Stax and the real black gospel music. One of my favorite records of all times is Ray Charles singing **Drownin' in My Own Tears.** It is live and it's the greatest performance I ever heard of anybody completely giving themselves free. If you are a singer, you say to yourself 'How can I ever be that great?' It's like Sam Cooke with the Soul Stirrers when you hear him sing you just want to quit, I mean, how can anyone be so good. At the same time it challenges you and that's what you want as a singer."

By the time Ray was eighteen years old he had already accumulated more than ten years as a performer and had worked with some of the top R&B artists of the time including Billy Preston, Vernon Green, Jackie Wilson and James Brown. With his new group he was now able to use what he had learned through the years, synchronizing his moves and dramatic expressions to his band. Barritone sax player Joe Urzua remembers being on stage with Jimenez "Out of all of the singers from East L.A. Little Ray was the only one that was a true performer." He said, "When he sang **I Who Have Nothing** he would go down on one knee, hold out one hand in front of him, close his eyes, with his hands he would mimic certain feelings and he would sing very emotional." To this day people that saw the Progressions on stage swear that Little Ray would break down and cry when he was singing **I Who Have Nothing.**

With the Progressions band built Jimenez took another idea from what he had learned through the years. "I put together my own revue called The Little Ray Revue." Says Jimenez, "I had a girl group called the Rayettes, I had two vocal groups the Four Clefs and the Epics, I wanted to create my own scene I wanted to do the Motown thing." The Progressions also had Clarence Playa a singer/guitarist from Delano who like Jimenez had come to Los Angeles looking for a break. Although he never recorded, Playa became a favorite in East Los Angeles "In Delano Clarence lived real close to me, he was a little older than me and he was a good singer so we always had this little friendly competition thing going."

At first Ray was going from gig to gig with his brother driving him around. "Every weekend I would do sometimes four shows a night. I would start of at the American Legion at 8:00 the very first show to go on." Recalls Jimenez, "I'd do five songs, get some money, my brothers would be waiting for me in the car. Then we'd head out to the Huntington Ballroom do a half hour set, so we still had two ours left. Then we'd go to the Kennedy Hall, then over to El Monte or Santa Ana." Once the Progressions joined him, his brother bought a hearse. "It was a '61 Buick." Recalls Urzua, "It had air suspension and the rollers for the casket were cool 'cause we could roll the equipment in. We could fit all the gear and three guys in there and the rest would go in cars."

In 1965 the group recorded Ben E. King's **I Who Have Nothing,** which became a hit for Little Ray but changed his life dramatically. Around the same time Cannibal and the Headhunters were touring with the Beatles and Frankie "Cannibal" Garcia asked Jimenez to join the Headhunters. "I already had my career and really couldn't leave what I was doing." He said, "Looking back I'm glad I did what I did but it would have been a good experience too. Later on they got signed with Seymour Stein and Date Records, which was part of Columbia." When Stein asked Garcia if he knew of anyone else Garcia suggested Little Ray. Ray signed with Columbia Records but this meant moving to New York. The allure of the Big Apple and the idea that he would be able to write and produce was too much of a temptation so he took the chance,

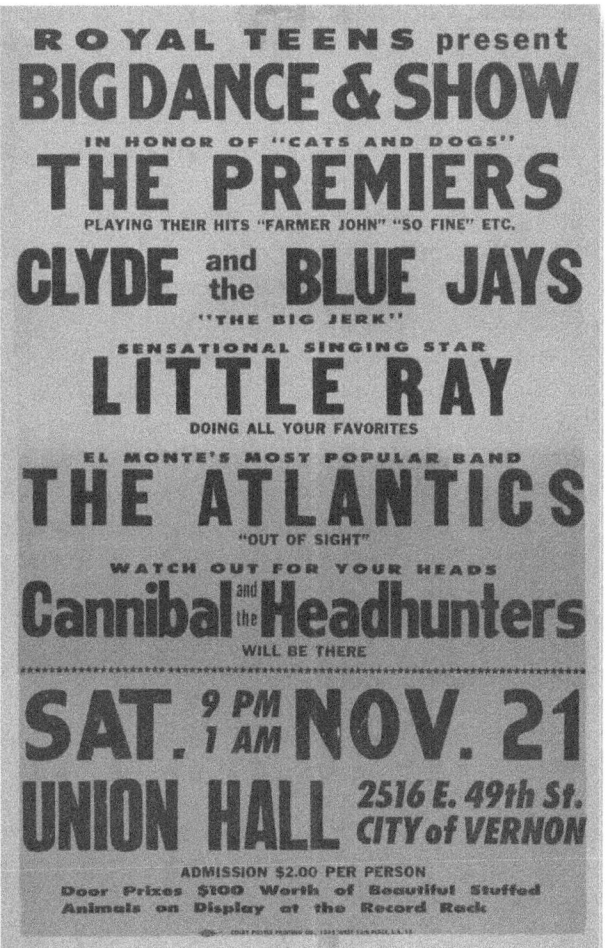

Poster courtesy of Jimmy Meza.

a chance that he now looks back on with some regret. "Looking back in time I'll be very honest with you I think it was a very bad mistake." He said, "I wish that I had stayed here because I had so much momentum going and people were dying to here something new from us. If I had good management I would have made the connection with Columbia but stayed in L.A. Had I stuck it out a little longer who knows where it would have gone. But then it became a survival trip in New York and it was hard. So when I got back in 1969 I had to start from scratch just trying to survive, all that I was thinking about was paying the rent and feeding the kids."

Little Ray was a star in East Los Angeles and people that had the opportunity to see and hear him and his band say they were one of the best around. He believes that people like Eddie Torres, Billy Cardenas and Eddie Davis put everything on the line to generate the excitement around the community at the time. "I have nothing but love for people like Eddie Davis and Billy Cardenas I'm very thankful that they were in our lives. They helped us all and if not me directly they did a lot for the community."

The San Gabriel Valley

The San Gabriel Valley, located approximately twelve miles east of Los Angeles, was a huge contributor to East Los Angeles sixties music scene. Starting in 1958 with the Story Tellers from San Gabriel the valley's musical contributions continued with groups like Doug and Freddy, the Atlantics, Righteous Rhythms, and the Royal Chessmen from El Monte, David and Ruben from La Puente, the Montclairs from Azusa and the Velveteens and the Casuals from Pomona. Other groups from San Gabriel were the Premiers, the In Crowd, the Occasions, the Monotones and the VIPs. The main artery into the valley from Los Angeles was Valley Boulevard, which was dotted with church, union, and military veteran halls used for dances.

There was Dead Man's Hall [*Sociodad de funeraria*] on San Gabriel Blvd. and Broadway in San Gabriel. A hall that was part of the local mortuary used by the community to raise money for the funeral expenses of community residents whose loved ones had passed away. Groups like the Premiers, Story Tellers, and the In-Crowd would perform free of charge as a community service. San Gabriel also had the Serbian Hall, which was a located on San Gabriel Boulevard and hosted several dances before it was demolished and replaced with a Serbian church. In El Monte there was the El Monte Teen Post, and Southern California's shrine to it's rock 'n roll past El Monte Legion Stadium, which succumbed to the wrecking ball in 1972 to make room for a post office. Farther east in La Puente dances were held at the Handball Courts, the Women's Club and the Diamond Horse Shoe. Several of the bands from the Valley discovered by Bob Keane and Billy Cardenas were performing at the Rainbow Gardens in Pomona, which was eventually burned down by a local gang member who was tired of getting turned away at the door.

The Velveteens

The Velveteens rise to stardom began in 1958 when twelve year old saxophonist Johnny Valenzuela joined a local rock 'n roll group from La Verne a bedroom community on the east end of the San Gabriel Valley. Valenzuela lived in nearby Pomona and initially would ride his bicycle to the rehearsals however, his father decided it was better if he drove him. Within a short period personnel in the group changed, becoming an all-Pomona group. As the group started to gain popularity in the community Di Brookings, a popular DJ from local radio station KASK started to announce where the Velveteens would be performing. "We were playing at the VFW, the Armory, Washington Park and the Rainbow Gardens a real popular place in Pomona," recalls Valenzuela. "We also did a lot of fund raisers for LULAC [League of United Latin American Citizens] of Pomona." Eventually Brookings, hooked the Velveteens up with local producer Paul Buff, who had the famed, Pal Studios in Cucamonga. The first record the group released was a single credited as Mary Lou Zuetta and the Velveteens titled **Oh Baby,** which featured the voice of Mary Unzuetta of San Dimas. Brookings plugged the song on her radio show and the local newspaper featured an article on the group. The band was back at Pal Studios the same year for a pair of instrumental recordings **Dog Patch Creeper** b/w **Johnny's Jump,** which Buff also released on his Emmy label. "I was thirteen," says Valenzuela. "I always said I was born at the right time. I was always playing music, stuff like **Autumn Leaves** but when I heard the words rock 'n roll and then I heard the music I thought, Wow!" Another female singer that started with the Velveteens was Shirlee Brooks who also lived in the *barrio* and was heavily involved with her church choir. Valenzuela knew that Brooks was going to be a star because she was very confident about who she was and what she was going to accomplish. After Brooks left the Velveteens she became the lead singer of the Shondells and recorded three singles for King Records in 1963 including their minor hit **Wonderful One.** Valenzuela recalls the day he met Brooks's replacement Terri Bonilla: "We still had Shirlee Brooks but we were looking for someone who could sing Spanish. We heard about Terri Bonilla who was singing with the Starlighters over in Ontario. It was 1959 and I was fourteen so we got my dad to drive us over to see her and her band perform." Valenzuela continues, "We approached her about singing with us and she said yea, then later she introduced us to her friend Lucy Duran who was from Chino and later on became Rosie of Rosie and Ron fame." With Terri singing lead the Velveteens went into Pal Studios and recorded two singles in 1960 **Bells of Love** b/w **You've Broken My Heart** for the Kerwood Label and **I'm Waiting** b/w **La Flor** for the Arc label. By 1960 the Velveteens popularity throughout Southern California had grown to the point that they were in demand at El Monte's Legion Stadium, the Big Union, Carpenters Hall in Boyle Heights and other locations in El Monte, La Puente, and Fullerton. While booked to perform at the Mexican Village at the 1960 Los Angeles County Fair they met Ray Quiñones who was also there to perform with a group from Lawndale, California called the Desires. "In 1960 we were booked at the fairgrounds and Ray [Quiñones] was there with a big vocal group. Well, we started talking and exchanging numbers. So they would book us at parties up around Hawthorne and Lawndale and we would book them on our side." Eventually Quiñones was incorporated into the Velveteens band.

While performing at the Rainbow Gardens in Pomona Bob Keane heard the Velveteens and approached Valenzuela's dad about recording for Del-Fi. "We were just kids." recalls Valenzuela, "So my dad handled it. We wrote and worked out **Bring Me Happiness** and **So Dearly** with Lucy Duran and Ralph Valdez and then we went over to Pal Studios for the recording session." Valdez had also been a member of the Desires and it was Quiñones who suggested that he be paired with Duran. Meanwhile in 1961, Lucy Duran had recorded a pair of singles on the Fifo Label. The ultra-rare **My Oh My** was with the Triangles, a trio that included Ruben Pando and Frankie

Gonzalez, and a single release titled **Oh Sweet Boy**.

Released on Keane's Donna label **Bring Me Happiness** was huge local success especially in Southern California and among Chicano record buyers. "**Bring Me Happiness** was number one on KFWB and **So Dearly** was number two." recalls Keane, "That was a big record." Valenzuela explains how the record ended up being a Rosie and Ron single, "Lucy Duran had a high pitched voice like Rosie [Hamlin] and the Originals. My dad came up with the idea for the name 'Rosie and Ron' because Rosie and the Originals were hot with **Angel Baby** and Ronnie and the Premiers had **Sharon** out so he wanted to capitalize on their fame and it worked." The popularity on **So Dearly** especially among Huggy Boy's audience prompted Huggy Boy to feature the Velveteens on shows that he was promoting, at the same time Valenzuela's father befriended Julian Herrera and started booking him at dances that the Velveteens were promoting. "We brought him from L.A. to play at dances we had in Pomona." recalls Valenzuela, "He stayed at our house over night and I don't care what people say he was all Chicano. He knew Spanish, he ate our food, and he loved our culture. I always felt that he never got the recognition that he deserves. I still say that Little Julian Herrera was the first [Chicano rock 'n roll star] and I'm talking about 1954-1955 with Johnny Otis. I remember as a kid watching him on TV when Johnny Otis had his show."

Another vocalist that Ray Quiñones brought over to the Velveteens camp was Pablo Venezuela who became the "Rene" of Rene and Ray in 1962. Once again the Velveteens along with Quiñones and Venezuela went over to Pal Studios and recorded **Queen of My Heart** a doo-wop ballad that became a local hit that besides having national appeal (number 76 on the *Billboard* charts) it was a big hit in Los Angeles climbing to number 5 on KFWB's music survey. In 1965 Terri and Johnny married and have been together ever since.

The Story Tellers

Around 1957 Alvin Sanchez and Ruben Ochoa teamed up with Nick Delgado to form the Pretenders. The trio had been members of the glee club at San Gabriel Mission High School. Both Alvin's father and Nick's father had also been performing together with a *trio Mexicano* traveling around California. Encouraged by the group's desire to pursue a career in music Alvin's mother purchased a piano and started to take the guys to voice lessons. "At that time we were listening to a lot of rhythm and blues," recalls Alvin Sanchez. "That's how we got started singing songs by Don and Dewey, Little Richard and Robert and Johnny. My dad was more traditional and every time we sang Little Richard stuff he would be making faces and tell us to turn it down, but he loved the ballads I guess because he sang with a *trio romantico*."

The Pretenders started performing at high school dances and then small local venues like Morgan Park in Baldwin Park and eventually were invited to perform with Bill Destri and the Destiny's. With Bill Destri they performed at the Long Beach Municipal Auditorium, Harmony Park Ballroom in Anaheim, Betty's Barn in Baldwin Park and the El Monte Legion Stadium, during this period they were joined by Ray Baez.

After a show at the Long Beach Municipal Auditorium, Nordy Beckman owner of Nordy's Records on Fairfax Avenue suggested that he become their manager. "He came over to our house," remembers Sanchez. "Discussed it with my parents and we decided to sign a contract with him." Beckman also suggested that the Pretenders change their name to the Story Tellers, which they did.

In late 1958 or early 1959 the Story Tellers went into the recording studio with Freddy Flynn & the Flashes and waxed their only single **You Played Me a Fool** backed with **Hey Baby**. The song started getting a lot of local airplay especially on the late night R&B programs like the one emanating from the famed, Dolphin's of Hollywood on Central and Vernon. Beckman was instrumental in getting Coca-Cola to sponsor a Story Tellers tour of California. "We actually toured by train," says Sanchez. "We went as far north as San Jose." Eventually Sanchez and Ruben Ochoa joined the Army leaving behind one highly sought after recording.

The Premiers

Nationally the biggest hit to come out of the San Gabriel Valley was the Premiers' **Farmer John,** the remake of Don and Dewey's 1959 R&B classic got its debut on June 20, 1964, and at least in Los Angeles it was still on the charts in early January of 1965. Once again the recording came with the help of Billy Cardenas and Max Uballez along with guitarist Andy Tesso. Unlike East Los Angeles where the Catholic schools were active in teaching music, San Gabriel was a little different. "East Los Angeles was like 85 percent Chicano," recalls Art Hernandez of the In Crowd. "In San Gabriel we were like 15 percent of the population so there wasn't anyone there trying to help us. The Premiers learned on their own watching some of the older groups like Frank Androti and the Blue Notes." Hernandez continues, "When the Premiers had their hit they [the school] didn't even make an announcement. I had a class with Lawrence [Perez] and one day he didn't show up, turns out they were on tour with Dick Clark. Among us Chicanos we were so proud of them but at school, they didn't really care."

The song that caught the attention of DJ Dick Hugg "Huggy Boy" was the "B" side instrumental titled **Duffy's Blues.** Initially the song became a part of Hugg's late night show, the revered DJ would spin it at midnight to signal the change of day. As it caught on, people started to flip the record and requests for **Farmer John** started to come in to KRLA and KFWB. At the same time Warner Brothers picked the record up for national distribution and it took off nationally.

Climbing to No.19 on the national charts and No. 3 on the local charts **Farmer John** gave the group a chance to tour nationally and kept the Premiers touring for two years. The military draft had its hand in the future of the Premiers. First to go was Zuniga who was drafted by the Army and replaced by former Rhythm Playboy Billy Watson. The Army's next target was Lawrence Perez who served a tour of duty in Vietnam. After returning home Perez rejoined the Premiers however, they were never given another chance to record.

The VIPs-El Chicano

With the VIP's we were doing a lot of rhythm and blues. We had Clarence Playa singing stuff like Wilson Pickett, and Otis Redding. I thought it was just a typical rock 'n roll band from the San Gabriel Valley so when I introduced *Viva Tirado* I was shocked when Freddie Sanchez said "yea! Let's do this." I suggested that we bring in a percussionist and start doing

some Mongo Santamaria he liked the idea. Meanwhile Mickey Lespron was getting into the Wes Montgomery style of playing so little by little we started to change the catalog. It just evolved into something different.

Bobby Loya- trumpeter
Blue Satins, VIP's, Tierra,
Thee Midniters

The VIPs were inspired by a mixture of R&B, jazz, and guitar based rock music. The group evolved out of a couple of bands from San Gabriel, CA. Bass player Freddie Sanchez led the VIPs which included San Gabriel High students guitarist Paul Palacio and drummer Danny Padilla. During this period Palacio had been giving Mickey Lespron guitar lessons. Since

Brothers; trumpeter Bobby Loya and saxophonist Tony Garcia. Clarence Playa in the background. *Author's archives.*

he was twelve years old Lespron had been jamming with his childhood friend Premiers guitarist Lawrence Perez. They studied riffs from blues classics like Freddie King's **Hide-A-Way.** "Back then all of the groups from East Los Angeles had big horn sections, Thee Midniters, the Blue Satins, the Enchantments and so on." Recalls Art Hernandez, "In San Gabriel we had to learn all that stuff on our own so there were these small five piece bands with maybe one sax until later on." Lespron who was attending Mission High School, joined the Monotones and eventually ended up with the In-Crowd. Sanchez recruited Lespron, drummer John de Luna, and keyboardist Bobby Espinosa (who had been performing with the Chicano surf group Mickey and the Invaders) into the VIPs. The group expanded its line-up in 1968 with the addition of a brass section, which included trumpeter Bobby Loya who had been with the Blue Satins, tenor saxophonist Tony Garcia and vocalist Clarence Playa who had been with Little Ray and the Progressions. According to Lespron, "It was Bobby Loya who introduced us to jazz and **Viva Tirado** which was performed by the horns at the break."

Bassist Billy Watson (former bass player of the Premiers and the Rhythm Playboys) had been working for Eddie Davis as an engineer and was turned on to the VIPs by Bobby Espinosa's brother Hector. With the blessing of Davis, Watson invited the group to Davis's Teron Recording Studios in Hollywood where during a jam session they recorded **Viva Tirado.** Davis was impressed with the demo, so he, Mario Paniagua and Billy Watson went to meet the group. The song was actually a composition written and originally recorded by L.A. jazz trumpeter Gerald Wilson. **Viva Tirado** was Wilson's tribute to Mexican bullfighter Jose Ramon Tirado, who would refuse to kill the bull he was fighting.

Bobby Loya describes how the song was introduced to the VIPs. "With the VIPs we were doing a lot of rhythm and blues. We had Clarence Playa singing Wilson Pickett stuff." He said, "Then I got a thrill when I went to the Lighthouse in Hermosa Beach to see trumpeter Gerald Wilson. That was a big, big Afro-American jazz band and I listened to them perform **Viva Tirado** and then I went and bought the album *Moment of Truth* and I thought 'Man that's a good tune,' maybe I can talk Freddie Sanchez and the band into playing it. I thought the VIPs were just a typical rock 'n roll band from the San Gabriel Valley so when I introduced **Viva Tirado** I was shocked when Freddie Sanchez said 'Yea! Let's do this.' I suggested that we bring in a percussionist and start doing some Mongo Santamaria. He liked that idea to, so little by little we started to change the catalog from the Wilson Pickett and Otis Redding stuff that Clarence Playa was singing to more of a Latin jazz feel. It just evolved into something different and with Mickey Lespron getting into the Wes Montgomery style of playing it just added a different dimension to it."

The evolution of the group continued as Loya, Garcia and Playa dropped out and percussionist Andre Baeza and female vocalist Ersi Arvizu replaced them. As the music scene around East Los Angeles shifted from the dance halls to the nightclubs the VIPs continued to be popular especially at Pico Rivera's Plush Bunny and in 1969 they became the house band at the famous Kabuki Club located in the Crenshaw District of Los Angeles.

Using the original title, Davis released a demo of **Viva Tirado** by El Chicano. Sanchez's steady bass line and Espinosa's smooth work on the Hammond Organ hold the tune together as Lespron's lead guitar provides the jazzy riffs à la Wes Montgomery. As the group's Latin rock version was starting to make some

Picture sleeve for European "Holland" release of **Viva Tirado**

right: **El Chicano** L-R:
Ersi Arvisu,
Micky Lespron,
Freddie Sanchez,
John DeLuna,
Bobby Espinosa,
Andre Baeza
Author's archives.

noise Eddie Davis got funding from Kapp Records to record an album. However, the VIPs wanted nothing to do with the name El Chicano so Davis was without a group. Eventually, Davis gathered a group of local musicians including Rudy Salas and started working on the album. Finally, after hearing their version on the radio Sanchez and the VIPs called Davis and were now ready to become El Chicano. "We were on our way to a gig in San Diego when we heard it on the radio." Recalls Espinosa, "and then the DJ said it was by a group called El Chicano." The term Chicano at least in Southern California was still more of a radical political statement popularized in the late sixties by Chicano youth united by a series of civil rights issues. The high school walkouts in 1968 where students demanded better education, the "Chicano Moratorium" of 1970 organized as a voice against American aggression and occupation in Vietnam, and Cesar Chavez's Farm Worker movement were all symbols of Chicano unity and pride. It was a difficult situation for Chicano musicians because politics had not been a part of their lives to this point. At first the VIPs didn't know how to embrace their new name, however as they toured the Southwest they realized that they had become a symbol of Chicano pride. Similar developments were under way throughout *Aztlán*.

CRAZY, CRAZY BABY

Texas Soul

"I was in the 10th grade at Crozier High when Fats recruited me as their bass player. Fats knew everyone around town Johnny Gonzales and Luther De La Garza who had the Hi-Ho. I was just sixteen and rolling along we played in Bridgeport, at the Hi-Ho and Johnny Gonzales's Zarape Ballroom. Fats was about 21, old enough to drink and drive I was just a kid so they never let me drive but I was there to play and for the girls. We were together for about a year in '68 then the group started to get their draft notices and that was it."

Paul Martinez bass player: Dallas [*Fats and the All-Stars*]

Central Texas: Dallas/Fort Worth

During America's soul years between 1962 and 1968 Chicano groups flourished throughout central and south Texas. Inspired by James Brown and the Memphis sound of Stax and Volt Records groups like Fats and the All-Stars, Sal de Leon and the Centennials, the Heartbreakers, Paul Rios and the Rivieras and the Night Creepers were the popular local teen groups during this period. The mid-sixties soul scene in central Texas was centered around the Dallas/Fort Worth area and many of the bands came from Croiser Tech High School located on Dallas's Westside. Thanks to Johnny Gonzales, Luther de la Garza and Zaragoza Escobedo these young soul groups as well as many of the traditional *ranchera* and *conjunto* groups of the region were able to get their music pressed on vinyl. Johnny Gonzales was considered the "godfather" of Dallas's music scene recording groups for his El Zarape, Tomi, and Gallito labels. "We were all like 15 or 16 years old and back then there was only one guy that would help any of us out and that was Johnny Gonzales," remembers Jesse Palma. "He would make a deal with the guys saying, 'Hell I'll record you guys, but you'd better practice as hard as you can because you only get one hour in the studio.' So we would play the song over and over and then pick the best one. Even then it wasn't that good, it was okay but it could have been better."

Luther and Lillian de la Garza's Capri Records and Zaragoza Escobedo's Mex-Melody Records were also instrumental in recording the music of Dallas, Fort Worth and the immediate region's Chicano musicians.

The three vocalists that left a huge mark on Dallas's short lived Chicano soul scene were brothers Joe and Jesse Palma and Clyde Alvarez. This trio

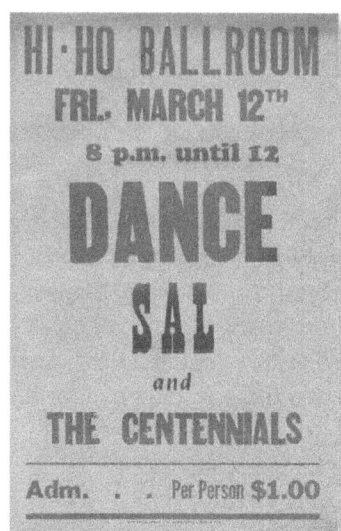

Early sixties at the Hi-Ho Ballroom L-R: Johnny Gonzales, Isidro Lopez, Roy Montelogo, and Lalo Ybarra. *Courtesy of Geno Reza.*

of young "soul brothers" are credited with much of Dallas's rhythm and blues out-put between 1965 and 1968. While at Crosier Tech High School Jesse Palma, and Clyde Alvarez were the lead vocalists for Sal de Leon and the Centennials a group that recorded several R&B covers including **Apples, Peaches Pumpkin Pie, Together** and **In a Moment**, all covers of popular soul singles that originated out of Philadelphia.

Meanwhile Joe Palma and Clyde Alvarez also fronted Paul Rios and the Rivieras with Alvarez taking on the Spanish recordings and Palma handling the English tunes like **She's My Woman, She's My Girl**, and **You Don't Know Like I Know**. Clyde Alvarez and the Palma Brothers eventually decided to form their own group calling themselves the Heartbreakers. "Sal De Leon and Paul Rios were a little older than us so we split from them because we didn't think they wanted to do the stuff we wanted like **Mustang Sally**," recalls Palma. "But we were young and we thought we knew everything."

This new generation of musicians was greatly influenced by soul super stars like Sam and Dave, Wilson Pickett and James Brown as well as other soul groups that were popular on the radio at the time. The Heartbreakers recorded two singles for Johnny Gonzales' Tomi label a cover of Sam and Dave's **Hold On I'm Coming** b/w **Going Out of My Head** and a cover of Cannibal and the Headhunters' **I'll Show You How to Love Me** a ballad written by Frankie "Cannibal" Garcia, which turns up as the flip side to the Headhunters' national hit **Land of a Thousand**

Dances from 1965. By 1968 the military draft had taken its toll on the group and the Heartbreakers was disbanded.

Dallas was also well known for its network of ballrooms and dance halls that catered to groups coming up from Corpus Christi, McAllen, Laredo, Houston, Austin and San Antonio, Texas. There was Johnny Gonzales's Zarape Ballroom, the Long Horn Ballroom, Luther de la Garza's Camelot and Hi-Ho ballrooms. In nearby Fort Worth there was Guys and Dolls, La Mona Lisa, the Manhattan Club and the Lakewood Casino. There was a distinct difference between Dallas and San Antonio as far as nightlife goes. Little Joe Hernandez who is from Temple, midway between the two centers, saw the differences. "Dallas was and still is today a bit more sophisticated (if you want to use that word) than San Antonio, of course San Antonio is the tourist attraction *todo el tiempo aye borlote en San Antonio* and it's not that way in Dallas. Dallas has a different atmosphere where there was a lot of Jazz clubs. San Antonio was more Mexican-ized, a lot of bars and a few ballrooms like Mi Ranchito but they didn't have, as far as I can remember big named ballrooms like in Dallas and Fort Worth but San Antonio had the music, a lot of groups came out of San Antonio."

The ballroom scene in Dallas was predominantly a Latin thing where most of the performers performed *rancheras* so things were jumping but not for the soul bands. Although soul music had greatly influenced many of the younger musicians it was *conjunto* music or *La Onda Chicana* that audiences wanted to hear. On the other hand recognition and respect from other musicians especially from the Mexican artists was an honor to those trying to do the rhythm and blues thing. The Rondels from Laredo were a popular group on the circuit and recorded for Capri Records as well as Carlos Guzman's Impacto label. Group leader Carlos Landin talks about being a soul group on the circuit. "We would tour or *caravana* as it was called with Vicente Fernandez, Mike Laure, Sonora Santanera, Cuco Sanchez, and groups like that. We thought man these guys have everything, they got *mariachis* and all that stuff and we would say to ourselves 'What do they think of us and our music?' We expected them to say 'who are these guy playing that crazy music.' On the contrary they would come to us and say 'we love your type of music it has so much soul.' So coming from people that we admired that was an honor. We were so unique because we could sound like the blacks, we could sound like the guero, and we could sound like the Mexicano and we blended all that together."

The military draft was also a factor in slowing Dallas's modest soul movement especially in '67, '68 and '69. As was the case in Los Angeles, San Antonio and Albuquerque many of the younger musicians who were fourteen, fifteen and sixteen years old when they started performing were turning eighteen by the time President Lyndon Johnson's 'Project 100,000' was in full swing. Initiated in 1966 the project's goal was to substantially increase the number of U.S. Soldiers fighting in Vietnam. This was done by lowering the qualification standards of the draft in order to scoop up those black, Hispanic and poor whites that were able to evade the draft due to lack of education. This fishnet approach also took many of the communities' most creative artists. After their tour of duty those musicians seeking to restart their careers found that *La Onda Chicana* had completely taken over the music scene in Texas leaving little or no room for music with English lyrics.

Junior and the Starlites from Waco, Texas. Cruz "Junior" Garcia standing at the Hammond M3. *Courtesy of Cruz Garcia.*

Jr. and the Starlites-Latinglows

Cruz Garcia started his career in music back in 1959 drumming with the R&B group Cruz Ortiz and the Flames. The group consisted of five Chicano musicians and a black singer. Between 1959 and 1965 the group recorded five R&B singles for the Fort Worth based Manco Records. "We didn't do anything in Spanish, everything we did were covers of R&B tunes like James Brown and stuff like that," recalls Cruz Garcia. As the Flames' run was coming to an end Garcia went from drums to playing the organ. "I played the Hammond M3 a smaller and less expensive version of the B3," remembers Garcia. "We didn't have the big sound systems back then so everybody that used the Hammond organ also used two Leslie cabinets stacked-up on top of each other so they could be heard in the dance halls.

Garcia, also known among friends as Junior formed his own group in 1966. "Jr. and the Starlites were just a bunch of local guys that went to school together," says Garcia. The group consisted of Garcia on organ, Joe "Chico" Ortega (vocals), Bird Tijerina (guitar), Johnny Quiñiones (bass), Johnny Gonzales (drums), and a horn section of Joe Lopez, Johnny Garcia and Nick Ramos. The Starlites' area of influence was West Texas. "We were popular mostly in the West Texas towns of Abilene, Lubbock, Midland,

Odessa and San Angelo," recalls Garcia. "And of course around Central Texas in Temple, Waco, Austin and Dallas."

Jr. and the Starlites recorded six or seven singles for Zaragosa Escobedo's Dallas based Mex-Melody Records including a wonderful version of Rene and Ray's 1962 Southern California classic **Queen of My Heart**. The Starlites take the lowrider classic and give it a Texas makeover, making it a must for Texas soul lovers. It was Joe Ortega who introduced the song to the group in fact Garcia believed all along that Ortega had written the song.

By 1969 the Starlites had broken up, with Joe Ortega joining Rocky Hernandez's Temple based Latinglows. After Rocky left the Latinglows to join his brother's group (Little Joe y la Familia) Garcia took over the group, which was now known as Cruz Garcia and the Latinglows. The band was now recording mainly Spanish songs which gave them a new base. "With the Starlites we got good airplay in West Texas but we didn't do that well in the south where it was mostly *Mexicanos*," remembers Garcia. "Now with the Latinglows we got airplay all over South Texas." After one album for Mex-Melody and three for Little Joe's Buena Suerte label the group broke up and Garcia toured with Little Joe as his soundman.

Little Joe and the Latinaires

Little Joe was born Jose Maria de Leon Hernandez in 1940 just south of Dallas in the rural community of Temple, Texas. The Hernandez family was big thirteen kids, and poor, his parents worked the cotton fields that surrounded their community. "My mom was always there, pregnant, pulling the (cotton) sack with kids riding on it and kids under the trailer *de algodón*."

Joe's formal education ended when he reached the seventh grade. His education in music came in the bicultural *barrios* of Temple that housed a mix of Mexican and black working class folk. "We were always real close to the African American." Recalls Hernandez, "The neighborhood other than my dad's family, grandfather and grandmother and a couple of sisters, and one other family was all black. We lived next to a black family and they matched us kid for kid so we would sleep over, listen to their records, eat their food and it was a big influence on me." It was in this enviroment that as a youngster he developed his taste for blues, jazz, rhythm and blues and the top-forty soul music that would help him and his brothers Jesse, Johnny and Rocky out of a life of poverty and into the hearts of fans throughout America.

In 1954 fourteen-year-old Joe and his cousin David Coronado formed a four-piece combo, David Coronado and the Latinaires, which featured Joe on guitar and vocals, Mike Barber on drums and two saxophones David Coronado (alto), no bass until Joe's younger brother Jesse joined the group. The band started playing local beer joints and bars musically crossing all of the boundaries that gave the community its flavor. "When we started playing one night might be an all black little joint, the next might be a totally white hillbilly crowd that wanted country western, and of course there was the Chicano shows and that's where we would mix it all up."

The Latinaires were performing at dance halls throughout South Texas and in 1957 while in Corpus Christi the group recorded their first single, an instrumental tune titled **Safari** for local DJ Genaro

Little Joe and the Latinaires at Johnny Gonzales's El Zarape Ballroom, Dallas Texas. Standing L-R: Cino Moreno, Raymond Flores, Tony Guerrero, Arturo Gonzales, Mike Rios, Luigi Navarro, Jaime Flores, Tony Matamoros. Seated L-R: Rocky Hernandez, Johnny Hernandez, Little Joe Hernandez, Bobby "El Charro Negro" Butler. Circa 1968. *Courtesy of Geno Reza.*

Left: Buena Suerte LP by "**El Charro Negro**" Bobby Butler.
courtesy of Nick Aguirre

Tamez's Torero label. David Coronado left the group in 1958 leaving Little Joe as the leader of the newly named—Little Joe and the Latinaires. That same year the group recorded **Little Girl of My Dreams** b/w **Ramona** for Manuel Rangel's newly formed Rival Records. Ten years earlier Rangel had formed Corona Records, the label that some consider to be the first *Tejano* record label to open its doors in the city of San Antonio. *Señor* Rangel was out in front once more this time with his Rival label, a label that he used to release English recordings by local Chicano R&B groups like Dimas Garza's Kool Dips, Sonny Ace and the Twisters and Tito and the Silhouettes.

Little Joe and the Latinaires had grown to a nine-piece band with three vocalists Joe, brother Johnny and Bobby "El Charo Negro" Butler and by 1964 were becoming very popular throughout Texas when Joe got the call from Dallas promoter Johnny Gonzales. "He called me and booked us over the phone, we played at a place called the Hi-Ho Ballroom, which was a big place back then, where all of the big band greats would play. After the show a well-dressed young man walked up to me and handed me an enveloped I think it was $150, I put it in my coat pocket and he said aren't you going to count it? I said 'nah, why would you want to cheat me when we agreed on something' and that was it."

After that meeting Little Joe and the Latinaires started recording for Johnny Gonzales's El Zarape record label issuing their first LP *Por Un Amor* in 1965. Although the group never cracked the national pop charts they had established a strong following both as a touring band and in record sales according to Hernandez *Por Un Amor* was popular in Mexico and Latin America and has sold around one million copies worldwide.

Hey, Paula

In 1965 the Latinaires added a female voice to the group. The addition of Paula Estrada gave the group more depth both in the Spanish *rancheras*, and in the English tunes that she performed. In 1965 the Latinaires and Paula recorded an excellent version of Barbara Lewis's **Hello Stranger**. Estrada who has a double major in business and Spanish with a minor in education from Howard Payne University also had an opportunity to record a number one national hit. "I was attending Howard Payne University in Brown-

Paula Estrada. *Courtesy of Crazy Chuy Hernandez.*

The Hi-Ho Ballroom has survived the test of time and is still standing just outside of Dallas.

wood, Texas. It's a small college and we didn't have much to do except get together on weekends and sing." remembers Estrada, "I would team up with a good friend of mine Ray Hildebrand and he's the one that wrote **Hey, Paula** the song that went to number one in the nation in 1962. But, back then and of course you know they discriminated against Hispanics. We sang the song but when it was recorded here in Fort Worth Jill Jackson who also went to school with us was used in the recorded version. That's where I lost my chance to be on a number one hit record."

Paula and her friends enjoyed attending dances that were held in the Fort Worth area. It was at one of these shows that she met Little Joe. "I went to see Little Joe who was performing at a little club here in Fort Worth called Guys and Dolls. I had never seen Joe, I was busy in college but I had been singing all my life so I loved music. Well my cousin was dating the organ player (Luis Pesina) in Joe's band, she knew the guys so she introduced me to them before the dance started. After the show we all went out to eat and Joe mentioned that they were recording a new record in Dallas. We started talking music and he said that they were looking for a female singer for the group and if I'd be interested. I didn't believe him but he called and said if I could make it down to Dallas for practice. My jaw dropped I couldn't believe he was calling me. We went up to Dallas to practice, and then to record and I still didn't believe it until the album came out and my picture was on it. That's how things got started with Joe. The first record that came out was a record called **Recuerdas Querido Amigo** and it was a duet that became a big hit here in Texas, **Hello Stranger** was further down the line. With that record people wanted to know who Paula was so Johnny Gonzales started booking me with Little Joe."

The mid-sixties was also a period of change for the Latinaires, after releasing more than a dozen English "soul" singles for Tear Drop, El Zarape and Tomi Records, the group turned to *la musica ranchera* with their first El Zarape album in 1965. **Por un Amor** was a huge seller and a major leap forward for what would become known as Tex-Mex, *La Onda Chicana* or *Tejano* music. The music that Sunny Ozuna describes as "a mix of all the influences that Chicano musicians had been absorbing since the late fifties; rhythm and blues, rock 'n roll, *conjunto* and *ranchera*."

The **Broken Hearts** L-R: George Soto, Frutoso "Fruit" Balderas, Ramon "Munche" Salazar, Jr., Bobby Gonzales, Rudy Machado, Gilbert Gonzales, Jimmy Solis, Jimmy Carrillo. Circa 1964.
Courtesy of Ramon Salazar Jr.

The Broken Hearts

Like many of the groups that made a huge impact on communities throughout *Aztlán* in the sixties the Broken Hearts got their start in the late fifties. Rudy and Ramon "Munche" Salazar grew up in the racially mixed *barrio* of Newton, located in Seguin, Texas. Like many of the small agricultural towns in Central Texas, Black and Mexican American families lived side-by-side sharing each other's culture. The Salazars' grocery store, which is still located on Newton Avenue and Avenue D and currently run by Ramon Salazar was the center of the community. George Soto lived down the street from the Salazars and was influenced by Rudy's guitar and harmonica playing so a couple of months after Munche bought a guitar, George bought one of his own. The three teens studied and practiced their instruments, inspired by the groups from San Antonio which, were playing English rock and R&B. The band, which now included Roco Rodriguez on drums and Johnny Ortiz called themselves the Playboys. In 1961 the band changed their name to the Broken Hearts. They had managed to gain some popularity with black audiences so they continued to add more blues and R&B tunes on their playlists. There were several black clubs in the community including the Ebony Club, Tony's Steakhouse, the Key Club and the Grapevine so there was plenty of work for the Broken Hearts. According to Salazar "One reason we preferred Black clubs was that they were willing to pay us," he said. " We hardly ever got paid when we performed in *las Cantinitas*."

Throughout the history of the Broken Hearts close to forty musicians performed with the group. As soon as they graduated from high school Uncle Sam was there waiting with his draft cards. The first to serve in the military was Roco Rodriguez in 1961. Fortunately there was an abundance of young musicians, which kept the Broken Hearts moving forward. Sometime in 1962 the Broken Hearts got their first chance in the recording studio. Thirteen-year-old Gilbert Gonzales and Tony Castillo had written a pair of tunes **Slowly, Slowly but Surely** and **Wherever My Darling**, which they recorded at Texas Sound Studios in San Antonio for Abe Epstein's Cobra Records. A contractual dispute developed between the group and Epstein, leaving the recordings on the shelf. Ironically, **Slowly, Slowly but Surely** was issued on Cobra by Henry and the Kasuals sometime later.

The group eventually landed with Ruben Ruiz's Rosina Records out of San Marcos, Texas located in the adjacent county to Seguin. With Rosina Records the Broken Hearts recorded the R&B ballad **Crying Over You** before going on to record a series of *Tejano* tunes. Their live performances were still a mix of blues, rock and Tejano music. However, their recordings after **Crying Over You** were strictly *Tejano*. The group recorded with Rosina, El Zarape, Key-Loc, Peerless and Little Joe's Buena Suerte Records. In 1965 one of the group's young singers Sixto Sanchez recorded **Me Piden** a song that became one of the Broken Hearts' most famous recordings climbing to number one on the Spanish language charts. The Rosina recording also became extremely popular across the border prompting Sixto to take a tour into Mexico a rarity for a Chicano group at the time.

As the Broken Hearts' reputation grew around Central Texas, word of their showmanship and versatility spread across the state and into the Midwest where a growing number of Mexican American migrant workers had moved to looking for work. The Broken Hearts like the Sunliners and dozens of Texas groups toured up and down the Midwest in their van. While returning back to Seguin from a dance in Abilene, Texas in November of 1967 the group got into a fatal accident, one that left their star singer Sixto Sanchez severely wounded. He died several days later in a San Antonio hospital. Sanchez who had recorded 40 singles during his short career had just turned twenty years old.

As the Vietnam war intensified, more and more of the musicians were being called up to serve in the military the once bountiful pool of musicians had dried up making it difficult for the Broken Hearts to keep mature experienced local musicians on their roster. Consequently, the group lost its local roots as musicians had to be recruited from out of town.

South Texas

A unique phenomenon in American popular music was the border town jive of southern Texas. The music that emerged from a string of towns that made up a triangle that stretches from Laredo to Brownsville on the Mexican border then up the gulf coast to Corpus Christi had a flavor all its own largely influenced by the rollin' drumbeat of Louisiana's blues and rock 'n roll, however it was a fusion of all of the cultures that called the border region home. As eccentric DJ and record producer Huey P. Meaux said of South Texas, "The reason why I had so many hits was that in this part of the country, you've got a different kind of people every hundred miles-Czech, Mexican, Cajun and black."

Meaux whose record companies included Eric,

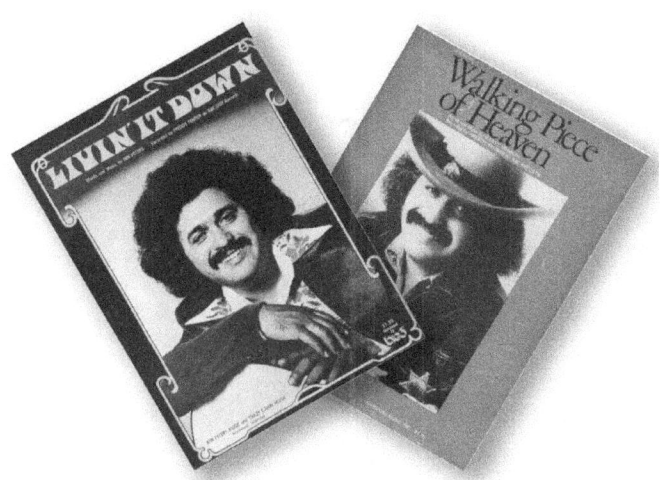

Freddy Fender was back on top in the seventies. He found a new fan base in the country music field with Before The Next Tear Drop *Falls* and a remake of his 1959 classic Wasted Days and Wasted Nights. *Author's archives.*

Crazy Cajun, Jet Stream and Tear Drop Records recorded dozens of Chicano artists from throughout Texas both in Spanish and English. He was instrumental in the resurgence of Freddy Fender's career in the seventies when he produced Fender's **Since I Met You Baby**, a remake of the 1959 classic **Wasted Days and Wasted Nights** and **Before the Next Tear Drop Falls** a country-western/Spanglish tune that went to number one in the winter of 1975.

Within the area of South Texas there exists a culture caught between Mexico and the rest of America, a buffer zone if you will, with a culture all its own. The music of this region was a reflection of this uniqueness and of the inhabitants of the region, gritty, and full of life.

During the forties and fifties the *conjunto* groups that emerged from the rural agriculture based communities that dotted the landscape were all American. Their lyrics may have been sung in Spanish, however their music was performed for American audiences from a variety of cultural backgrounds. The generation that followed this group of musicians fused what they had learned from their elders with the rolling beat, funky horns and jazzy guitar licks coming from New Orleans and the Louisiana zydeco and swamp rockers.

Although there were some aspects of soul music found in South Texas's music scene it was the more up-tempo rock 'n roll beat that was a favorite of the groups. Bandleader Noé Pro recalls his early inspirations: "I had my very first band in the late fifties in Corpus Christi we were playing in the style of Oscar Martinez, Bobby Galvan and Isidro Lopez and then I went into the army in 1960." He said, "I was gone for a couple of years. Then I ended up in Brownsville in 1962 and someone told the bandleader of a little group called Los Blue Valiants that I was a drummer and a singer. They offered me a job and all we did was rock 'n roll English stuff you know stuff that was on the radio at the time." Pro, the son of Mexican immigrants, whose grandparents immigrated to Mexico from Italy recorded at least ten English rock 'n roll singles for an array of record labels in the early sixties.

Freddy Fender, Bobby Galvan, Oscar Martinez and Noé Pro were more than likely inspired by New Orleans than by Philadelphia or Chicago. The origins of their inspiration is revealed in the music they produced. Not as glamorous and with a harder edge than the more sophisticated sounds of Dallas and San Antonio. All one has to do is listen to Bobby Galvan's **Do the Bear**, Noé Pro's **You Drive Me Crazy**, Vine

Noé Pro and the Blue Valiants. Noé played drums and sang. *Courtesy of Noé Pro.*

Cantú's **Born to Be a Loser** or Freddie Martinez's **Walking the Dog** to realize that this style of Chicano soul was a style all its own.

A few local entrepreneurs saw the need for the recording and distribution of this music and developed several record companies to meet this demand. In San Benito Paco Betancourt had Norco Records, which released singles of Freddy Fender, Noé Pro, Johnny Jay and the Pompadours and the Prophets. Arnoldo Ramirez's McAllen based Falcon Records also released singles by Freddy Fender, as well as René and René and Los Dinos. Ramirez also had ARV, which waxed records by George Jay and the Rockin' Ravens, accordion wizard Esteban Jordan, Ray Camacho, Freddy Fender and Noé Pro. Also in McAllen was Jimmy Nichols's Pharaoh Records who besides Noé Pro, released singles by the Cruisers and Johnny Jay and the Pompadours. The Gulf Coast town of Corpus Christi produced several popular groups like Vince Cantú and the Rockin' Dominoes who recorded on Johnny Herrera's Fox label, Johnny Canales and the hard rocking Bobby Galvan and Oscar Martinez.

Thirty-two years before Selena (Quintanilla) y Los Dinos were riding the charts with several hit records her father Abraham was singing with a group called Los Dinos. Los Dinos were one of the smoother more polished groups from the region. They had adopted

Although they were popular it was difficult for a Mexican American group to get their music played on the radio. The black stations wouldn't play their music because they were not black and the Spanish station wouldn't play their music because it was black music. Tired of the struggle the group called it quits in 1968.

West of Corpus Christi Laredo's Carlos Landin and the Rondels were cutting records for Carlos Guzman's Impacto label as well as the Dallas-based Capri Records. The Rondels were inspired by the funkier Southern soul of Sam and Dave, Wilson Pickett and Otis Redding and recorded a soulful version of Johnnie Taylor's **Love Bones**. The Rondels' lead singer Ricco was African American. "Ricco was black but he sang in Spanish," recalls Landin. "I mean if you listen to him on **Aye Mama** you would think he was Chicano. But with him we could play R&B and sound like it. I mean he gave us depth." The Rondels were one of those groups that became popular with Mexican audiences throughout America. "Back then it was hard for Hispanic groups to record." He said, "We finally recorded our first album with Carlos Guzman's Impacto Label out of McAllen. It blew us away. After that we started to get calls from Chicago, Detroit, Ohio, Indiana, Milwaukee, Denver, and then over to California from San Jose to San Francisco, Bakersfield, Los Angeles, and all the way down to the southern town of Indio."

Like many of the musicians that made the road their way of life the Rondels got tired and weary and eventually decided to retire to a simpler way of life. "We were on the road for about seven years and the band was made up of musicians from all over Texas." Recalls Landin, "I had guys from San Anto, Dallas, Corpus, and Houston. When Los Dinos broke up we got all of their *pitos* (horns). We had two suburbans

Los Dinos 1964. Clockwise from left: Ray Villareal, Johnny Cadena, Seferino Perales, Bobby Lira, Abraham Quintanilla, Manuel Hernandez, Danny Contreras, George Martinez. *Courtesy of Joe Silva.*

the three part harmonies *de los trios romanticos* coming up from Mexico and incorporated that with the similar harmonies of the soul groups from Chicago, Philadelphia and the Motown sound. Bobby Lira, Abraham Quintanilla and Seff Perales used their three part harmonies much like the Royal Jesters were doing in San Antonio making them extremely popular in the region. From 1962 through 1968 they recorded a number of singles and several albums that were a blend of popular soul tunes and Mexican standards.

and we traveled some hard road. When we stopped traveling we were at the top of our careers and it was so hard to adjust. I mean having to go to work for a hundred dollars a week after making two grand or so a week. But we wanted to be civilians, we were just tired."

The Tex-Mex Influence: ? and the Mysterians

For anyone who is familiar with sixties Tex-Mex soul the first 3 bars of thirteen-year old Frank Rodríquez's Farfisa organ intro to **96 Tears** have San Antonio written all over them. Not true, how about the vibrant Chicano community of Saginaw, Michigan? Actually, there are several strong connections between the Mexican American community in Saginaw and the rural communities of southern Texas. Ever since the signing of the Bracero Treaty of 1942 Mexican immigrants have been making their way across Texas into the Midwest. There was a constant demand for agricultural workers and factory laborers caused by the demands of World War II.

The Bracero Program came to an end in 1963, farmworkers who had dedicated their best efforts during America's time of need, suddenly found themselves being asked to get out even though there was still a demand for agricultural workers in the midwestern states of Indiana, Wisconsin, Ohio, Illinois and Michigan. Meanwhile in Texas the introduction of the mechanical harvester displaced many *Tejano* cotton pickers, which created a migration of workers into the Midwest to fill the void left by the end of the Bracero Program. In 1966 alone 129,000 migrants left Texas for the Midwest fields. At first they were looking for seasonal work however, as some found work in the factories they established small communities with strong Mexican roots.

This migration also established something that might be considered the "Menudo Circuit" for the many *conjunto* bands and *orquestas* coming out of San Antonio, Corpus Christi, Dallas, Laredo, Seguin and Austin. Throughout this route there was a circuit of ballrooms and dance halls that catered to these immigrant workers and the many bands that followed them seeking work for themselves. The bands headed north to homesick *Tejanos* who welcomed a little homegrown music.

By the mid-sixties the younger groups, which had set aside the accordion and the music of the *conjunto* and had developed their own style of soul music, were also becoming popular on the circuit especially among second and third-generation immigrants that had settled along the way. Groups like the Sunglows, Little Joe and the Latinaires, Rudy Tee and the Reno-Bops, Sunny and the Sunliners and the Rondels made their way up north in Winnebagos, reworked school buses and old station wagons.

? and the Mysterians' 96 Tears was origially released on the Pa-Go-Go label. Owned by Jose "**PA**to" Gonzales, Rudy Tee **GO**nzales, and Manuel "Red" **GO**nzales.

? and the **Mysterians.** *Author's archives.*

Having a booking agent that they trusted made for a better situation. For Rudy Tee, Pato Gonzales was a good man to work with. Jose "Pato" Gonzales and his wife Lillian owned a grocery store in Saginaw, Michigan. Besides the store they booked bands coming up from Texas for dances around the Saginaw Valley and co-owned Bego Records with Paulino Bernal.

On one such trip Pato loaned Rudy Tee $1,000 and told him, "I want you to start your own record label." But according to Rudy Tee there was one condition. "He was the one who told us, 'There's a little group that's been hanging around that I want you to record."

This was the beginning of the short-lived Pa-Go-Go label. Pa-Go-Go stood for PAto-GOnzales-GOnzales and was owned by Jose "Pato" Gonzales, Rudy Tee Gonzales, and Manuel "Red" Gonzales later on Paulino Bernal from McAllen, Texas became a partner. ? and the Mysterians had been performing at teen dances, and sock hops and had opened for groups like Conjunto Bernal, Carlos Guzman and Los Fabulosos Cautros around the Saginaw Valley.

The group felt they had a hit with a song Rudy (?) Martinez had written titled **96 Tears** and they had been going around trying to get someone to record them. "We went out to Bay City, about 15 minutes outside of Saginaw, and there was a backroom studio (Art Shields Recording Studio), and that's where I recorded them," recalls Rudy Tee. The group at the session consisted of Rudy (?) Martinez (vocals), Eddie Serrato (drums), Bobby Balderrama (guitar), Frank Rodriguez, Jr (organ) at the time the group didn't have a bass player so Rudy Tee used his bass player Fernando Aguilar.

The group's roots go back to 1961 when twelve-year old Bobby Balderrama, his uncle Larry Borjas and Robert Martinez started jamming together. The group was playing popular instrumental rock tunes because no one was willing to step up and sing, that is, until Rudy Martinez joined the band. In an interview with Larry Rodarte of *Mi Gente* magazine Balerrama recalls how the group got its name. "My nephew Larry and I were watching a Japanese movie about space invaders who were called Mysterians, Larry said that it was a great name. I tried it for a whole week before I realized he was right." While performing for a fundraiser for the American G.I. Forum the Mysterians met David Torres, a Saginaw area artist who offered to manage the group. Balderrama continues "He gave us each a letter X Y Z, and he gave Question Mark his name." When the group went to see DJ Bob Dell at WTAC Dell asked Rudy Martinez his name, Martinez replied 'Question Mark' Dell said it had a ring to it and announced us as ? and the Mysterians over the radio, that's how we got our name."

There are two stories on how the record broke, according to Rudy Tee, "Michigan was the hardest state to break a record and Pato's wife Lillian went to the radio stations and told them they were being prejudiced because we're Chicanos, well they started playing it and it hit; she's the one that made it hit. Once it broke in Michigan *no hombre!* It started to break everywhere." In an interview with Larry Rodarte for *Mi Gente* magazine (?) remembers having to do the footwork "In the sixties WTAC of Flint was the power station. I took Bob Dell the record, he played it and said it wasn't any good and threw it in the trash. We were already playing at Mount Holly, a teen spot for WTAC, drawing huge crowds and making $125 a night." The Mysterians decided to take matters into their own hands. They stopped doing shows for WTAC and rented a hall in nearby Denton and for eight weeks they packed the place. Their fans started requesting **96 Tears** by phone and through a letter writing campaign. To make it big they would have to get the record played in Detroit. "I always had confidence in my song. This booking agent from Detroit heard the song and liked it. I told him that if he took it to Detroit, and made it a hit, then I would make him my manager." Once in the hands of popular Detroit DJ Tom Shannon the record started to take off. In order to meet the demand of 15,000 records the group had to sign with a larger record label.

Rudy Tee also remembers trying to get ? and the Mysterians an appearance on one of San Antonio's popular teen shows. "I remember going to Don Couser he had the *Swing Time* program *y le deje* "Don, they are going to be in town, put them on." He said, 'no Rudy I have someone else booked' and I told him 'Don, these guys are going to be big.' Within a month they came to town I got them to play at Patio Anda Luz, Vince Cantú and the Rockin' Dominoes and the Reno-Bops opened up for them we had a big crowd, well Don Couser called me asking me to get them on his show and I told him 'Sorry I can't, the best that I can do is send you some videotape.'"

Offers were coming in from all of the major labels. The group signed with Cameo-Parkway Records who had not had a record in the top forty since Chubby Checker in 1964. By October of '66 **96 Tears** had reached number one on the national charts making ? and the Mysterians the only all Mexican American band to achieve such heights. Unfortunately for the group the contracts that they signed left them out in the cold and we re-visit that old line "I never made a cent from that record."

Sam the Sham and the Pharaohs

On the rough streets of Dallas's Westside *barrio* a group led by Omar "Big Man" Lopez was trying to make a little noise. The Pharaohs were a ragtag group of street smart musicians; Carl Menke, Russell Fowler, Domingo Samudio and sixteen-year-old Vincent Lopez. By some accounts as many as three of the band members were on probation.

This was 1961 and Big Man and the Pharaohs were rockin' and rollin' on Dallas's nightclub circuit. Problem was the clubs were only paying $5.00 a night per man. After their 1962 recording (an instrumental titled **I Don't Know**) failed to sell the band called it quits.

Sometime in 1963 Vincent Lopez moved to Louisiana to work with an R&B group called Andy and the Nightriders. The Nightriders were tearing it up at the Congo Club, off of Highway 171 just across the state line in Leesville, Louisiana. Halfway between Shreveport and the swamp country of Lake Charles, the Congo Room was a magnet for a hardy mix of swampers and Cajun folk (or gun and knife folk) that would come from as far as one hundred miles away. This was a perfect setting for an eccentric, charismatic, rockin' bluesman so when the Nightriders lost their keyboard player Vincent Lopez called his old friend Domingo Samudio. Sam had just purchased the organ and was getting acquainted with it, however Lopez insisted. What Sam lacked in his finger-work he made up for as a singer and an entertainer. This is where Samudio evolved into Sam the Sham.

The Nightriders packed their bags and headed north looking for greener pastures in the birthplace of rock 'n roll— Memphis, Tennessee. The band takes up residence as the house band for the Club Diplomat and proceeded to get the joint jumping. When Andy Anderson the band's leader and Vincent Lopez decided to return to Louisiana Samudio took over as the group's leader and changed the name of the group to Sam the Sham and the Pharaohs. The new line-up now included David Martin, Jerry Patterson, Ray Stinnett and Butch Gibson. Meanwhile, Sam bought a 1952 Packard hearse; the funeral wagon or "Black Beauty" as she was known traveled some hard road as she carried the group and the tools of their trade as they moved back and forth between Texas, Louisiana and Tennessee.

Finally, in 1963 Sam the Sham and the Pharaohs recorded their first single **Betty and Dupree**. The following year they tried again with the release of **Haunted House**. Both singles failed but the band was in hot pursuit of fame and gold so they kept on rolling the dice.

By the end of 1964 they had recorded their third single a nonsense lyric rocker titled **Wooly Bully** pressed on the "XL" label. In the spring of 1965 the single with that crazy Tex-Mex intro *"Uno, dos, one, two, tres, quarto . . ."* was picked up by MGM Records and debuted on the *Billboard* charts in April. It did not take long for the crazy Mexican in sheik's clothing to go number one in Los Angeles and number two across the country selling three million units along the way. Sam the Sham was a throwback to the original R&B rockers like Fats Domino, Little Richard and Chuck Willis (who may have given him the turban idea) and his hard driving shouter came at a time when rock 'n roll had been pacified by the likes of Herman's Hermits and the Beatles. It would take fourteen months and a series of so-so singles to get back to the top of the charts with **Little Red Riding Hood**. Although, MGM Records kept the group busy recording songs with silly novelty themes they were rock 'n roll from the word go.

The El Paso Sound

Although El Paso itself did not produce many R&B recording groups it was one of the most influential cities in the Chicano Southwest, placed halfway between San Antonio and Los Angeles, El Paso was the crossroads for many groups touring through the Southwest or as far as some groups would venture out from their respective regions. Through the efforts

CHICANO SOUL

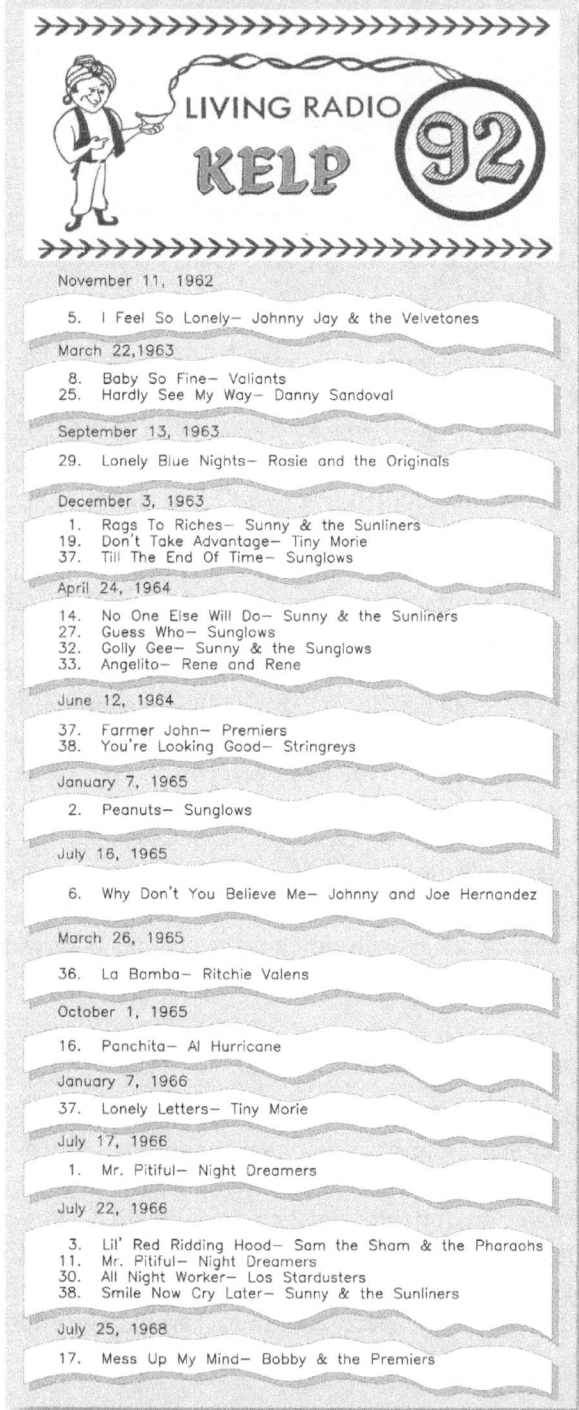

Through the efforts of local disc jockey Steve Crosno the air-waves of El Paso became a tapestry of music, both Spanish and English from throughout Aztlán and mixed with the rich music of Black America. Radio station KELP's music surveys throughout the sixties was heavy with "Chicano Soul" groups. Shown are just a few of the singles that KELP's listeners were enjoying in the sixties.

of local disc jockey Steve Crosno the air-waves of El Paso became a tapestry of music both Spanish and English from throughout Aztlán mixed with the rich music of Black America. Radio station KELP's music surveys throughout the sixties were heavy with "Chicano Soul" groups: from San Antonio Sunny & the Sunliners, Rudy and the Reno-Bops and the Sunglows were top tune regulars; Albuquerque's Sheltons, Al Hurricane and Tiny Morie were well received; Los Angeles groups who left their mark in El Paso were Thee Midniters, the Premiers, and the Blendells. Noé Pro, Freddy Fender, and René and René represented *El Valle de Tejas* and of course Little Joe and the Latinaires who made their way west from Temple, Texas were and still remain extremely popular in the region. Bobby and the Premiers, the Valiants, the Night Dreamers, the Jives and the El Paso Drifters were some of the local groups that benefited from Steve Crosno's radio and television shows as well as concerts promoted by the eccentric and extremely popular DJ.

Steve Crosno's career in radio began around 1957 while he was still attending Union High School in Las Cruces, New Mexico. Within two years Crosno would become the program director and popular DJ for KELP, El Paso's number one radio station. What Crosno created in his ten years at KELP was affectionately known as the "El Paso Sound." With his hands on the pulse on the community Crosno silenced the drums of racism through his programs. The music he played and his unique sense of humor gave the youth of El Paso a place of their own. Between 1962 and 1970 his televised dance show, *Crosno's Hop* on KELP channel 13 was so popular that according to music-store owner George Reynoso "Locally, the shows ratings equaled or surpassed those of Dick Clark's *American Bandstand*.

One of the first doo-wop styled recordings to come out of El Paso was **Cradle Rock,** a tender ballad by the Rhythm Heirs, Evelyn and Virgie Gallegos the latter penned the lyrics with the popular children's lullaby as a template. The rare 1958 recording was released on Calvin Boles' Yucca label based in Alamogordo, New Mexico, which is 150 miles north of El Paso. The song re-surfaced in 1963 when brothers Benny and Joe Rodriguez of the popular East Los Angeles duet the Heartbreakers recorded **Cradle Rock** for Bob Keane's Donna label. Another early El Paso recording was Johnny Trujillo and the Knightsmen's 1961 recording of **Darlin' Why?**

El Paso Premiers

By 1966 one of the most popular local groups was Bobby Rosales and the El Paso Premiers. They came together on the Eastside of El Paso back in 1958, at the time Jaime Rosales was the group's saxophone player. When the band's piano player dropped out Jaime threw his kid brother eleven-year-old Bobby name in the hat. Rosales remembers those early years as fond memories. "My brother started playing in a band back in 1958, the band was called the Premiers. They lost their piano player and he told them 'Hey, my kid brother plays piano.' They invited me to practice and right away they took me in. Our first gig was in San Elizario a small town just south of El Paso. We played there in small adobe places that you can't believe could fit a band and the people; they were a lot of fun." Eventually guys started to drop out, changing the makeup of the group. Bobby was on piano, Jaime on sax, Angel on drums and the group had a pair of vocalists Gilbert Mendez and an African American named James Patterson who was serving in the military. By 1963 several musicians had dropped out and the band was ready to call it quits, prompting Rosales to step up and take over. From that moment on the group was known as Bobby and the Premiers.

In 1966 Bobby and the Premiers went into the recording studio with DJ Steve Crosno. They had prepared one song for the session **Let Me Call You Darling** with James Patterson on lead vocals. Crosno who was set to release the record on his Frog Death label, caught the group by surprise when he asked for another song for the "B" side. "I told Crosno to give me about 20 minutes" remembers Rosales. "And in that time I wrote **This Is the Beginning** music and all. I was nineteen-years-old at the time and I just started going out with this girl who ended up being my wife, that was my inspiration for the song." An instant hit in El Paso **This Is the Beginning** went to number one and stayed there for eleven weeks. For many of the groups that were coming up during this period rhythm and blues with the big horn arrangements was the thing, the soul music of Otis Redding, Sam and Dave, Wilson Pickett and James Brown and much of this sound can be heard in the El Paso Sound. The Premiers became regulars at the Basin Street East, a club located in a black neighborhood dubbed the "Black Society" and situated just outside the limits of El Segundo Barrio. By 1966 there were several R&B groups that had formed, creating a bit of excitement in the community. Before long everyone was looking forward to the battle of the bands. "We had the Night Dreamers with Sonny Powell, the El Paso Drifters, the El Paso Chessmen and the Premiers and between us it was a constant battle." Recalls Rosales, "we all wanted to out do each other especially at the battle of the bands, which was held at the El Paso Coliseum."

While touring through Eastern Texas in 1968 Bobby and the Premiers went into Robins Studios in Tyler, Texas and recorded two singles for C.L. Milburn's Souled Out of Texas record label. **Mess Up My Mind** a funky horn laden tune patterned after Otis Redding's **Can't Turn You Lose** was backed with the soulful ballad **What about One More Time**. The same session also produced a second single **Man about Town** b/w **Gotta Have a Reason** both highly sought after by soul record collectors.

By the early seventies Rosales and his whole group had moved to Pico Rivera a suburb east of Los Angeles where the group was a regular at the Plush Bunny as well as headlining at the Hollywood Palladium. Through the years the Premiers were the back up band for soul sensations James Brown and Stevie Wonder as well as touring on several soul revues that included Etta James, the Drifters and J.J. Jackson. El Paso's soul groups produced no national hits and except for a few record collectors and soul music fans very few people even know that they existed however, those that grew in mid-sixties El Paso cherish the memories and the music of that time.

Jives

Towards the end of the El Paso Sound era there was one band that was still creating excitement in El Paso and throughout Texas. A family enterprise called the Jives. The band was formed in 1968 by Charlie, Al-

El Paso, TX was as far east as **Thee Midniters** would venture.

bert and Donnie Miller, their uncle Tony Gomez and cousins Rudy and Barney Magaña. "The only ones that had any musical training were Rudy and Barney," recalls Tony Gomez. "Charlie was singing real nice and he got a hold of an old guitar, I rented a bass and we got Rudy and Barney to play with us." After a

The **Jives'** third album for Foy Lee's Tear Drop label. *Making Time* was released in 1973.

few informal sessions in the family living room they decided to start practicing in earnest.

Tony Gomez was thirty-two years old, while the rest of the group were fifteen and sixteen years old. Ultimately, he became the band's guardian as they performed at house parties and local dances. The Jives stuck to a rhythm and blues format, covering soul standards of the period and as they began to develop musically they entered the battle of the bands at Bowie High School, going up against some of the better-known groups like the El Paso Drifters. As word spread about this new R&B group that was creating a little excitement around town the Jives were invited to perform at Fort Bliss. "We started playing at the NCO clubs and man they loved us," remembers Gomez. "Especially the black soldiers."

Local promoter Joe Stevens, who had been booking all of the big groups from San Antonio started booking the Jives for local gigs and eventually passed on word to Chester Foy Lee of Tear Drop Records that this group was hot. According to Gomez "Foy Lee flew down to meet us and decided to give us a chance." He said, "He wanted us to work out six originals and four standards." Lee had the group fly down to Corpus Christi for the recording session. Their first album *Espera Un Tantito* contained two English R&B tunes and eight in Spanish. The biggest hit from the album was **Mi Gordita** a *polka* that climbed up San Antonio's Hit Parade to number one in 1969. Also on the first album was **El Segundo** an instrumental tune that paid tribute to *El Segundo Barrio* a historic neighborhood in El Paso. As the group started touring to promote the album it started to sell all over Texas, New Mexico and Arizona.

By the Jives' third album *Making Time* they had grown to an eight-piece band with a heavier horn section and a polished sound. They were also doing less rhythm and blues tunes and more *polkas* (something that Foy Lee had suggested) and Spanish songs. "If you notice from the first to the second album, from the second to the third, and the third to the fourth there is a great improvement in our sound." Says Gomez, "We were amateurs in the beginning and by the fourth we were seasoned and more professional."

By 1973 seventeen-year-old Charlie Miller wanted to call it quits. He was tired of playing in the clubs and salons and wanted to get into the popular rock field. The group had just finished their fourth album and Foy Lee pleaded with them to stay together. He felt that they had a big future in the Tejano field. However, they had made up their mind to disband. Charlie Miller went on to form a rock band called Windfall and although the Jives albums continued to sell the band would never perform together again.

Houston

Houston is situated on the eastern end of South Texas about one hundred and twenty-five miles from the Louisiana state-line. Although the city had a substantial Mexican American community, musically it was so multi-cultural that *La Onda Chicana* did not push into the city until the late sixties. Some of the earlier Chicano groups to call Houston home were Jesse Casas and the Crystals, Little Jesse and the Rockin' Vee's, the Exiles and Johnny and the Del-Hearts. They came up between 1960 and 1963 and were typical rock 'n roll combos. During the mid-sixties groups like the Stardusters, Neto Perez and the Originals, Big Lu y los Muchachos, and Rocky Gil and the Bishops had bigger bands or *orquestas* that were inspired by Sunny and the Sunliners.

Vocalist Jesse Casas was going to Stephen F. Austin High in 1960 when he joined a local group called the Crystals. "That band was all guitars and Isidro Rodriguez on drums," recalls Casas. "Everybody wanted to play guitar and nobody wanted to play bass." Eventually Tony Tostado played the bass lines on his guitar. Although the Crystals stayed together until 1971, they only recorded one single, a ballad titled **Tell Me**.

The Rockin' Vee's were also around during this period and consisted of the Villanueva Brothers; Jesse, Oscar and Ray, Alfred Luna, Tony Tostado and Gilbert Fernandez. This is the group that Sunny Ozuna recruited to be the first Sunliners band. The Vee's

The **Stardusters** and **Bobby and the Premiers** at the El Paso Coliseum. *Courtesy of George Reynoso.*

Six rare singles that were recorded by Houston based groups. **Los Stardusters** LP. *Courtesy of Joe Silva.*
Los Muchachos LP- the group later teamed up with Big LU.

stayed with Sunny for about six months before he put together the band that would stay with him for the next ten years. "In the summer of 1963 I got a call from Villanuevas," remembers Jesse Casas. "Sunny had left the band to form another Sunliner band and Jesse was starting a group called the Stardusters." Sunny had taken Tony Tostado with him so Frank Ardela became the Stardusters' bass player. This group recorded one single **It Must Be the Girl** for Huey P. Meaux's Pic 1 record label. Several years later a group called Los Stardusters were recording for Tear Drop Records. However, thay may have been unrelated.

Sunny and the Sunliners were the only *Tejano* band for along time that would venture into the multi-cultural cauldron that is Houston. One of the reasons was that they left a big impression on the black community and DJ Skipper Lee Fraiser used them to draw in the Mexican American audiences. "Because there were so many musical taste here in Houston a lot of the *Tejano* bands wouldn't even come here," says Casas. "When Sunny and the Sunliners started coming here all they would play was R&B, then later they started playing stuff like **La Cacahuate**. Now they were awesome the music was powerful, the way they dressed, everything. I'm glad we never opened up for them we would have been blown away."

The legendary **Rocky Gil and the Bishops** were one of Houston's top Chicano R&B groups. *Courtesy of Joe Silva.*

SOUL SIDE OF THE STREET

Phoenix and Albuquerque

> "Even now when you hear Chicano music being played here in New Mexico as opposed to Tejano music there is a distinct difference. During the mid-sixties I used to visit a buddy of mine in L.A. named Bobby Espinosa, and we'd go see Little Willie G and Thee Midniters, Little Ray, and the Premiers. My grandparents lived in City Terrace Park, and I used to go back and forth. So I'd come back from L.A. with these records and we would all sit around listening to them. Well we started doing something's like "Midnight Hour" and add a little something, our own flavor then someone else would copy us and we would then have the Albuquerque sound. I brought back from L.A. what I had heard Thee Midniters and Little Ray doing with the horns. No one was using trumpets and trombones here until I brought them in."
>
> Freddy Chavez-vocals-keyboards [Thee Chekkers]

Phoenix

Hadley Murrell started broadcasting soul music over the airwaves of Phoenix in the early sixties from AM station KCAC, a small station located on the Southside of town. The station's first location was in a small shopping center on Broadway Road (the same Broadway that Dyke and the Blazers were paying tribute to in **Funky Broadway**) and Central Avenue. Murrell started with a late night oldies show, which became popular with the Southside's Chicano population. As Hadley told John P. Dixon in an interview, "My audience was 80 percent Chicano and 20 percent black. I grew up in a Mexican neighborhood and most of my friends were Mexican. The records I liked were the records they liked." Hadley whose on-air line was "Hadley, who loves you madly" and on-air moniker was "Hadley Madly" was also spinning records for local high school dances and eventually started adding local rhythm and blues bands to his shows.

Those Fabulous Jokers had been around since 1962 first performing as the Night Owls with most of the members being from South Mountain High. When the Night Owls broke up Tony Neibles and Bobby "Soul" Frajo formed Those Fabulous Jokers taking the name from a local hang out called the Joker Lounge. "Between the Jokers and the Majestics we pretty much influenced the younger groups," recalls drummer Sandy Flores. "Which was good because we influenced Chicano and American Indian musicians who got inspired and started their own bands. We were all doing a lot of soul music, you know R&B, we weren't doing Chicano music."

With Hadley using the Jokers for his shows and

The group shortened their name to the **Jokers** after their first recording. *Courtesy of Sandy Flores.*

Handbill for a show at the Abell Hall in Phoenix featuring recording artists **Those Fabulous Jokers**. *Courtesy of Sandy Flores.*

acting as their manager the group quickly picked up a large following and Hadley stopped spinning records and started promoting other local bands and artists like Roy and the Dew Drops. Flores recalls the group's following among Chicano teens. "We had a big following especially from the *Chicanada* in the sixties." He said, "Every Tuesday night it was teen night at the Riverside Ballroom, which was on Central Ave. and it would be packed with twelve, thirteen hundred kids. Then everyone would cruise down Central across the river to the Arctic Circle for hamburgers, shakes and to just hang out. When we showed up the people would come around and treat us real special."

The Jokers were also popular at the Calderon Ballroom a venue known for their Saturday and Sunday dances featuring popular Mexican music. However, the popularity of rhythm and blues among the Mexican American community was so strong that they started booking various soul revues touring the country. "We opened up for Ike and Tina Turner, Marvin Gaye, Bobby "Blue" Bland and the Ikettes," says Flores. "It was a great experience for us."

In December of 1964 Murrell went into Audio Recorders with Those Fabulous Jokers and produced **The No No** b/w **Frankie's Jerk** for his Madley label. At the suggestion of Madley Those Fabulous Jokers changed their name to the Soulsetters and recorded the James Brown classic **Out of Sight** which was produced by Murrell for Randy Woods's Onacrest label.

The Soulsetters on stage. *Courtesy of Sandy Flores.*

As the Soulsetters' popularity grew and the membership changed, they were teamed up with soul singers Freddi (Fred Gowdy) and Henchi (Marvin Graves). Between 1968 and 1975 they released a steady stream of soul stompers and funk tunes for a variety of record labels including Bell, Reprise and MoSoul. The Soulsetters eventually made Boulder, Colorado their home base and Hadley started booking them at all of the big celebrity functions in the ski resorts of Boulder, Aspen, Vail, and Big Bear, Colorado. The group also performed in San Francisco and Los Angeles. As Hadley put it, "Wherever there was celebrity money they were there."

Meanwhile back in Phoenix, Hadley was looking for another band to replace the Soulsetters so he picked up another young Chicano band, which he felt had a lot of potential. Hadley signed Roy and the Dew Drops to his Wind Hit label in 1967 and released one single of the group. The Dew Drops recorded a cover of Sunny Ozuna's **The One Who's Hurting Is You** b/w **I'm Gonna Hurt You** like many of these singles **I'm Gonna Hurt You** did not get much airplay out of the general region, however though the years they have become extremely popular on England's Northern Soul Scene and among record collectors.

The departure of the Soulsetters left a void in the community however the foundation had been laid and the younger musicians were determined to continue the soul trend. In 1966 Sandy Flores was approached by his younger brother and some friends who were trying to form a band. "They were all between twelve and thirteen years old and I was nineteen so I was basically working from scratch," recalls Flores. "Then we started playing at Jerry Paisno's Swing City, which was Jamaica East when the Soulsetters were playing there. So we became the house band and opened up for Jackie Lee, the Ronettes and other soul acts." The Soulsations caught the attention of Mike Lenaburg who released a song Flores had written called **Soul Skate** on his Out Of Sight label. The song was picked up by a radio station in Tucson located about one hundred and fifty miles south of Phoenix, as **Soul Skate** caught on it became a huge hit. "We were booked at the Club La Jolla in Tucson and it was amazing to see the line around the street when we showed up." Unfortunately Tucson was the only place it caught on and the record's life was short lived.

In Chicano communities all over the Southwest the Vietnam war played a huge role in the demise of the local music scene. In 1967 Flores joined a steady stream of young men being called up by Uncle Sam to fight in Vietnam. The Soulsations continued performing until 1970. When Flores was joined in Viet Nam by his brother Tony. As the Vietnam war escalated the draft got a hold of more and more of the musicians ending a lot of the community's live music scene. As the musicians started to return in the late sixties and early seventies things had changed and live music was slowly taking a back seat to disco music.

Albuquerque

Unlike Los Angeles and San Antonio, Albuquerque's soul scene did not really get off the ground until 1965 and before anyone outside of New Mexico could really take notice of what was known as the "Duke City Soul Sound" it was gone. Most of these recordings were done by groups whose members were still in high school and were inspired by the Motown Sound,

The **Majestics** with Freddie Chavez on keyboards. *Courtesy of Freddie Chavez.*

James Brown, Wilson Picket and Los Angeles's Eastside Sound. By 1967 the military draft had decimated the groups, and the record labels either folded or turned their sights on a different music genre.

There were four record labels working out of Albuquerque between 1965 and 1970. Dave Bohnam's Red Feather Records, which recorded a variety of music including country, frat rock and a couple of the Chicano soul groups like the Bristols and Thee Chekkers. Bennie Sanchez's Hurricane Records was formed to promote her three sons Al Hurricane, Tiny Morrie and Baby Gaby. However, Hurricane Records did release some nice soul singles by Tommy G and the Charms, and Freddie and the Starlighters. John Wagner and Dick Scovels's Delta and Look labels had the Sneakers, Saliens, Chekkers, David Nuñez and Freddy Chavez on their roster.

In the south valley it was Dick Stewart's Lance Records, which was one of the most successful Albuquerque labels with the "Duke City Soul Sound." Lance's stable of groups like the Sheltons, Rudy and the Soulsetters, and Doc Rand and the Purple Blues kept the label busy through the late sixties. Dick Stewart sums up the music scene in Albuquerque like this "At the time when soul was in its infancy in Albuquerque, the genre's fan base was mostly that of

Look recording group **Thee Chekkers**. *Courtesy of Freddie Chavez.*

the Hispanic population which was in the majority on the West Side. Anglos, on the other hand, were in the majority on the East Side and their preference was for the British influenced psychedelic and folk rock."

Freddie Chavez

One of the most influential artists of this teen sound was Freddie Chavez, who by the time he was a student at Albuquerque High School had already been lead singer for several of the local bands. "I started at the age of eleven with a group called Freddie and the Flames," recalls Chavez. "I was the guitar player and we had this little group but we weren't so good, we couldn't get any gigs. But we'd hang around the other groups mainly the Majestics, which I ended up joining. We did one gig for like $5.00 for the whole group, we lasted for about six months." At the suggestion of the Majestics' leader Chavez learned to play the piano and eventually purchased a small electric piano. Meanwhile, he was spending summers at his grandmother's home in East Los Angeles's City Terrace neighborhood where he was able to attend dances and shows featuring the sounds of Little Ray and the Progressions, Thee Midniters and the VIPs. Eventually he developed a friendship with Bobby Espinosa who was then the keyboard player for the VIPs.

Chavez, a multi-talented musician, went on to record with several of Burque's top groups as well as record **They'll Never Know Why** a solo effort that is rated number 59 of the 500 top soul recordings on England's northern soul scene. His connection to Los Angeles and his friendship with keyboardist Bobby Espinosa of El Chicano fame was extremely influential in defining Albuquerque's soul sound. "I brought back from L.A. what I had heard Thee Midniters and Little Ray doing with the horns," recalls Chavez. "No one was using trumpets and trombones here until I brought them in."

Thee Chekkers

Thee Chekkers were already an established group in 1966, having recorded a pair of singles including a cover of Freddy Fender's **Only One** for Red Feather Records with David Nuñez as their lead singer. Sometime that year Nuñez enlisted in the Army Reserves and Freddie Chavez who was still attending Rio Grande High School stepped up to fill in as vocalist. At the time John Wagner and Dick Scovels had a recording studio located at 900 Fourth S.W. and were

Lance recording group **Rudy and the Soulsetters.** *Courtesy of Dick Stewart.*

putting out singles by local groups on their Delta and Look labels. With sixteen-year-old Chavez fronting the group the Chekkers went into Wagner studios with a pair of songs written and arranged by Chavez. All of the influences that Freddie Chavez had accumulated for the past five years came out on these two sides from the up-tempo horn driven **Lack of Love** to the soulful ballad **Please Don't Go** you could swear these were straight out of Detroit's soul machine of the sixties. According to Chavez only 500 copies of **Lack of Love** were pressed. Chavez's follow up solo effort **They'll Never Know Why** was, like his first release, poorly marketed and failed to get any air-play at all even in Albuquerque. Although Chavez is well known and respected in Burque for his work, the lack of proper management and marketing kept him from becoming a well known singer.

Lance Records

Lance Records was formed in 1966 by Dick Stewart to record and promote his own group King Richard and the Knights and other folk and psych rock bands from the Albuquerque area and eventually landed several of the area's hot Chicano R&B based groups. As Stewart recalls, "We were playing frat rock/garage band instrumentals that were popular for a while then the soul thing started to pick up steam on the westside of town." Tommy Bee an American Indian musician who had previously fronted a group called Tommy Bee and the Stingers started to bring some of the local groups to the attention of Stewart. Bee had been promoting shows and saw the professionalism and the following that these young groups had. "In 1966 we put out **I Who Have Nothing** by the Sheltons and it became a big regional hit," recalls Stewart.

CHICANO SOUL

After the Sheltons, Bee kept coming to Lance with new groups "He kept bringing the groups and we kept on recording them Rudy and the Soulsetters, Doc Rand and the Purple Blues and Love Special Delivery." Lance Records became the number one soul label in New Mexico and did it with Chicano groups. Lance Music Enterprises expanded into a regional distributor and booking agency, and in 1966 Stewart put out a monthly newsletter the *Lance Monthly* which covered Burque's local rock 'n roll scene. The region that was covered by Lance's groups went north to Santa Fe south to Las Cruces, across into El Paso, and across the Arizona border to Tucson and Phoenix and the small towns within that region. The groups performed their distinct style of Southwest soul in towns like Deming, Gallup, Clovis, and Socorro, New Mexico.

Sheltons

> *By the time the recordings were released on the Lance label, George's (Lucero) phone was ringing off the wall with gigs, Back then, in the mid-sixties, radio stations and DJs were very helpful. They played a lot of the local groups and more than half of the local groups were on Lance. Having our own music being played on the radio was great!. . . . We had lots of support like this. . . . Many of the local DJs (Lew Jones, Bobby Box, Al Tafoya, Bill Prevetti) were now operating teen clubs and teen dances. There was plenty of work for everybody.*
>
> Ray Avila [Sheltons]
> Mike Dugo interview for the Lance Monthly

Albuquerque soul singer **Tommy "G" Gonzales** Nashville, Tenn. 1966. *Courtesy of Dick Stewart.*

The Sheltons came together in the summer of '65 while Steve Lucero (vocals, sax, keyboards), George "Bud" Lucero (guitar), and Toby Romero (drums) were still attending high school, Steve Lucero was at Washington High and George and Toby were at Albu-

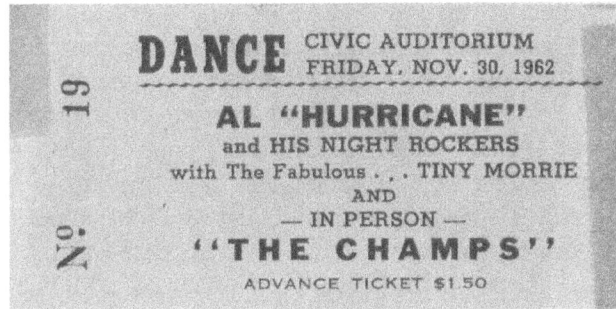

Ticket for a 1962 dance featuring **Al Hurricane**, **Tiny Morrie** and the **Champs**.

querque High School. By the fall of '65 the trio was joined by Ray Avila (bass), and Robert Elks (guitar) and in January of '66 they added a second horn player Ed Sanchez (tenor sax). Inspired by James Brown, Wilson Pickett and the Motown Sound the band put together a set of songs and started to work Burque's night club scene. The group caught the attention of local A&R man Tommy Bee who was looking for groups to fill Dick Stewart's roster at Lance Records.

The Sheltons's first single was recorded at Dell Studios and later used John Wagner's studios located at 900 4th S.W. where Stewart was renting office space for his Lance Records operation. The first of the two Lance singles **Find It** b/w **Yesterday's Laughter** got the group some air-play on the local radio stations KQEO and KLOS but it was their second 1967 release **I Who Have Nothing** b/w **Knock On Wood** which kicked off the "Duke City Soul Sound" and made Albuquerque the regional soul center.

It is possible that the Sheltons were inspired to record **I Who Have Nothing** by Thee Chekkers who had included the song on their playlist. Chavez would bring the records back from Los Angeles and the musicians from the various groups would sit around listening to the Premiers, Thee Midniters and Little Ray. Before long the Sheltons were playing **That's All** and Thee Chekkers were playing **I Who Have Nothing.** By the time the Sheltons went into Lance Records they had mastered the Little Ray classic and were ready to record it. "Stevie Lucero was borrowing my organ, trying to get the sound down," recalls Mike Sanchez of Rudy and the Soulsetters. "He was about fifteen years old and was a very talented musician he played the sax, organ, and he sang. Anyway we'd all sit around and ask each other hey, how do you play this or how did you get that sound. We were all trying to learn together."

The Sheltons walked away from the more dramatic version by Little Ray and completely rearranged the song with the keyboards as the dominant rhythm instrument and a strong horn section that gave the record a real Southwest feel to it. Fifteen-year-old Steve Lucero's vocals are exceptionally strong making this version of the Leiber and Stoller classic one of the best. The single stayed on top of the regional charts from October to December of 1967, just as the single was set for national distribution on Dot Records Uncle Sam stepped in. This was the during the peak of the Vietnam War and as members of the group turned eighteen they qualified for the military draft. First called up was George Lucero, then Ed Sanchez, then Ray Avila.

Another group to come out of Albuquerque High School was Tommy G and the Charms, led by one of the better soul singers in the area Tommy Gonzales. Not only could Tommy G handle the ballads like **Please Don't Fool with Me** but he was quite comfortable with the deeper soul groovers he was performing like James Brown's **I Want You So Bad** or the Brown inspired **I Know What I Want** which was written by Tiny Morrie, two songs initially released on Hurricane Records before being leased to Hollywood Records.

The war and the changing landscape of music contributed to the demise of the Duke City Soul Sound. "By the late sixties things were changing it wasn't just the war situation, although the war did affect us." Mike Sanchez confides "It was also like we were getting to the point where we were starting to grow. We started to see what else was going on in music and some wanted to change and others didn't, things finally fell apart." As the Charms started to get their draft notices the group disbanded and Gonzales joined the Chekkers until they were also called to serve leaving him without a group. In the early seventies Gonzales resurfaced with a psychedelic rock group called Mud who recorded for EMI.

Al Hurricane

Although the Sanchez brothers Al "Hurricane," Amador "Tiny Morrie" and Gabriel "Baby Gaby" were synonymous with the great Spanish music of northern New Mexico they were also influenced by and played along side early rhythm and blues stars like Fats Domino, James Brown, Jimmy Clanton and others. Al Hurricane was born to Jose and Bennie Sanchez in 1936. From an early age he earned the nickname Hurricane because he always seemed to be destroying what ever was in his path, knocking down things as he ran through the house. Before long his mother would say *"Aqui viene mi Hurricane."* Years later "Hurricane" also described his on stage persona as a hard rockin' guitar player.

Around 1956 Al formed a group called the Sentimentalists. This was at a time when the big band sound still had some popularity but things were changing fast as rock 'n roll had arrived and for a young guitar player it was a chance to be part of something new. Al changed the name of his group to Al Hurricane and the Night Rockers. With this Al's industrious mother, Bennie Sanchez decided it would be cheaper if they owned their own facility rather than renting a place for the Night Rockers to perform in. With that, the Sanchez family opened the Hurricane Palladium on Central Ave.

The Night Rockers' first release came in 1957 with **Hey! Let Me Tell You** backed with **You're the Girl For Me** a single released on the family owned Hurricane label. The single featured the vocals of Tiny Morrie backed by the Night Rockers.

One of the biggest hits for the band was Tiny Morrie's 1966 recording of **Lonely Letters**. The song was popular throughout New Mexico, Arizona and west Texas. Bennie Sanchez took Morrie to Hollywood and got a national distribution deal with Dot Records.

In November of 1969 Al and his band were returning from a show in Denver, CO, A winter storm had left a skin of ice on a bridge in Walsenburg, CO. Al, who was driving lost control of the car he was driving and drove off of an embankment. Everyone in the vehicle survived. However, Al suffered several serious injuries and a decision was made to remove his right eye. This didn't stop Hurricane it only changed his appearance as he was now performing with a patch over his right eye.

Through the years the music of Al Hurricane, Tiny Morrie and Baby Gaby has evolved and moved away from rock 'n roll and more towards the *rancheras* and *cumbias* that have made them international stars. However, it was rock 'n roll that inspired them to make music their life.

YO SOY CHICANO

Brown Pride

"The Movement changed the environment in the barrio. Everybody was talking about *La Raza* and *la causa*. The dances had tapered off and it seemed like everyone was going their own way. I, myself got involved with David Sanchez the Brown Berets we used to meet at the Calypso on Brooklyn and Mott. After Catalina Island (In 1972 the Brown Berets occupied Catalina Island and claimed it for Mexico) I joined the CCM (Chicano Committee Movement de Aztlán). We worked to change the political situation in East Los Angeles."

Johnny Jay Jimenez- Promoter

Political Awakening

By the mid-sxities Mexican Americans had been growing increasingly impatient with their status in American society. Fed up with being economically and politically marginalized, the Chicano generation, to a significant degree, was becoming increasingly militant as well. President Lyndon Johnson's Great Society programs and the Civil Rights Act of 1965, which were designed to lift African Americans and other oppressed minorities out of poverty, simply were not living up to their exalted promise. It was a matter of "too little, too late." A number of factors created a turbulent cauldron of social consciousness and political activism. It sometimes boiled over. That energy spread across the country, sometimes resulting in defiant clashes with authority. Even the step of calling themselves "Chicanos" was an act of assertiveness and new-found identity for Mexican Americans.

The years of being essentially locked out of America's political and economic mainstream had nurtured a counterculture among Chicanos that was influenced by the anti-war, civil rights, labor rights and Black Power movements in the late sixties. That struggle spawned unrest and, in some cases, forceful confrontations with police in Texas, California, New Mexico and Colorado. Protests demonstrations and marches spread to Chicago, Minneapolis, Seattle and practically every other city with a sizeable Mexican American population.

Young Chicanos began to define themselves and their goals in ways that were in sharp contrast to the perspectives of their parents and grandparents. For example, a longstanding organization called the League of United Latin American Citizens (LULAC)

El Chicano at the Watts Summer Festival 1974. *Courtesy of Mickey Lespron.*

consistently urged Mexican Americans to assimilate into the dominant Anglo culture in order to achieve political and economic gains and to attain acceptance by the mainstream society. By the late 1960s the youth-driven Chicano movement stood for a rejection of some of those tenets, especially the goal of any type of cultural absorption into the mainstream. Chicanos wanted progress and success on their own terms.

Some of those goals were codified in two seminal documents. The first of those, adopted in 1966 at the Denver Youth Conference hosted by activist Rodolfo "Corky" Gonzalez's Crusade for Justice, was "El Plan Espiritual de Aztlán." The second document was adopted three years later by a group called the Chicano Coordinating Committee on Higher Education and was called "El Plan de Santa Bárbara." Both of those called for Chicano self-determintion and urgent political action. They focused on the notion of "Aztlán"—a sort of spiritual birthplace of the Chicano.

During these heady times Chicanos were asserting their pride in their heritage as an indigenous people and they were rejecting the negative connotations that had been cast upon them by Anglo American society. The goal was not to pursue some pie-in-the sky total break from Anglo American society. It was to embue Mexican Americans with a new and legitimate pride in their heritage and their capabilities to achieve. This renewed pride and sense of self-identity among the new Chicano generation also led to a change in the popular music they were creating—music that drew upon and celebrated their cultural heritage.

Texas: Returning to the Past

Chicano musicians were ready for a change in the music they were creating. The years they spent performing rhythm and blues and rock 'n roll were also used as a period of development and training. However, for the most part, they had been imitating African American musical styles and it was now time for them to use their knowledge and creativity to develop a sound that was culturally closer to home.

By far the most influential musical form among the Texas groups during this transitional period was the *ranchera*, which was brought back into the mainstream of *Tejano* music by Sunny Ozuna and Little Joe Hernandez during the mid-sixties. In both cases *ranchera* music was fused with the intricate rhythms and horn arrangements that the Sunliners and the Latinaires had developed with their R&B tunes. Another indicator of this cross pollination can be discerned as far back as the early sixties when it was not uncommon for *Tejano* artists to record English-language R&B style records followed by a *ranchera*, *corrido* or *conjunto* style recording. For example, in 1963 the Royal Jesters recorded **I Want to Be Loved** and **Love Me** two of their most popular releases.

Mexican Revolution de Ruben Ramos: *Viva La Revolucion Mexicana*, El Zarape 1075 [1972] members from the Alfonso Ramos and Roy Montelongo orchestras. *Courtesy of Joe Silva.*
Yaqui: Playboy 127 [1972] Originally recorded as the Impalas and the Slauson Brothers. *Courtesy of Brown Bag Productions.*

During the same timeframe they recorded **Poco A Poco** and **Compañera**. This revealed the unique ability of the Chicano band to cross back and forth between the two cultures.

This "bi-musical" formula was also used by the Sunglows, Sunny and the Sunliners, Rudy Tee, Junior and the Starlites, the Broken Hearts, Carlos Landin and the Rondels, Freddie Fender, Gilbert and the Blue Notes, Rudy Tee and many others. This can be attributed to the influences coming from the rural, working class communities of South Texas where *ranchera* and *conjunto* music were extremely popular. Unlike Los Angeles, San Antonio is comparatively small and many of the bands were dependant on nearby rural communities for work. This was a two-way dependency because the kids in these communities also wanted to hear big city rock 'n roll, while the older folks demanded "their" music. By the late sixties there was little demand in these rural areas for anything other than *música Tejana*.

Los Angeles: Latin Rock and Latin Jazz

In Southern California this phenomenon of dual language releases never really caught on among the rock 'n roll groups although the influences were surely there. Several groups including the Salas Brothers, Terri and the Velveteens, the Perez Brothers, El Chicano and Thee Midniters did record in Spanish. However, by the late sixties it was the Afro-Cuban influences of Latin-jazz rather than *música norteña* and *rancheras* that dominated Los Angeles's transition

El Chicano: *Revolucíon* Kapp 3640 [1971] Originally performed as the VIPs. **Tierra**: 20th Century 412 [1973] Brothers Steve and Rudy Salas spent the previous ten years as the Salas Brothers. *Courtesy of Brown Bag Productions.*

from R&B to Latin rock. The Latinization of Los Angeles's rock groups may have been implanted into the psyche of several influential musicians as far back as 1958 through Bill Taggert's music program at Salesian High School on L.A.'s Eastside. Through his program he introduced his young students to standard jazz. As jazz itself was fused with *música tropical* and the Afro-Cuban rhythms of Mongo Santamaria, Cal Tjader and Perez Prado, it became a popular music form in Los Angeles and was then effortlessly incorporated into the R&B and rock format as Taggert's students developed.

Chicano nationalism, political awareness, and the civil rights and anti-war movements all contributed to the late-sixties cultural renaissance in Los Angeles's Chicano arts community. This was also an engaging transitional period for fans of the Eastside sound. By 1968 live music shifted away from the safe confines of community ballrooms to the more liberating and free-wheeling outdoor venues popularized in San Francisco by the hippie movement which seemed to sprout overnight. Gone was the desire for well-groomed musicians in white shirts, ties and dark suits.

Strident political activism in the form of school walkouts, sit-ins and anti-war marches was a call-to-arms throughout the Southwest. Musically, Thee Midniters responded first with an instrumental tune which trombonist Romeo Prado composed during the height of the 1968 school walkouts. The song titled **Chicano Power** was released on Eddie Torres's La Raza label and really emphasized the Latin jazz roots that several of the group members had an affinity for.

During the 1968 "blowouts" or school walkouts Steve Salas was attending Lincoln High School, where a year later he would become student body president (after which he was accepted at Stanford University). "When we walked out of high school, it was one of the more glorious moments of my life, because we were standing up for what we believed in," recalls Salas. "I don't care what anyone says. For us, the people that were involved, we knew what we were standing up for. It wasn't like 'Hey! Let's get out of class.'"

The school walkouts in 1968 were another pivotal event in the burgeoning Chicano Movement. Thousands of students from the four Eastside high schools—Garfield, Roosevelt, Lincoln and Wilson—boycotted classes over several days. They were protesting inferior school facilities and the dearth of educational opportunities. It was yet another defiant act rooted in an emerging zeal for social change. With this political awakening a new era in Chicano music was born.

El Chicano

With the release of **Viva Tirado** the VIPs were the first group to be put in the national spotlight in the late 1960s. The VIPs became El Chicano, but the name change didn't happen immediately. When Eddie Davis released the single he did so without the consent of the VIPs and released the record using a different name for the band—El Chicano. The VIPs' initial reaction was one of anger. "At first the VIPs were offended that someone (Eddie Davis) had taken something that they had created and put it on the radio under another name," remembers Steve Salas of Tierra. "They didn't want to represent the group (El Chicano) and I don't blame them. But they came around and it has worked for them. They took a negative and worked it into a positive."

"The heat was on Eddie Davis to come up with a group to represent El Chicano," recalls Rudy Salas. That led to some confusing scurrying around. Rudy Salas recalls: "The demos he sent out were credited to a group called El Chicano. He started to get some response with it so he talked to the VIPs, they didn't want anything to do with changing their name. They were a band called the VIPs. So Eddie Davis all of a sudden had a record that he sold to MCA, which was getting airplay but he had no group. Meanwhile Kapp Records, which was a subsidiary of MCA, gave Davis a budget to go into the studio and record an album."

Davis decided to put together another group that would become El Chicano. "Eddie called around and got some musicians including myself to go into the studio and start working on an album," recalls Rudy Salas of Tierra. "We were going to represent El Chicano. Well, a few weeks into the thing the song started to do real well on the charts, so the guys from the VIPs came to us and said, 'Hey that's our song,' and rightly so."

To the traditional first generation Mexican immigrant the term "Chicano" was something too radical for them to accept readily. To the traditionalist it was a dirty term, a pejorative name. Mexican American veterans of World War II and those from their generation were generally conservative and viewed themselves as proud red-blooded Americans and the idea that their children and grandchildren were in the streets demonstrating against American foreign aggression and demanding their civil rights was disquieting and difficult to comprehend.

Ersi Arvisu, El Chicano's lead vocalist saw "Chicano" as a radical, anti-American term that depicted Mexican Americans as something akin to com-

Jonny Chingas LP 1980 after nearly 35 years of being one of the unsung heroes of the Chicano rhythm and blues scene in Los Angeles, Rulie Garcia finally got his hit.

munists wearing brown berets and running around dangerously with guns. "I felt that the name Chicano was harsh," Arvisu says. She adds: "When you said 'Chicano' it was like the movement. It wasn't that we were a band of Mexican Americans, it was like we represented the movement. We didn't want to be characterized as revolutionaries."

However, once the VIPs realized that the name El Chicano had propelled them to the forefront of the growing Chicano pride movement they belatedly embraced their new name. Not only the name but, the concept of the political and social change. That acceptance was made evident by the title of their second album, *Revolución*. Yet, such decisions revealed the political sensitivity associated with the era. Some criticized the group's second album for the cover art.

The cover featured the band superimposed onto a photo, standing behind Mexican Revolutionary War leaders Emiliano Zapata and Pancho Villa sitting in front of a bombed out building with the American flag on the left side of *el General* Pancho Villa. The inclusion of the American flag behind the Mexican revolutionary heroes was considered political blasphemy among the more radical circles. Although they had a number-one hit song in Los Angeles and would record nine albums with some exceptional recordings on them, El Chicano never caught on in other areas of the Southwest where people expected them (because of their name) to play *rancheras*.

However, like the enormously talented groundbreaking San Francisco Bay Area group Santana, El Chicano helped to open the door for a growing number of west coast musicians that were already headed down the Latin rock/Latin jazz path. In several ways **Viva Tirado** was pivotal in creating this new sound that would become synonymous with East Los Angeles.

What Rudy Salas and the musicians that were assembled by Eddie Davis created in the studio was a series of Latin-jazz instrumentals that focused on Rudy Salas's guitar playing. "I always played the guitar mainly to accompany my brother and myself, but I never played it while with the Jaguars," Salas says. "Mario Paniagua was the lead guitar player and Frank Chavez was the rhythm guitarist back then. It wasn't until 1968 when Mario left the band and we became Six-Pak that I moved up to lead guitar, then I heard Carlos Santana and I knew which way I was going with our music." Not wanting to waste the masters of those experimental recordings, Eddie Davis released them under a series of group names such as One G Plus Three, Tocayo and Hummingbird 4.

Little Joe y la Familia

> "We've kind of segregated ourselves, we've become too ethnic with what they call *musica Tejana* today, with the accordion and all that and less bi-lingual. For Sunny and I coming up in the rock 'n roll era we had to play half our shows doing cover tunes of what was happening because that's what the kids wanted to hear. That's why the crowd was always a mixed one, black, white and Chicano."
>
> Little Joe Hernandez- band leader
> Temple, Texas [Little Joe Y La Familia]

La Raza was hungry for artists who identified with their newfound Chicanismo. Mexican Americans were eager to embrace art and music unique to Chicano culture. Little Joe and the Latinaires realized this after spending time in San Francisco watching Malo and Santana. These two successful bands, regarded by some as "Chicano/hippie" groups, were performing a powerful, pulsating blend of rock and soul with heavy Afro-Cuban rhythms and percussion. Enlightened by what they had witnessed in San Francisco, the Latinaires shed their suits, let their hair grow and changed their name to Little Joe y la Familia. The group shifted away from black-influenced R&B and embraced the more traditional *ranchera* style that dominated La Familia's first album.

Although today Little Joe laments somewhat the isolationism that was created during the late-sixties, he recalls those days fondly. "I've always been attracted by a mixed crowd," he said. "But we've kind of segregated ourselves, we've become too ethnic with what they call *música Tejana* today, with the accordion and all that and less bilingual. For Sunny and

Courtesy of Max Uballez.

I coming up in the rock 'n roll era we had to play half our shows doing cover tunes of what was happening because that's what the kids wanted to hear. That's why the crowd was always a mixed one, black, white and Chicano."

By 1968 the *ranchera* and the music of the *conjunto* had returned to the forefront throughout Texas and there was little demand for rhythm and blues so the bands adjusted and gave the people what they wanted. Fortunately for Augustine Ramirez, Johnny Canales, Carlos Landin, Latin Breed and Los Dinos they never really strayed too far from their roots and the adjustment was really more of a choice. Sunny Ozuna reflects on the development of *La Onda Chicana*: "A lot of the wording and the language that we used either in English or Spanish was more of they way we *Tejanos* think and it kind of found its own way back." He said, "The *norteño* and *conjunto* was already here and the accordion has been here forever. The accordion to the *conjunto* or anything Hispanic, whatsoever, is like the steel guitar to country music. It's there no matter what happens. We've pushed it back, moved it to the side, brought it up to the front, we've done everything to the poor accordion especially when the keyboards came up front."

Macondo

In Los Angeles Max Uballez took what he had started with the Romancers and continued the evolution of his music with his new group Macondo. "With Macondo I took some funky groove tunes I had written and we added the Latin instrumentation on top of it," explains Uballez. "Macondo was more of a Latin funk band. You might call it 'The Romancers go Latin.' When I began putting the band together in 1971 the band included myself, Bob Hernandez and Manuel Rodriguez, the foundation of the Romancers band." Uballez continues, "We were working more in a guitar-based funk direction and we added Fred Ramirez on keyboards. Fred is a great Latin/jazz keyboardist. So we began to learn Latin rhythms and added Lee Pastora on congas and Eddie Caicedo on timbales. This was a natural evolution because most of my material always had a slight Latin edge to it. Listen to **Slauson Shuffle** we had a cowbell and if you add congas and timbales you have Latin-rock. Maybe the **Slauson Shuffle** was the first Latin rock tune?"

Tierra

It was inevitable through all that had been occurring both musically and politically for the six years or so leading up to 1971 that a group from East Los Angeles would emerge that would speak eloquently and artistically to the issues at hand. This group was Tierra. It was the right group at the right time. It combined a social consciousness with unquestionable musicianship and innovative artistry. Tierra was formed and led by two brothers who started singing professionally when they were still in elementary school. They honed their skills as rock musicians in the 1960s when they were teenagers.

Rudy and Steve Salas's careers run parallel with the peak years of East Los Angeles's music renaissance and the political dynamism that created an opening for positive social awareness. As pre-teens the Salas brothers were already performing as a mariachi duo in the Lincoln Heights area, just east of downtown Los Angeles, when they met guitarist Mario Paniagua, leader of the Jaguars. "We lived on Clover Street in Lincoln Heights," remembers Rudy Salas, "and the homeboys from Clover would walk around the neighborhood with acoustic guitars singing and my uncle Turi (Art Brambila) put that little combo together, and they started playing at the local fiestas and stuff like that. So our first live entertainment outside of the family came from these pachucos singing rancheras—it was pretty cool."

Rudy and Steve had already developed an ear for music and were starting to mimic the harmonies of *los trios románticos* like Los Dandys and Los Panchos when Rudy got his first guitar. After performing at some family functions things quickly developed for the Salas brothers. "A family friend used to book the

The original members of **Tierra** L-R: Steve Salas (vocals, bass, trombone), Rodarte Torres Jr. (keyboards, trumpet), Rudy Villa (sax, flute, vocals), Rudy Salas (vocals, guitar), Conrad Lozano (bass), seated Kenny Roman (drums). *Courtesy of Brown Bag Productions, photographer: Rudy Rodriguez.*

music for the church bazaar," Rudy Salas said. "So she got us to do a couple of songs and then things took off for us. My brother was eight and I was ten."

The Jaguars started as the Percussions while the band members were attending Lincoln High School and consisted of Mario Paniagua, Anthony Carroll, Adrian Sansone and Frank Chavez. At a small neighborhood church bazaar where the Salas brothers were singing in Spanish, Paniagua went up to them after their performance.

"They were looking for some vocalists for the band so they came up to us," recalls Rudy. "Mario started speaking Spanish to us, but we told him, 'We don't speak Spanish' so he told us that he was looking for some singers and he liked our harmony." After discussing it with their parents and agreeing that Paniagua would take care of them, the Salas Brothers started to learn English-language pop songs. Rudy continues, "My parents had a lot of trust in Mario. He was only a teenager himself but he was very responsible and he made sure we were taken care of."

As the Salas Brothers, with the backing of the Jaguars, they recorded the first single for Eddie Davis's Faro Records. It was a harmony duet titled **Darling (Please Bring Your Love)** released as Faro 614. That same year the Jaguars had a local hit with an instrumental ballad titled **Where Lovers Go** followed by a Mario Paniagua composition titled **One Like Mine** by the Salas Brothers.

Meanwhile, Art Brambila had gone to work for Capitol Records as a materials buyer for their printing department, an executive position, which gave him some contacts. During East Los Angeles' music renaissance of the mid-sixties Brambila tried to get the attention of music executives at Capitol. "I tried to convince them (Capitol Records) to look into the music from the Eastside," recalls Brambila. "But I was totally ignored. I was just a kid from the Eastside who happened to get a good executive job at a record company."

Everything changed as a result of the National Chicano Moratorium on August 29, 1970. It was a transformative event for the Chicano Movement. And, ultimately for the music performed by Mexican Americans. It was billed as a demonstration against the war in Vietnam and the idea that poor, working class men from the Chicano community were being used as cannon fodder to fight an illegal and unjust war. It began as a peaceful demonstration which drew more than 25,000 marchers who made their way along Whittier Boulevard in East Los Angeles. But on that hot summer day it eventually turned into a scene of chaos and violence. Many who participated in the demonstration described an unprovoked attack on the marchers by helmeted police officers who began clubbing young men and women and began firing tear gas projectiles into the crowd, creating havoc. It ended in a deadly confrontation. The national spotlight was on the "Chicano issue."

The march ended with a huge rally at Laguna Park (now named Salazar Park). Documentary film footage reveals now infamous scenes of police officers clubbing and otherwise attacking young demonstrators. Several people were killed including journalist Ruben Salazar who was a columnist for the *Los Angeles Times* and news director for Spanish-language television station KMEX. Using a launcher that looks like a bazooka, an L.A. County sheriff's deputy fired a tear gas projectile at Salazar's head from ten feet away, killing him instantly. Months later a Los Angeles County coroner's inquest ruled that Salazar had "died at the hands of another." Yet, no one was ever prosecuted for the death of Ruben Salazar, who became something of a martyr to the Chicano Movement. Those events shocked the nation and propelled Chicanos, however briefly, into the spotlight of the country's news media.

"Now we were front page," remembers Brambila. "The following Monday I was called into the executive offices. They wanted to know about what this kid from the Eastside had been telling them about and the music from across the bridges. So I rattled off some names of groups and they asked me to be a scout. They said, 'Use our resources and do whatever you want.' All they asked for was first choice in what we produced."

Inspired by the success of El Chicano and San Francisco's Latin rock groups Santana, Malo, Sapo and Azteca, Rudy and Steve Salas assembled a group of top musicians from Los Angeles and started performing together as Maya. Maya was was made up of the Salas brothers, Danny Lamont on drums and Jimmy Espinosa on bass. The experiment lasted about one year before Steve and Rudy were left without a band. In 1971 a new group of musicians was assembled: David Torres, Jr. (now with the Poncho Sanchez band) on keyboards, Kenny Roman on drums, Rudy "Bub" Villa on sax and flute and Conrad Lozano (now with Los Lobos) on bass. Without a name, they started working on original material, much of it written by Rudy, Steve and David Torres.

During the same period veteran Eastside musicians George Ochoa (Slauson Brothers), Eddie Serrano (Cannibal and the Headhunters), Ray Regalado (El Chicano), and Ronnie Reyes (Thee Impalas) came together as Yaqui, a socially progressive rock group with a lot of raw talent.

Another group vying for a chance at a recording contract was Tango, an extension of Mark and the Escorts, a group led by Mark Guerrero. The Escorts recorded a pair of singles that Billy Cardenas sold to Creshendo-GNP in 1965. Mark Guerrero, the son of legendary Mexican American singer/songwriter Lalo Guerrero, was only sixteen at the time. Unlike the older groups who were covering R&B and soul tunes, young Guerrero was inspired by the Beatles and the other mid-sixties British Invasion groups. When things started to change in 1967 Mark and the Escorts changed their name to the Men from S.O.U.N.D. and eventually started getting gigs on the west side of town. "Most of the bands stayed in East L.A. and went through the changes," recalls Guerrero. "Our situation was different. Around 1967 I started getting more into Cream, Vanilla Fudge, Neil Young and that kind of sixties rock. We started playing at Gazzari's and other places outside of East Los Angeles in 1968. Then we got we signed by Kapp and then A&M. So went more into the Hollywood scene."

Brambila was instrumental in getting Tierra, Yaqui and Tango signed with major record labels. "I bought the contract for Tierra from Mario Paniagua," recalls Brambila. "I wanted to get some recognition so I took a chance. I told my wife, 'I have ten thousand dollars in the bank and I want to be a record producer, so I have to take chances,' and she supported me. So I bought the contract from Mario Paniagua for my two nephews (Rudy and Steve Salas). They wanted something that was true to the community so they came up with the name Tierra. I also had Yaqui, Mark Guerrero and Carmen Moreno on contract."

However, the age-old challenge for Chicano groups was marketing with all its attendant difficulties. It was particularly difficult to market something new and untried. For example, in what category do you insert a new genre of music that has potential in several categories? One of the hurdles these groups had to overcome was the fact that most mainstream radio stations had no idea how to handle a group with a Latin name, a problem that Chicano artists had confronted since the emergence of Ritchie Valens.

After nearly twenty years of hard work and perseverance Tierra produced a national hit record in the late 1970s. They did it by going back to their R&B roots, covering **Together**, a hit song from 1967 by a popular soul group, the Intruders. Steve Salas on **Together**. "By the seventies we were no longer performing one Latin song, one R&B tune, one rock song and so on," recalls Salas. "We were taking elements of all of this music and creating a new branch of rock music. That's what **Together** was all about. Letting the music pour out of the musicians and not worry about the parameters, let all of the ingredients of your lifetime surface. There was no arrangement. My brother (Rudy) brought the song to rehearsal, we all knew it so everyone knew where to go with it. Nobody dictated nothing to anybody, everybody just fell into place, it was just magic and by far our biggest hit."

CONCLUSION

Wherever you go in the Chicano Southwest you can find remnants of this much-overlooked 1960s Chicano soul scene. Many of the unsung heroes and the music they created are still cherished by their local communities and it is not uncommon on any given weekend to get a glimpse of the past. In Los Angeles Thee Midniters, Tierra and El Chicano are still performing their brand of Latin-rock, as are dozens of musicians, both from that era and those that chose to continue their soulful tradition. In San Antonio soul singers Joe Jama and Ernie Garibay continue the tradition with their groups 100 Proof and Cats Don't Sleep. Arturo "Sauce" Gonzales and the Westside Sound, Dimas Garza, Charlie Alvarado, Sonny Ace, J. Jay and Mr. Entertainment Rudy T. Gonzales still make the occasional stage appearance. Nationally Sunny Ozuna and Little Joe still take their show on the road. And there is a growing number of younger groups like Los Lonely Boys from Austin and Rocky Padilla, Rich Garcia and the Midnight Cruzzers from Los Angeles that are determined to keep this music form alive.

DISCOGRAPHY OF RECORDINGS

Abel and the Starliners Combo
San Antonio, TX
Abel Hernandez
Chico 18   You Know I Love You / Chicken Hop Twist [1962]
see: Rickie and the Keys

Sonny Ace and the Twisters
San Antonio, TX
Sonny Ace (Domingo Solis) (vocals), Martin Linan (tenor sax), Mike Rodriguez (tenor sax), David Spiller (alto sax), Gene Noriega (drums), Tony Villarreal (guitar), Ralph Mendez (bass)
with the Dell-Sharps
TNT 153   If My Teardrops Could Talk / Swinging Stroll [1958]
TNT 140   I Love Her So / Darling of Mine [Al Reed]   [1958]
with the Twisters
Atlantic 2364   Wooleh Booleh / Chilli Pepper [1965]
Cobra 006   When You're Smiling / Gypsy [1963]
Cobra 011   Devil or Angel / Fever [1963]
Cobra 214   Amor Que Malo Eres / La Traidora [1963]
Cobra 1112   Cuatro Copas / Cuatro Vidas [1963]
Cobra 1113   Anymore / Stand-by Love [1964]
Cobra 1133   Little Girl / Little Spark [1964]
Cobra 2224   Wooleh Booleh / Chili Pepper [1965]
Cobra 4444   You'll Tear Our Dreams Apart / Oh Marie [1965]
Gigolo 061   If My Teardrops Could Talk
Jox 028   Gotta See My Baby Tonight / Lucille [1963]
Rival 01   Tamales / Take My Love [1959]
Rival 02   So Lonely / Oh Little Girl [1959]
Rival 06   Just a Gigolo-Ain't Got Nobody / Really [1960]
Rival 08   Just You and Me / [1960]
Sunglow 107   Easy Rocking / Dreamer Boy [1963]
Sonny   Blue Monday / Here Is the Song
LP: Sonny Ace [Discos Grande 4003]

Dee Adra (Lori Cantu)
Corpus Christi, TX
Dynamic 113   Don't Need a Reason / Without Regret [1966]

Rickey Agary (Aguirre)
San Antonio, TX
Bel Canto 728   Everybody Needs Someone / part 2 [1959]
see: Ricky and the Keys

Lonnie Aguilar and the Latin Souls
Fort Worth, TX
Lonnie Aguilar, Paul Martinez (sax)
Capri 218   Mama's Pollo / Me Despido De Ti [1971]

Al and the Exclusives
San Antonio, TX
Jox 015   Please Forgive Me / Breezy [1963]

Alfred and Joe and the Noblemen
Los Angeles, CA
Alfred Garcia & unknown
Kay-Gee 101   Darling Dear / Soul Shuffle [1964]

Ambertones
Los Angeles, CA
Danny Medina, Eddie Delgado, Henry Hernandez, Mike Sandoval, Jimmy Alvarez, Charles Muñoz
Dottie 1129   One Summer Night / Chocolate Covered Ants [1965]
Dottie1130   I Need Someone/If I Do [1965]
GNP-Crescendo 329   Charlena / Bandito [1964]
Newman 601   Clap Your Hands / Cruise [1966]
White Whale 242   You Don't Know Like I Know / Ninety-Nine & a Half [68]

Ambrose and the Royal Bops
San Antonio, TX
AAA xxx   I'm in the Mood for Love

Apollo Brothers
Los Angeles, CA
Ruben Guevara, Paul Amarillas
Cleveland 108   My Beloved One / Riot [1961]
Locket 108   My Beloved One / Riot [1960]

Jack Arnold and the Chalecos
San Antonio, TX
Wild Cat 0009   Chulita / Target [1959]

Arturo and Pat with the Invaders
McAllen, TX
Arturo Longoria
Pharoah 134   Oh Yes Tonight / So Tenderly and Faithfully

Atlantics
El Monte, CA
Jimmy Meza (guitar), John Meza (bass), Manuel Garcia (guitar), Jim Hughes (drums), Frank Ascolese (trumpet), Mike Quinvilla, Carmen Caudillo (vocals)
Rampart 643   Beaver Shot / Fine, Fine, Fine [1965]
Rampart 647   Sloop Dance / Sonny & Cher [1965]

Hank Ayala and the Matadors
Weslaco, TX
Hank Ayala; lead, Manuel Pena: high tenor, Eddie Ramirez; second tenor
Back Beat   530   Betty Jo / Handsome [1960]

Aztlan
Brawley, CA
Thomas Valles
Aztlan 8234   You Say You Love Me / Should I Take You Home

B.P. and His Royal Tones
Hurley, NM
A-OK 1000   Love and Be Loved / Lorica

Baby Gaby with Al Hurricane's Band
Albuquerque, NM
Gabriel Sanchez, Al Sanchez, Amador Sanchez
Hurricane
6980   I'll Be Crying Teardrops over You / When I Walk Out That Door
LP: Canta Pepito Y Otras [Hurricane 10013]
See: Tiny Morie, Al Hurricane
Johnny Ballad and the Zodiacs
Wildcat 0016   My Song / Another Day [1959]
Wildcat 0017   I'll Gamble / Search For Love [1959]

Eddie Benavides Y Los Jesters
Los Lunas, NM
Eddie Benavides, Bennie Valenzuela, Armando Velasco, Johnny Torres
Los Jesters 1004   Just a Dream / Let the Four Winds Blow

Gil Bernal
Los Angeles, CA
American 1034   I'll Come Back to You / Keep Those Wandering Eyes Off My Baby
Imperial 66332   Man (The) / Tower of Strength [1968]
Spark 102   Easyville / The Whip [1954]
Spark 106   Strawberry Stomp / King Solomon's Blues [1954]

Big Lu Y **Los Muchachos**   see Los Muchachos with big Lu Valeny

Big Man and the Pharaohs
Dallas, TX
Omar "Big Man" Lopez, Domingo Samudio, Carl Medke, Russell Fowler & Vincent Lopez
Pharaohs 1083   I Don't Know / Stand By Me (Little Russell/Pharaohs) [61]
see: Sam the Sham and the Pharaohs

Big Ralph and the Gigolos
San Antonio, TX
Ralph Sanchez (Tenor Sax), Patricio Elizondo (sax), Albert Flores (vocals, Keyboards), Benny Torres (bass), John Torres (guitar)
Cobra 3333   Through Right and Through Wrong / Big Man [1964]

Bip and Bop
Los Angeles, CA
Emanuel Perez, Billy Guy
Aladdin 3287   Ding Dong Ding / Du Wadda Du [1955]

Blendells
Los Angeles, CA
Mike Rincon (bass), Ronnie Chipres (drums), Rudy Valona (lead guitar), Don Cardenas (sax), Tommy Esparza (rhythm guitar), Sal Murillo (vocals)
Rampart 641   La La La La La / Huggies Bunnies [1964]
Reprise 0291   La La La La La / Huggies Bunnies [1964]
Reprise 0340   Dance with Me / Get Your Baby [1965]
see: Vaqueros

Blue Satins
Los Angeles, CA
Mike Gomez, Louie Lopez, Pete Ventura, Raul Suarez, Frank Estrella, Frank Mezquita, Bobby Loya, Charles Lueras, Robert Perez, John Betancourt
Scarlet 501   You Don't Know Me / My Wife Can't Cook [1963]

Bobby and the Hurricanes
Shallowater, TX
Disco Gilguero 114   El Jerk / Sufres Porque Quieres

Bobby and the Premiers
El Paso, TX
Bobby Rosales (vocals, piano), James Patterson (vocals "Let Me Call You Darling"), Jaime Rosales (sax), Angel (drums)
Souled Out 36201   Mess Up My Mind / What about One More Time? [1968]
Souled Out 36202   Man about Town / Gotta Have a Reason [1968]
El Paso Premiers
Death Frog 66/2   This Is the Beginning / Let Me Call You Darling [1966]
Bobby Rosales and the Premiers Orchestra
B Rosales Records xxx   El Pajarito / Si Pudieras Darme Tu Amor

Joe Bravo
San Antonio, TX
El Zarape 284   Black Coffee / Aguna Que Viene Asi Abajo
El Zarape 288   Teardrops from My Heart / Cuantas Veces
El Zarape 342   Amor de Pobre / [1967]
El Zarape 384   It's Okay / Aunque Me Hagas Llorar [1968]
El Zarape 450   Ain't Got No Money / Quien Te Dijo
as Joe Bravo and the Sunglows
Sunglow 127   It's Okay / Ninety-Nine Plus One [1966]
Sunglow 130   Does He Remind You of Me / Think It Over [1966]
Sunglow 172   Please Call Me Baby / Tres Flores [1967]
LP: Te Regana Tu Senora [Sunglow 118]

Please Call Me Baby [Sunglow 126]
Playboy 70 [El Zarape]
see: **Sunglows, Little Joe and the Harlems**

Bristols
Albuquerque, NM
David Nuñez (vocals)
Red Feather 1339   Only to you / Do the Continental [1965]
see: **Thee Chekkers**

Broken Hearts, Los
Seguin, TX
Ramon "Munche" Salazar, Sixto Sanchez, George Soto, Frutoso "Fruit" Balderas, Bobby Gonzales, Rudy Machado, Gilbert Gonzales, Jimmy Solis, Jimmy Carrillo
Mike Gonzales, Knolle Turner
El Zarape 179   Porque Soy Como Soy / Cuando Nadien Te Quiera
Key-Loc' 1016   Hay Illusiones / Facinacion
Key-Loc' 1028   Si Fueras Mia / Sique Llorando
Rosina 147   Crying over You / Thrill Up on the Hill [1964]
Rosina 172   Palabras de Cielo / Once in a While (inst) [1964]

Brown Brandy
San Antonio, TX
Joe "Jama" Perales (vocals, bass), Henry Parilla (organ), Rudy Palacios (guitar), Larry Gonzáles (drums)
Personality 1262   That's the Way It Is / Vote [1972]
see: **Royal Jesters, Casino Royal, Revells, Sunny & the Sunliners, Little Henry Lee, Henry and the Laveers**

Brown Brothers of Soul
see: **Rulie Garcia, Jonny Chingas**

Brown Sugar
Omega 4416   Since You Went Away / Yo Te Quiero Mucho [1975]

Brown Sugar Band
Sugar 100   Night Time Lady / Get Up and Shake Your Stuff

Bobby Butler and the Latinaires
Temple, TX
Little Joe and the Latinaires
Tear Drop 3219   Next Time You See Me / My World Is Empty without You [1966]

Ray C and His Valiants
El Paso, TX
Raymond Carreon (lead vocals)
S.A.M. 118   Baby's So Fine / All Your Love [1963]

Joe Camacho
Victoria, TX
Crystal 102   On the Outside Looking In / My Girl

Ray Camacho and the Tear Drops
Fresno, CA
Ray Camacho, Mike Flores, David Duran, Hank Mendoza, Tom Gonzales, Manuel Palafox, Jesse Luna, Boni Valdez, M. Cervantes
Copper State 1078   I Told You So / Lonely Town [1966]
Copper State 1093   Volveras / El Pollo de Carlitos [1966]
ARV 5018   She's So Good to Me / Sunshine Superman
RCP Cal   Tough Talk / One Mint Julep
LP: **The International....[California Records 1001]**
    Salsa Chicana [California Records 1005]

Johnny Canales
Corpus Christi, TX
Guti1 02   Lost / Hey Jude
Penco 116   Johnny B. Goode / I Am Sorry

Cannibal and the Headhunters
Los Angeles, CA
first group: Frankie "Cannibal" Garcia, Joe "JoJo" Jaramillo, Bobby "Rabbit" Jaramillo, Richard "Scar" Lopez second group: without Richard Lopez
Aries 1001   Dance by the Light of the Moon / Means So Much [67]
Capitol 2393   Get on Up (Get the Courage) / Means So Much [1967]
Date1516   Land of 1000 Dances / La Bamba [1966]
Rampart 642   Land of 1000 Dances / I'll Show You How to

Love Me [65]
Rampart 644 Here Comes Love / Nau Ninny Nau [1965]
Rampart 646 I Need Your Loving / Follow the Music [1965]
Rampart 654 Please Baby Please / Out of Sight [1966]
LP: Land of 1,000 Dances [Rampart 3302]
 Land of 1,000 Dances [Date 3001]

Vince Cantú and the Rockin' Dominoes
Refugio, TX
Cozy 104 Hold My Hand / Slow Glow [1962]
J.W. Fox 103 Hold My Hand / Slow Glow [1962]
J.W. Fox 108 Born to Be a Loser / Blowout [1962]
J.W. Fox 111 By My Side / St. James Infirmary [1962]

Carlos Brothers (Shadows)
Wilmington, CA
Jimmy Carlos, Pete Antoniano
Del-Fi 4112 Tonight / Come On, Let's Dance [1959] w/R. Valens
Del-Fi 4118 It's Time to Go/ Little Cupid [1959]
Del-Fi 4145 It's Time to Go / La Bamba [1959]
Zen 106 I Realize / Meet My Town [1963]
As the Shadows
Del-Fi 4109 Under the Stars of Love / Jungle Fever [1958]

Jesse Casas and the Crystals
Houston, TX
Jesse Casas (vocals), Mike Garza (guitar), Armando (guitar), Tony Tostado (bass), Jesse Ruiz (sax), Bill Flores
Geno 12348 Tell Me / Anything Goes [1961]
See: Stardusters

Casino Royale
San Antonio, TX
Joe "Jama" Perales (vocals), Fernando Arragua (vocals), Tommy Zumudia (vocals), Henry Medrano (drums), Robert Gomez (guitar), Ruben Olivares (keyboard), Louie Ornelas (sax), Harry Salinas (trumpet), David Sanchez (trumpet), Richard Navarro (trumpet)
Key-Loc' 1029 To Be My Girl / Memories of Yesterday [1970]
Key-Loc' 1039 Nobody Loves You but Me / I Want a Girl [1970]
Key-Loc' 1043 Live and Learn / Get Yourself Together [1971]

Key-Loc' xxxx I Feel Forgotten / I'll Be Back Again [1970]
Satin 128 Don't Mistake Me for a Fool / Return of the Prodigal Son [66]
see: Royal Jesters, Eptones, Joe Jama

Al Castana and the Primettes
San Antonio, TX
Garu 105 I Need and Love You / Eat 'Em Up in '69 [1968]

Ramiro Cervera Orchestra
San Antonio, TX
Splendor 19 Every Day

Changes
San Antonio, TX
Joey 5007 Feel So Bad / Glamour Boy
Zaz 257 And I'll Love You Forever / Say You'll Be Mine

Charlie and the Jives
San Antonio, TX
Charlie Alvarado (sax), Arnold de la Garza (guitar), Jesse Garza (bass) vocalist: Randy Garibay, Bobby Taylor, Benny Easley
Harlem 111 For the Rest of My Life / Bobby Socks & Tennis Shoes [1959]
Harlem 115 Mercy Baby / Come On [1960]
Hour 101 I'm Leaving It All Up To You / Scratchy [1961]
Hour 102 Seven Steps To An Angel / Ubangi Stomp [1962]
Hour 104 Coffee Grind / Pt 2 [1962]
as Charlie's Jive Quintet
Dynamic 108 Lora Jean / Taste of Soul [1966]
as Benny Easley with Charlie and the Jives
Worlds 123 Kiss Tomorrow Goodbye/ You Say You Love Me [1963]

Charlie and the Jives see: **Jives**
El Paso, TX

Chavez and Chaney see: **Jaguars**
Los Angeles, CA

Freddie Chavez
Albuquerque, NM
Look 5010   They'll Never Know Why / Baby I'm Sorry [1968]
FCP 2001   I Just Go through the Changes / I've Got It Made Now
Mother Lode 4000   You've Been Wrong So Long / It's My Turn to Boogie with You
see: Thee Chekkers

Cheaters
Victoria, TX
Henry Garcia
JBJ 1001   Please Come Home / Cheating
Jolo 101   Call A Cheater / How Much
Jolo 102   He's Been Fooled / I Don't Know How
Gizmo xx   Call a Cheater / How Much

Chekkers, Thee
Albuquerque, NM
Look recording: Johnny Armijo (drums, leader), Freddie Chavez (vocals, keyboards), Jackie Ayala (sax), Alfred Gabaldon (trumpet) Joe Costales (bass), Alfred Romero (guitar)
Red Feather recording: David Nuñez (vocals), Jerry Pacheco (bass)
Look 5007   Lack of Love / Please Don't Go [1966]
Red Feather 18122   Only One / Sentimental Reasons [1966]
see: Freddie Chavez, Dave Newman, Bristols

Chili Peppers
San Antonio, TX
Armando Almandarez (vocals), Chucho Perales
Golden Crest 105   Don't Say Goodnight / South of the Border
Golden Crest 122   I Love to Eat Chili

Johnny Chingas see: Rulie Garcia
Los Angeles, CA

Chuck and the Dots
Laredo, TX
Laredo 114   I Need You / Dance to the Music

Chris and Cathy see: Chris Montez
Los Angeles, CA

Gilbert Cisneros Meets the Saints
Dant 101   Little Girl of My Dreams / Swing to the Sway

Commands
San Antonio, TX
Dan Henderson (vocals), Sam Pebbles (vocals), Jack Martinez (vocals), Vic Montes (guitar), Pete Granato (bass), Roger "Pache" Ruiz (drums), Rudy Palacios (guitar), Johnny Zaragosa (organ), Sugar Bear (tenor sax)
Back Beat 570   Hey It's Love / No Time for You [1966]
Dynamic 104   Hey It's Love / No Time for You [1966]
Dynamic 111   Don't Be Afraid to Love Me / Around the Go-Go [1966]
Dynamic 114   Chain Gang / Must Be Alright [1966]
Dynamic 123   I've Got Love For My Baby / Too Late to Cry [1967]
Dynamic 123   Too Late to Cry / A Way to Love Me [1967]
see: J.J. and the Dell-Tones, Dino and the Dell-Tones

Cruisers
McAllen, TX
ARV 5004   Just Having Fun / Lucky Man
ARV 5010   Movin' Man / Children Playing in the Sun
Impacto 178   Can't Believe It / Down by the River [1968]
Pharaoh 125   An Angel Like You / [1962]
Pharaoh 128   Another Lonely Night / Please Let Me Be [1962]
Pharaoh 148   Oh! Sweetness / The Fire Is Gone [1962]
Pharaoh 155   Celina / Baby Doll [1962]

Czars
San Antonio, TX
Key-Loc' 1020   Get Down / Get Down Part 2 [1967]
Key-Loc' 1023   Be Mine Forever / Tell Her with Your Eyes [1967]

Danny and the Counts
El Paso, TX
Danny Parra
Coronado 136   You Need Love / Ode to the Wind [1966]
Frog Death 4   It's All Over / For Your Love [1965]

Danny and the Dreamers
San Antonio, TX
Danny Escobedo (guitar), Jimmy Treviño (aka: Jimmy Edward) (vocals, sax, bass), Bobby Galvan (organ), Gilbert Sanchez (vocals), Pete Garza (bass), Rudy Hetler (drums), Mando Peña (guitar), Gene Chavez (trumpet)
Dreamer 101   I've Just Got to Forget You / O Heart [1965]
Dreamer 102   Baby Something's Wrong / Come Back to You [1965]
Dreamer 103   Hey Little Girl / Eternal Love [1965]
Tear Drop 3158   Ask the Lonely / Think Nothing about It [1966]
see: Lovells, Latin Breed, Jimmy Edward

Danny and the Sessions see: Danny Segovia
San Antonio, TX

Danny and the Tejanos
San Antonio, TX
Danny Martinez
Pa-Go-Go 112   Sweet Thing / What's the Word [1966]
Tear Drop 3148   Oiga Compadre / Por Tu Dulce Amor [1965]
Tear Drop 3164   My Love / Mustard Greens [1966]
as Danny and the Texans
Cobra 001   Rockin' Johnny Home / Old Reb

David and Ruben
La Puente, CA
David Robles, Ruben Robles, and Arthur Robles backed by The Romancers band and Ralph Ventura Mariachi group
Rampart 662   Girl Of My Dreams / (I Love Her So Much) It Hurts Me [1969]
Warner Bros 7316   Girl of My Dreams / (I Love Her So Much) It Hurts Me
see: Little D and the Bel-Aires, Majestics

Ricky Davila and the Laveers
San Antonio, TX
Teens Choice 101   You Were My Everything / The Day I Found You
see: Doc and Sal

Del-Fi's Combo
Robstown, TX
1001 101   Let's Start All Over / Worthless Love [1963]

Del-Rays
Houston, TX
Delreco 101   Fannie Mae / Should I Ever Love Again

Del Rios
Houston, TX
Big H 613   The Vines of Love / Sessions [1957]

Delcades (Bob and the Delcades)
Corpus Christi, TX
Robert Flores
Fox 0102   Singing Heart [1963]
Fox 0107   Dream Girl / A New Day [1963]

Sal de Leon and the Centennials
Dallas, TX
Jesse Palma (vocals), Clyde Alvarez (vocals), Joe Martinez (vocals), Sal de Leon (piano, organ), Ralph Atilano (bass), Paul Rios, Jerry Maldonado, Ben Martinez, Butch Lopez (drums), Gilbert Solano (guitar), Mauricio Gonzales, Mike Mora, Luis Casrtellajano, Jesse Martinez, Paul Martinez, Mike Martinez, Joe Luna
Capri 102   Together / Apple, Peaches, Pumpkin Pie [1968]
Capri 109   Que Bonita Amor / Asi Quiero Quererte [1968]
Capri 169   Segue Llorando / Siempe Junto a Ti [1969]
Capri 174   In a Moment / Never Gonna Give You Up [1969]
El Zarape 158   Amor De Alma / Amor Mio
see: Heartbreakers, Paul Rios and the Rivieras

Dell Kings featuring Carl Henderson
San Antonio, TX
Carl Henderson (vocals), Randy Garibay (vocals), Jimmy Casas (bass), Frank Rodarte (sax), Rocky Morales, Cleto Escobedo (sax), Richard Garza (drums)
Renco 3002   Big Mistake / Just Remember [1962]
see: Lyrics, Pharoahs, Los Blues

Dell-Tones see: J. Jay & the Dell-Tones, Dimas Garza
San Antonio, TX

Dimas III see: Dimas Garza
San Antonio, TX

Dino and the Dell-Tones
San Antonio, TX
Dimas Garza (vocals), Vic Montes (guitar), Bobby San Miguel (guitar), Johnny Saragosa (keyboards), Roger "Pache" Ruiz (drums), Pete Granato (bass), Ricky Martinez (sax)
Cobra 219   Mi Ultima Carta / Peor de los Caminos [1964]
Cobra 1112   Sticks and Stones / Living End [1965]
Cobra 1117   Daydream / Slapstick [1965]
Cobra xxx   La Media Vuelta / Ruega Por Nosotros [1964]
Jox 031   Don't Leave Me Baby / I'm Gonna Run [1964]
see: Dimas Garza, Royal Jesters, Lyrics, Commands, J.J. and the Dell-Tones

Diamantes, Los
Horoscopo 5004   Baby Giving Good Loving / Triunfal

Dinos, Los
Corpus Christi, TX
Bobby Lira, Abraham Quintanilla, Seff Perales, Joe Garza (drums), Floyd Hannan (organ), Johnny Cadena (guitar), John Joslin (trumpet), Louis Flores (trumpet), Rudy Perales (bass), George Ramirez (sax), Sylvester Ramirez (sax)
Epitome 119   A Love As Sweet As Yours / Ride Your Pony [1965]
Falcon 1613   Tierra Mala / Abrigando Su Tumba [1967]
Falcon 1643   Amor y Corazon / La Maquina [1967]
Fox 0101   Twistin' Irene / Darling, Oh Darling [1962]
Fox 0105   Happy Fool / Lover's Holiday [1962]
Fox 1010   So Hard to Tell / [1963]
Fox 3000-2   Darling
Fine 001   It's Good to Know / (Won't You) Give Me a Chance
Fun 101   Our Love's about Over / [1964]
Van 03265   Baby Come On In / This Is My Story
LP: Sock It To Ya [Bego 1044] 1967
  El Tracalero [Bernal 2003]
  Bobby Lira y Los Dinos: De lo Viejo a lo Nuevo
  [Bernal 2032]
  Con Esta Copa [Falcon 2019]
  Los Dinos [Falcon 2088]

Doc and Sal
San Antonio, TX
Ricky Davila, Sal Martinez
Dynamic 121   Laughing to Keep from Crying / Can't Get You Off of My Mind [68]
Dynamic 122   Cry and Wonder Why / My Dream [1968]
see: Ricky Davila and the Laveers

Bobby Domino
Los Angeles, CA
Bobby Dominguez
Donna 1339   Your Love for Me / Marilyn [1961]

Dorris and Maxine
Albuquerque, NM
Hurricane 6978   I Made Him Blue / Two Wrongs Don't Make a Right

Doug and Freddy
El Monte, CA
Doug Salma (Salamanca), Freddy Ruiz
Rendezvous 111   A Lover's Plea / I Believe in Love [1959]
K&G 100   Need Your Love / Campus Girl [1961]
Finer Arts 1001   Take a Chance on Love / And I Know You're Lyin' [1961]
see: Memories

Dreamliners
San Antonio, TX
Sylvia Wilburn, Cecilia Silva, Claire Peralta
Cobra 013   Just Me and You / Daiquiri by the Velvederes [1965]
Jox 037   Best Things in Life / From One Fool to Another [1965]
Jox 042   A Shoulder to Cry On / The Lonely Fool [1965]

Dukes
San Antonio, TX
A. Salinas (vocals)
Jeanie's 115   Just One More Time / Girls First (Mujeres Primero)

Lucy Duran
Ontario, CA
Fifo 109   Oh Sweet Baby / I Tried to Make You Understand
see: Rosie and Ron, Triangles

Dupremes
San Bernardino, CA
Dupreme 72282   I'm So Happy / So in Love with You
Dupreme   Misery / Madison St

Eddy and the Upsets
Phoenix, AZ
Eddy Dimas, Arthur Castro
Dektr 4166   El Mosquito / La Montanesa [1966]
Dektr 4168   I Got News / Cry, Cry, Cry [1968]
Dektr 42973   La Vieja Seca / El Mitote [1967]
La Bamba 42974   El Mitote / La Vieja Seca [1966]
with Jud Baker
Rebelde 4710   Chicano Blues / Ls Valentines De Tucson

Jimmy Edward (Treviño)
San Antonio, TX
G.C.P. 1026   If You Need Me / Memories
G.C.P. 1064   Mucho Corazon / Siempre Junto A Ti
G.C.P. 1070   The More I See You / Palabras De Mujer
Texas Best 5005   In The Still Of The Night / I'm Sorry [1979]
as Little Jimmy Edward & the Dreamers Band
Key-Loc' 1024   Slapping Some Soul On Me / Just A Dream [1967]
Key-Loc' 1033   Chiquito Pero Picoso / Razon Para Emborracharme [67]
Mr. G 1004   Cajita De Flores / Esta Noche La Paso Contigo
LP: Solo [GCLP 128]
see: Lovells, Danny and the Dreamers, Latin Breed

El Chicano
Los Angeles, CA
1969-1971 Ersi Arvisu (vocals, percussion), John DeLuna (drums), Bobby Espinosa (organ), Mickey Lespron (guitar), Andre Baéza (conga, percussion), Freddie Sanchez (bass)
1974 Bobby Espinosa (keyboards), Mickey Lespron (guitar), Andre Baéza (congas, percussion), Hector 'Rudy" Regalado (vocals, drums, timbales, percussion), Jerry Salas (guitar, vocals), Eddie Rodriguez (drums, percussion, vocals), Brian Magness (bass)1975 replace Brian Magness with Joe Perreira
Black-Jack xxx   Sabor a Mi   bootleg issue only [1972]
Gordo 703   Viva Tirado / part II [1970]
Kapp 2085   Viva Tirado / part II [1970]
Kapp 2099   Coming Home Baby / Eleanor Rigby [1970]
Kapp 2129   Cubano Chant / Viva La Raza [1970]
Kapp 2150   Don't Put Me Down / Sugar, Sugar [1971]
Kapp 2173   Brown Eyed Girl / Mas Zacate [1972]
Kapp 2182   Satisfy Me Woman / Señor Blues [1972]
MCA 40104   Tell Her She's Lovely / Se Fue (Mi Chachita) [1973]
MCA 40136   Brown Eyed Girl / Mas Zacate [1973]
MCA 40240   You've Been Wrong So Long / El Cayuco
MCA 40391   Might As Well / Put on a Show
Royal Family 1001   Groovin' / same
LP: Viva Tirado [Kapp 3632] 1970
   Revolución [Kapp 3640] 1971
   Celebration [Kapp 3663] 1972
   El Chicano [MCA 312] 1973
   Cinco [MCA 401] 1974
   The Best of Everything [MCA 437] 1975
   Pyramid of Love and Friends [MCA 2150] 1976
   This Is El Chicano [Shadybrook 33-005] 1976

El Paso Drifters
El Paso, TX
Coronado 143   All in My Mind / In the Midnight Hour [1966]

El Paso Premiers see: Bobby and the Premiers

Enchanting Enchanters
East Chicago/Gary, IN
Ben-Mo_Keith 685   No One in This World / Boss Action [1969]

Enchantments, Thee
Los Angeles, CA
Eddie Serrano (vocals), Steve Lopez (lead guitar), Bobby Brambila (rhythm guitar), Larry Torres (bass), Tom Lawrence (organ), Frankie Lee (drums), Ray Oliande (sax), Gil Perez (sax), John Madrid (trumpet)
Faro 620   I'm in Love with Your Daughter pt. 1 / pt. 2 [1965]

Entertainers
San Antonio, TX
Danny Escobedo (guitar), Fernando Hernandez, Bobby Solis, Pete Garza (bass)
Amber 1969   I Can't Do Enough / We Don't Need No Music [1969]
Amber 1970   Does Anybody Really Know What Time It Is / Mama Lo-Lo [1970]
see: Danny and the Dreamers

Al Epp and the Pharaohs
San Antonio, TX
Abe Epstein, with the Pharaohs: Randy Garibay, Duke Anthony, Joe Perez, Oscar Cavasos, Richard Garza
Wild Cat 0018   My Dream Girl / Breaking My Heart [1959]
see: Pharaohs

Eptones
San Antonio, TX
David Mares (vocals), Joe "Jama" Perales (vocals), Robert Gomez (guitar)
Cobra 114   Encanto / Ten Compacion
Jox 063   Making Me Cry / Sweet Tater Pie [1967]
Jox 070   A Love That's Real / No One Else but You [1967]
see: Royal Jesters, Joe Jama, Revells, Casino Royale

Albert Esbirdo and the Majestic Four
Los Angeles, CA
Tina 1009   Ain't No Big Thing / La Bamba

Ethics with Rocky Gil
Houston, TX
Geno 12310   Funny / Do the Slop
see: Rocky Gil and the Bishops

Sherman Evans with Cruz Ortiz and the Flames
Waco, TX
Sherman Evans (vocals), Cruz Ortiz, Cruz Garcia (drums)
A-O-K 101   There's Gonna Be Some Crying / Looking for My Baby [1962]
Manco 1036   There's Gonna Be Some Crying / Looking for My Baby [1962]
Manco 1046   Secretly / Cuban Refugee [1963]
Manco 1049   Yo-Yo Twist / I Don't Care [1963]

Exiles
Houston, TX
Gapoca 210   Por lo Pronto / La Prieta Ingrata
Gapoca 247   For Your Precious Love / Don't Cry No More

Face Of Blue
San Antonio, TX
Silver Luck 101   No Use for Me to Cry / Moon of June

Fats and the All-Stars
Dallas, TX
Edward "Fats" Fuentes, Mando Benavides, Manny Cisneros, Paul Martinez
Capri 121   Wild Onions / No Me Importa [1968]

Freddie Fender (Freddy Fender, Baldemar Huerta, Scotty Wayne)
San Benito, TX
As Baldemar Huerta
ABC 12370   Talk to Me / same [1978]
Argo 5375   A Man Can Cry / You're Something Else for Me [1961]
ARV 5083   She Thinks I Still Care / Crazy Arms [1974]
ARV 5146   El Rock De La Carcel / No Seas Cruel [1977]
Bego 02   Tu Amor y El Mio / Fuiste a Acapulco
Crazy Cajun 2002   Waiting for Your Love / Before the Next Teardrop Falls [1974]

Crazy Cajun 2011   Wasted Day's and Wasted Nights / Caminto [1974]
Crazy Cajun 2014   I Love My Rancho Grande / No Toguen Ya [1975]
Dot 17540   Before the Next Teardrop Falls / Waiting for Your Love [74]
Dot 17607   You'll Lose a Good Thing / I'm to Blame [1974]
Duncan 1000   Holy One / Mean Woman [1959]
Duncan 1001   Wasted Days and Wasted Nights / San Antonio Rock [59]
Duncan 1004   Since I Met You Baby / Little Mama [1959]
Duncan 1022   Crazy Baby / Wild Side of Life [1961]
Goldband 1214   Carmela / My Train of Love
Goldband 1264   Bye, Bye Little Angel / Oh, My Love
Goldband 1272   Me and My Bottle of Rum / Three Wishes
Ideal 2109 Diablo Con Atifaz / Cuando Calienta el Sol [1963]
Ideal 2148   Todo Me Amor
Ideal 2168   Dime / Las Cerezas [1965]
Ideal 2176   Buscando un Carino / Que Salarete
Ideal 2290   No Estas Sonando/A Bailar El Perro
Ideal 2355   Que Tal Amor / Porque Eres Tan Mala [1966]
Montel 2002   Crazy Baby / Rose Marie
Norco 100   Love's Light Is an Ember / New Stroll [1963]
Norco 102   Never Trust a Cheating Woman / You Made Me Cry [63]
Norco 103   Coming Home Soon / Going Out with the Tide [64]
Norco 104   Just A Little Bit / You Made a Fool of Me [1964]
Norco 106   Ooh Poo Doo Dah / You Don't Have to Go [1964]
Norco 108   In the Still of the Night / Three Wishes [1965]
Norco 111   Lover's Quarrel / Donna [1965]
Pa-Go-Go 115   Cool Mary Lou / You Are My Sunshine [1966]
Talent Scout 1002   Crazy Baby / Wild Side Of Life [1961]
Talent Scout 1010   Something on Your Mind [1962]
Talent Scout 1013   Wasted Day's and Wasted / Sweet Summer Day [1962]
Talent Scout 1014   You're Something Else For Me / A Man Can Cry [62]
as Scotty Wayne
Talent Scout 1007   Lonely Night / Find Somebody New [1961]
Talent Scout 1008   Only One / I'm Gonna Leave [1961]
Talent Scout 1009   Pretty Baby / Sweet Summer Day [1962]
Talent Scout 1011   You Told Me You Loved Me / Roobie Doobie [1962]
as Baldemar Huerta con los Romanceros
Falcon 45626 Hay Amor / No Seas Cruel (Don't Be Cruel) [1957]
Falcon 45646   Cantando los Blues / Puerta Verde [1957]
Falcon 45656   Los Ojos de Pancha / Si Estuvieras a Mi Lado [1957]
Falcon 45666 Marianne / Adios a Jamaica [1957]
Falcon 45717 Ese Sera El Dia / En Medio de una Isla [1957]
Falcon 100   Holy One / [1958]
Falcon 1036   El Twist / Botecito de Vela [1960]
as Baldemar Huerta con el Conjunto de Rafael Ramirez
Falcon 45723 Enriqueta / Rock de la Prison (Jailhouse Rock) [1957]
as Freddy Fender con Los Personalities
Falcon 1459   Un Gato de la Cola / Te Acusa el Corazon [1965]
as Freddy Fender and the Comancheros
Ideal 2253   Majia de Amor (Magic of Love) / Anillo de Diamante [1965]
Chico 149   Crazy Cat / Just Because
Chico 150   Te Vi Llorando / Aunquen Me Hagas Llorar
as Freddy Fender con los Barbarians
Ideal 2094   Despeinada / Para Madura [1963]
as Eddie con los Shades
Ideal 1870   No Estas Aqui / Alcapulco Rock [1959]
Ideal 1882   Que Soledad / Tequila Rock [1959]
as Freddy Fender
Imperial 5059   Holy One / Mean Woman [1960]
Imperial 5659   Wasted Days And Wasted Nights / Mean Woman [1960]
Imperial 5670   Wasted Days and Wasted Nights / I Can't Remember When I Didn't Love You [1960]
Instant 3332   Some People Say / Today's Your Wedding [1972]
as Freddy Fender and Noel Vill
Norco 107   Bonie Maroni / The Magic of Love [1965]
Sock-O 101   Bonie Maroni / The Magic of Love [1965]
as Boo and the Girlfriends
Talent Scout 1010 Something on Your Mind / You Got What It Takes [60]

Bob Flores
Impala 123   Jeanie

Bobby Flores
Whiz 604   Everyday I Have to Cry / Hey Girl, Please Listen

Danny Flores aka Chuck Rio
Los Angeles, CA
RPM 491   Trying to Forget / No Matter What You Do [1957]
as Danny Boy Flores
Kent 300   Don't Go Pretty Baby / All of Me
with Eddie Atwood and his Goodies
Surf 5028   Hot Saki / [1958]
with the Champs
Challenge 1016   Tequila / Train to Nowhere [1958]
as Chuck Rio
Flair 103   Big Boy [1962]
Jackpot 48016   Margarita / [1959]
Saturn 402   Kreschendo Stomp / [1963]
Tequila 103   If You Were the Only Girl in the World / [1960]
Danny Flores and the Chumps
Tequila 4099   La Bamba / Malagueña Salerosa
LP: Go Champs Go! [Challenge 601] 1958

Ree Flores
Riverside, CA
M&H 9343   Look into My Heart

Freddie and the Starlighters
Albuquerque, NM
Freddie Barela
Hurricane 6979   Long Lonely Years / Mobil Lil [1966]

Ricky G and the Dreamglows
Corpus Christi, TX
Rose 1   Fire

Ricky G and the Rhythm Rockers
Corpus Christi, TX
Marco 711   Take Me Back / Traveling Twist

G Robert G (Robert Gomez)
San Antonio, TX
Clown 106   But That Was Then / Private Number
see: Casino Royale, Eptones, Revells

Tommy G and the Charms
Albuquerque, NM
Tommy Gonzales
Hollywood 1109   I Want You So Bad / I Know What I Want [1966]
Hurricane 6991   Hey, Hey! (You're Too Much) [1966]
Hurricane xxx   Please Don't Fool with Me / Don't Cry
Ranwood 838   I Know / Blow the Ashes Away

Willie G (Garcia)
Los Angeles, CA
Willie Garcia (vocals), Rudy Salas (vocals, guitar), Steve Salas (vocals), Mario Paniagua (guitar), Frank Chavez (rhythm guitar), Anthony "Beaver" Carroll (bass), Adrian Sansone (drums), horns ????
Gordo 702   Brown Baby / Lonely Lullaby [1969]
see: Thee Midniters, Jaguars, God's Children

Bobby Galvan
Corpus Christi, TX
Impala 136   Do the Bear / I am the Greatest [1962]

Johnny Gamboa and the Crowns
Los Angeles, CA
Star Revue 1003   Why Lover / She's Never There [1960]

Felix Garcia
Rosco 411   Two Tacos / Crazy Fingers [1958]

Gloria Garcia with Ike & Tina Turner Revue
Los Angeles, CA
Innis 3001   No Puedes Extrañar / Konnki Cookie [1966]

Jay Garcia
San Antonio, TX
G.C.P. 1058   Sincerely (Spanish) / Tres Veces

Rulie Garcia aka Ruly Garcia, Jonny Chingas
Los Angeles, CA
Billionaire 100   Candy Is Dandy / Prescription-Rock and Roll [1979]
Billionaire 1027   Poquito Soul / Santo Clos [1979]
Dore 859   Earthquake / Be My Brother
as Garcia Brothers
Ruly 698   Doin' the Babalu / Buzz, Buzz, Buzz [1964]
as Brown Brothers of Soul
Raza 1027   Cholo / Poquito Soul [1971]
Specialty 698   Cholo / Poquito Soul [1971]
as Jonny Chingas
Billionaire 1983   Hairy Situation / I Want to Marry You
Billionaire 1995   Young Stuff / (same)
Billionaire 2010   Show Me How to Dance / I Want You to Have My Baby
Billionaire 2011   Show Me How to Dance / I'm Looking for an Automatic Lover
Billionaire 2060   Pachuco Walk / Those Oldies
JDC xxx   Samba
as Rulie Garcia and the East L.A. Congregation
Billionaire 1027   Sabrocito/ Be My Girl Blues [1972]
United Artist 51104   Sabrocito/ Be My Girl Blues [1972]
United Artist XW264   Que Pasa (What's Happening) pt 1 / pt 2 [1973]
as Rulie Garcia and the Katinga
Billionaire   Cholo/ The Ghost of Mr. Hughes
LP: Pachuco vol. 1 [Billionaire 1980]
     Love Drops [Billionaire]

Randy Garibay
San Antonio, TX
E.A. 551   Brown Eyed Girl / Let Them Talk

Dimas Garza (Dimas III)
San Antonio, TX
Mr. G 1003   No Llores
Mr. G 1008   Just a Moment / Why Am I Treated So Bad
as Dimas III
Clown 101   You Succeeded / Just a Friend [1965]
Clown 102   I Won't Love You Again / So Funny [1965]
Clown 105   So in Love / Not the Right Time [1966]
as Rick and Mann featuring the Sonics

Garu 101   As Time Goes By / Me Quiero Enamorar
as Dimas Garza y el Barrio
Garu 113   El Ciego / Sin Compromiso
Garu 115   Ola / Un Buen Partido
Garu 117   Salamon / Sinceridad
LP: Los Sunglows de Dimas Garza [Disco Grande 4042]
     Dimas [Mr. G 5002]
See: Lyrics, Royal Jesters, Dino and the Dell-Tones

Genotones
Casino 52261   Counting Stars / City Lights [1958]

Rocky Gil and the Bishops
Houston, TX
Fidencio Garza-Rocky Gil
Big Shot 001   Me and You
Jet Stream 813   Built Like A Brickhouse / The Pleasures Of My Woman
Tear Drop 3101   It's Not The End / [1965]
Tear Drop 3118   La Medallita / Un Adobe Y Cuatro Velas
Tear Drop 3132   El Vasilon / Nuestro Dia Vendra
Tear Drop 3150   I'm So Cruel / Dancing In The Streets
Tear Drop 3166   El Cisne / La Justicia De Amor
Tear Drop 3174   Buscando un Cariño / Al Pie de un Crucificio [1966]
Tear Drop 3181   Everyday of My Life / It's Not the End [1967]
Tear Drop 3193   Polytechnic Mambo / Las Gueras [1967]
Tear Drop 3199   Soul Party / After the Party [1968]
Tear Drop 3235   Oily / Looking for a Lover [1969]
LP's: The Two Sides of Rocky Gil & the Bishops [Tear Drop 2012]
     El Fantastico [Tear Drop 2016]
     Soul Party [Tear Drop 2022]
     Rocky Gil & the Bishops [Latin Soul 4003]

Gilbert and the Blue Notes
San Antonio, TX
Gilbert Rodriguez
Red Top 504   A Thousand Miles Away / La Bamba [1963]
Rosina 131   Out of Sight / Beer Barrell Polka [1964]
Rosina 176   Mexican Shuffle / Lloras en Navidad [1964]
Tear Drop 3165   Amigo Amigo / Dimelo de Frente
LP: Yo Soy Aquel [Tear Drop 2020]

God's Children
Los Angeles, CA
Willie Garcia, Ray Jimenez
UNI 55266   Lonely Lullaby / Hey, Does Somebody Care

Goldtones
Goldtone K-47   Night Owl / Walking the Dog

Frank Gonzales and the Palisades
Las Cruces, NM
F-G 1000   Love You Forever / Dance to the Palisades [1961]
F-G 1001   Let's Make Up / Sweet Little Surfing Girl [1961]

Rudy Tee Gonzales see: Rudy and the Reno-Bops

Julio Gutierrez
Vico 1003   Fun-K-City / Revival

Gilbert Guerra and the Skylighters
Dallas, TX
Gilbert Guerra, Jimmy Esparza, Cecilio Rodriguez, Frank Ibarra, Jimmy Flores, Santos Robles, Moses Rosales, Ernest Guerra
Tear Drop 3079   You're So Fine / Romona [1965]

Rudy Guerra
San Antonio, TX
Sunglow 121   Shake A Plenty / Still Love You [1964]
see: Sunglows, Sunny & the Sunliners, Latin Breed

Carlos Guzman y los Fabulosos 4
Corpus Christi, TX
Bego 01   I Knew You When / Crying Time
Bego 330   96 Lagrimas / La Justicia de Amor
Bego 372   El Tren
LP: [Bego 1016]
  [Bego 1019]

Heartbreakers
Los Angeles, CA
Benny Rodriguez, Joe Rodriguez
Brent 7037   I'm Leaving It All Up to You / Corrido Mash [1963]
Donna 1381   Cradle Rock / Everytime I See You [1963]
Linda 114   Please Answer / She Is My Baby [1964]

Heartbreakers
Dallas, TX
Clyde Alvarez, Jesse Palma, Joe Palma, Rick Alvarez, Ralph Atilano, Mike Mora, Trino Palma, Tommy Perez, Luis Rivera, George Solares, Alfonso Maldonado, Gabino Villanueva, Al Villanueva
Tomi 118   Going Out of My Head / Hold On I'm Coming [1967]
Tomi 121   I'll Show You How to Love Me / Mustang Sally [1967]
see: Sal de Leon and the Centennials, Paul Rios and the Rivieras

Henry and the Kasuals
San Antonio, TX
Henry Peña, Gordy Saldivar, Frank Lujan
Cobra 1124   Slowly, Slowly but Surely / Workout [1965]
Cobra 1130   Forever / Funny, Funny, Funny [1966]
Cobra 1134   Love and Run Away / Little Girl (Of My Dreams) [1966]
Cobra 1138   Ace un Año / El Destrampe
Cobra 1139   I'll Come Running / Only One
Cobra 1154   Te Regana Tu Señora / La Hija de Oralia

Johnny Hernandez & the Sinceres w/Little Joe & the Latinaires
Temple, TX
Buena Suerte 944   Confidential / By the Time I Get to Phoenix
El Zarape 122   Why Don't You Write Me / Crazy Baby [1963]
Good Luck 007   My World Is Empty without You / And I Wait
Tomi 132   Bring It Up / Love Is a Hurting Thing [1966]
As Johnny Hernandez y Aztlan
LP: Tomate Una Copa [Chicano Records Of America] 1976

Rocky Hernandez w/ Little Joe and the Latinaires Band
Temple TX
Buena Suerte 937   Security / La Yerea Mala (Roy Montelongo)
LP: Triste Pensamento [Buena Suerte]

Tony Hernandez and the Latinliners
Dallas, TX
Capri 246   Yesterday Is Gone / Placing Pictures [1972]

Little Julian Herrera and the Tigers
Los Angeles, CA
Dig 118   Lonely, Lonely Nights / In Exchange for Your Love [1956]
Dig 137   Symbol of Heaven / Here in My Arms [1957]
Eldo 130   Lonely, Lonely Nights / In Exchange for Your Love [1963]
Essar 1012   Lonely Lonely Nights / I Want to Be with You [1963]
Emmo 3302   Your Careless Love / You Will Cry
Iris 137   Symbol of Heaven / Here in My Arms
Starla 6   I Remember Linda / True Fine Mama [1958]

High Seas
Adrian Torres
D-M-G 4000   We Go Together / Sunday Kind of Love [1960]

Freddy Hill
San Antonio, TX
Fernando Aguilar with Rudy and the Reno-Bops
Ru Tee Hit Record 101   Mr. Lucky / Mr. Hurt [1968]

Houserockers
Corpus Christi, TX
Fred Sanders, Sunny Hinojosa, Billy Guy, Roy Tipton
Fun 102   Say You'll Be Mine / Cook It [1964]

Baldemar Huerta see: Freddie Fender

Hummingbird 4
Los Angeles, CA
Rudy Salas (guitar)
Rampart 721   Cho Cho San / part II [1972]
see: Salas Brothers, Six Pak, Tierra

Hunk Of Funk
Commerce City, CO
Luis Sanchez (vocals), R. Martinez, R. Apolinar
Infal 205   Chicano Brother / Llorras

Al Hurricane and the Night Rockers
Albuquerque, NM
Al Hurricane (sax, guitar), Tiny Morrie (vocals, sax), Baby Gaby (sax), Joe Polanco (guitar), George Quintana (bass), Henry Ramirez (drums), Herman Padilla (sax)
APT 25049   South Bend [1960]
Challenge 9127   Lobo / Racer [1961]
Hurricane xxx   Hey! Let Me Tell You / You're the Girl for Me [1957]
Hurricane 6965   Panchita / La Mula Bronca [1966]
Hurricane 6968   Sentimiento / Mi Saxophono [1966]
Hurricane 6981   Maldita Suerte / Con Lagrimetas [1966]
see: Baby Gaby, Tiny Morrie

Impalas, Thee
Los Angeles, CA
Al Anaya (vocals), Ronnie Reyes (guitar), Joe Alvarez, Willie Alvarez, Ruben ?
Gee-Kay 1003   Power Glide / Rosalie (Slauson Bros)
Whittier 502   Yes I'm Ready / Band of Gold [1966]
Whittier 506   Come on Up / Oh, Yea Whittier [1966]
see: Thee Midniters, Yaqui

In Crowd, The
San Gabriel, CA
Art Hernandez, Grover Berumen, Bobby Esparza, Larry Vallejo, Richard Hernandez, John Gonzales, Joe Perez, Ray Diaz
Living Sound 4   Monkey Time / Quiet Village

In-Set, Thee
Los Angeles, CA
Cal-Omen 101   My Heart Cries / They Say

Irene (Irene Soto)
Los Angeles, CA
Baronet 12   Forget / Don't

Ivorys
Los Angeles, CA
Sparta 01   Why Don't You Write Me / Deep Freeze

J.V. and the Velvetones
San Antonio, TX
Joe Tinajero
Sinclair 101   That Day She Went Away / Move It On Out

Jade
Los Angeles, CA
Century City 512   Brown and Beautiful / The Siesta Is Over [1970]
Century City 512   Brown and Beautiful / VIVA! (Viva Tirado) [1970]

Jaguars
Los Angeles, CA
Manny Chavez and Sonny Chaney, Val Poliuto, Charles Middleton
Aardell 0006   You Don't Believe Me / Be My Sweetie [1956]
Baronet 1   The Way You Look Tonight
Ebb 129   Hold Me Tight / Piccadilly [1958]
Ebb 142   Never Let You Go / I'll Make a Bet [1958]
Original Sound 6   Thinking of You / Look into My Eyes [1959]
R-Dell 011   The Way You Look Tonight / Moonlight and You [1956]
R-Dell 016   I Love You Baby / Baby, Baby, Baby [1957]
R-Dell 045   I Wanted You / Rock It Davy, Rock It [1958]
R-Dell 117   Girl of My Dreams / Don't Go Home [1960]
Rendezvous 159   Fine, Fine, Fine / It Finally Happened
as Chavez and Chaney
Spry 122   Be My Love / Piccadilly Rose [1960]
Blast-Off 100   Be My Love / Piccadilly Rose [1964]
as Frankie and Johnny (Manny Chavez and Sonny Chaney)
Sabrina 331   My First Love / Do You Love Me [1959]
Liberty 55271   My First Love / Do You Love Me [1959]
as the Miracles
Cash 1008   You're an Angel / A Gal Named Jo [1955]
as the Sevilles
Cal-Gold 172   Don't You Know I Care [1962]
Galaxy 727   Baby / Creation [1963]

J.C. 116   Charlena / Loving You (Is My Desire) [1960]
J.C. 118   Louella [1961]
J.C. 120   Fat Sally [1961]

Jaguars
Los Angeles, CA
Mario Paniagua (lead guitar), Frank Chavez (rhythm guitar), Anthony Carroll (bass), Adrian Sansone (drums)
Faro 618   Where Lovers Go / Discover a Lover [1964]
see: Six Pak, Salas Brothers

Joe Jama with the Royal Jesters Band
San Antonio, TX
Joe Perales
Freddie 261   Guerita Preferida b/w Siete Dias
G.C.P 10398   Angelito / Soy Feliz [1970]
Optimum 101   I've Got Soul / My Kind of Woman [1969]
Optimum 102   Sleep Late My Lady Friend / My Life [1969]
Optimum 103   Phases of Time / Down, Down, Down [1970]
see: Revells, Eptones, Casino Royale, Royal Jesters, Brown Brandy

George Jay and the Rockin' Ravens
McAllen, TX
George Bali
ARV 5001   Gee Baby / Dancing in the Street [1967]
ARV 5012   Greetings (This Is Uncle Sam) / Another Lonely Night [1967]
Dynamic 112   Say That You Love Me / You Don't Know Me [1967]
Falcon 1583   El Pachuco / Mi Peden
Peerless 016   La Pachuca / Necesito Tu Amor
Rave 101   Cross My Heart / You Took My Love [1960]
Rave 104   True Love / Sticks and Stones
As George Jay y Los Ravens
Balli 111   Gina / As Life Goes On
LP: Me Piden... [Falcon 2046]
    George Jay [Falcon 3012]

J. Jay and the Dell-Tones
San Antonio, TX
Jay Martinez (vocals, guitar), Pete Granato (bass), Roger "Pache"

Ruiz (drums),
Ricky Martinez (alto sax), Danny Morin (tenor sax), Johnny Zaragosa (keyboards)
Cobra 004   Wrong Side of the Tracks / If I Cry a Little More [1963]
Cobra 1121   The Best Man Cried / Golly Gee
Cobra 5555   Too Late to Forgive / Just a Matter of Time [1963]
see: Dino and the Dell-Tones, Commands

Johnny Jay and the Pompadors
Corpus Christi, TX
Johnny (Jay) Mendez, Benny Mendez
Benja 102   You Lied / Just You and Me [1963]
Norco 101   Love of My Life / While I Play You Dance [1963]
Pharaoh 103   You Drive Me Crazy / I Feel So Lonely [1962]
Pharaoh 105   I Want You So, I Need You So / She's Gone and I'm All Alone [1962]

Sammy Jay and the Tiffanaires
San Antonio, TX
Hi-Note 1025   Candy Kisses / I Hope You Won't Hold It Against Me [63]
Princess 4021   Candy Kisses / I Hope You Won't Hold It Against Me [63]
Princess 4032   Blue Tears [1965]
Tear Drop 3054   Come Closer to Me / La Tentacion
Tribe 8311   You're Driving Me Insane / Never Let Me Go [1965]

Jives (Charlie and the Jives)
El Paso, TX
Charlie Miller (vocals), Donnie Miller (rhythm guitar), Albert Miller (sax), Tony Gomez (bass), Bobby Lujan (trumpet), Cruz Garcia (organ), Rudy Magaña -Johnny Valdez (trumpet), Barney Magaña - Bobby Olan (drums)
Tear Drop xxxx   Espera un Tantito / Mi Gordita [1968]
Tear Drop 3264   Fuiste el Primero Amor / Te la Llevaste [1968]
Tear Drop 3267   Love / I Want You [1968]
as Charlie and the Jives
Tear Drop 3278   Sad Girl / No Tiengo Dinero [1972]

LP: Espera Un Tatito [Tear Drop] 1968
   The Jives [Tear Drop 2027] 1968
   Making Time [Tear Drop 2028] 1971
   No Tengo Dinero [Tear Drop] 1972

Johnny and Gene
San Antonio, TX
Jox 023   It's You I Love / Baby You Know [1964]

Steve (Esteban) **Jordan** and the Jordan Brothers
Elsa, TX
Steve Jordan, Bonnie Jordan, Sam Jordan
ARV 5005   Run for Your Life / Turn On Your Lovelight [1966]
ARV 5006   Squeeze Box Man / La Bamba [1966]
ARV 5009   Ain't No Big Thing / If You Love Me Like You Say [1966]
ARV 5013   You Keep Me Hanging On / Would You Believe [1967]
Falcon 1672 Squeeze Box Man / Hazte Garras
Falcon 1772 You Keep Me Hanging On / Contigo en la Distansia
ID 223   Ain't No Big Thing / La Bamba [1965]
LP: El Gran Steve Jordan y los Hermanos Jordan [Falcon 2058]
   La Bamba [Falcon 2082] 1965

Junior and the Preludes
Anaheim, CA
Gabriel Lopez (vocals), Ray Amezcua (bass), Mickey Hernandez (lead vocalist), Joe Escobar (sax), Bill Newton (trumpet), Gene Wing (trumpet), Art Galvan (drums)
DeMarco 561   Somebody Help Me / Do You Remember
LP: One Night [S&R]
   Junior and the Preludes [S&R 818]

Jr. and the Starlites
Waco, TX
Cruz "Jr" Garcia (keyboards), Joe Ortega (vocals), Johnny Quiñiones (bass), ? Tejerina (guitar), Johnny Gonzales (drums), Nick Ramos (trumpet), Johnny Garcia (sax), Joe Lopez (sax)
Mex-Melody 101 This Is My Story / Hang Over (La Cruda) [1965]

Mex-Melody 111   Juanita / Paloma Querida [1965]
Mex-Melody 116   Panchita / No Hay Que Llorar [1965]
Mex-Melody 121   Queen of My Heart / Tres Suspiros [1965]
Mex-Melody 130   Cu Curru Cu Cu Paloma / Te Voy a Complacer [1966]
see: Latinglows, Cruz Ortiz and the Flames, Sherman Evans

K-Men
Stockton, CA
Angel R. Martinez
Quality   I Who Have Nothing / Getting My Feet on the Main Drag, Joe

Knightsmen
El Paso, TX
Johnny Trujillo (vocals), Sue Black (vocals)
Bocaldun 1005   Darling Why / Pistol Packin' Mama [1961]

Kool Dips
San Antonio, TX
Dimas Garza (vocals)
Rival 04   Trying to Forget / Down in the Alley (inst) [1960]
see: Dimas III, Lyrics, Royal Jesters, Dino and the Dell-Tones, Dimas Garza

La Conexion Mexicana
El Zarape 485   Somebody Loves You / Whenever You Have the Time

Larry and Mike
Los Angeles, CA
Era 3135   So Long Little Buddy [1964]
Picadilly 500   Queen of the Starlight Dance / We Fell in Love [1963]

Latin Breed
San Antonio, TX
Jimmy Edwards (lead vocals), Rudy Guera, Gibby Escobedo, Donald Garza (horn), Frank Perez (horn), Pete Garza (bass)
G.C. 5001   I Turned You On / Rainy Day
G.C. 5003   Hard to Handle / Danny Boy
G.C.P. 1004   Baby / Gavelina O Paloma [1978]
G.C.P. 1069   Marantha / Tomando Mil Copas [1978]
LP: De Rudy Guera [GCP]
  Oye Corazon [GCP 103]
  Return of.... [GCP 106]
  Mas Latin Breed [GCP 108] 1974
  Minus One [GCP 111] 1974
  USA [GCP 115] 1975
  Power Drive [GCP 124] 1976
  Latin Breed [GC 133] 1977
  De Tejas [GCP 142] 1978

Latinglows, Los (Cruz Garcia and the Latinglows)
LP: Los Laurelles [Buena Suerte 1016]
see: Jr. and the Starlites

Latintones
San Antonio, TX
Alex De Leon
LT 681127   Lies, Lies (Margie & Alex) / I'll Never Forget Her (Alex De Leon)

Marky Lee
El Zarape
262   She's Looking Good / Augustine Ramirez Soul Serenade

Leggeriors
Los Angeles, CA
Sal Padilla (guitar), Bobby Hernandez (lead guitar), Johnny Gonzales (vocals), Ernie Castillo (vocals), Richard Bernal, Danny Dominguez (drums), Frank Uballez (drums), Frank "Burns" Quemada (bass), Phil Ruiz (tenor), Hector Contreras (piano)
Goliath 1351   Flame of Love / Justine [1963]

Ray Liberto
San Antonio, TX
Dot 15848   Wicked, Wicked, Woman / Calling Margie [1958]
TNT 156   Wicked, Wicked, Woman / Calling Margie [1958]
TNT 172   I Want You to Love Me Tonight [1959]

Michael Liggins and the Super Souls
Phoenix, AZ
Mighty 6901   Loaded Back / Get to Steppin' [1969]
Mighty 7001   Loaded to the Gills / pt. 2 [1970]

Lil' Lavair and the Fabulous Jades
San Bernardino, CA
Ralph Payan (guitar), Delbert "Lil' Lavair" White (vocals), Dwight White (bass), Nathan White (organ), Juan "Malo" Macias (drums), David R. Wood (tenor sax), David Alvarez (trumpet), Dennis Byas (trombone), Alfred Aguila (alto sax)
Lennan 1264   Cold Heat / [1968]

Lil' Migul's Golden Five
Migul Chacon
Golden 2168 Funky Feeling / Tu Ausencia [1970]

Lindy and the Lavells
Albuquerque, NM
Lindy Blaskey
Lavette 5001   Wine, Wine, Wine / Meet Me Tonight in Your Dreams [1963]
Space 001   What Chance Have I

Liserio and the Blues Aspect
San Antonio, TX
Jose H. Liserio
High Tower 101   I Want Your Lovin' / Love Me in the Morning

Little Artie and the Pharaohs
Millwaukee, WI
Artie Herrera
Cuca 1142   My Symphony / Fox and the Hound [1963]
Cuca 1157   It Puzzles Me [1963]
Cuca 1162   Foxy Devil [1964]

Little D and the Bel-Aires
La Puente, CA
David Robles (vocals, drums), Kay Lavell (vocals), Ellie Lavell (vocals), Danny Berumen (guitar), Arthur Robles (sax), Bobby Bentancourt (sax)
Raft 604   Are You My Girl / Scratch [1962]
see: David and Ruben

Little Gil and the Nightmares
Gil Gonzales
San 1507   Could This Be Love / Moving Late

Little Henry and the Laveers
San Antonio, TX
Henry Parilla (vocals, organ)
Cobra 003   What to Do / Keep Twistin' [1963]
Cobra 012   Break It to Me Now / I Don't Want No Woman [1963]
Laveer 640710   Whip It on Me / Georgia [1963]
Little Henry and his Pa-Go-Go Band
Pa-Go-Go 117   Masquerade Is Over / Hello Young Lovers
Little Henry Lee with the Sunliners Band
Gismo 1002   Only to Be Hurt / I Need Your Love
Gismo 1007   Better Use Your Head / I Want Somebody
Key-Loc 1037   She's a Woman / Give Me a Little Loving
Key-Loc 1042   Como Los Meros Hombres / Ya No Te Quemes
see: Sunny and the Sunliners, Little Henry and the Laveers, Sounds

Little Jesse and the Rockin' Vee's
Alice, TX
Jesse Villanueva (drums), Oscar Villanueva (guitar), Ray Villanueva (sax), Tony Tostado (bass), Gilbert Fernandez (sax), Alfred Luna (organ)
Sunglow 108   My Love for You / Got to Have Heart [1963]
see: Sunny & the Sunliners

Little Joe and the Embers
Houston, TX
Discos Jeesna 009   Soul Finger / Happy Sax

Little Joe and the Harlems
San Antonio, TX
Joe Bravo (vocals), Bones Aragon (drums)

Tina 1   Crying in the Chapel / Putting Me Down [1963]
Tina 2   On My Knees / To You Makes No Difference [1963]
Tina 3   I Can't Forget You / My Baby Left Me [1963]
see: Sunglows, Joe Bravo

Little Joe and the Latinaires (Little Joe y La Familia)
Temple, TX
Joe Hernandez, Johnny Hernandez, Rocky Hernandez, Bobby Butler, Cino Moreno, Raymond Flores, Tony Guerrero, Arturo Gonzales, Mike Rios, Luigi Navarro, Jaime Flores, Tony Matamorros, Paula Estrada on "Hello Stranger"
Buena Suerte 935   Los Ojos de Pancha/ La Malaguena
Corona 5207   Little Girl of My Dreams / Ramona [1960]
El Zarape 104   Cross My Heart / Tell Me What I Did Wrong
El Zarape 128   Hi-Ho Polka / Cada Vez Que Te Miro
El Zarape 146   Bola Negra / Quinto Patio
El Zarape 162   Pa Que Me Dice Cosas / Ojitos Verdes
El Zarape 274   Dream Lover / All Night Worker
Rival 11   Little Girl of My Dreams / Ramona [1958]
Tear Drop 3122   Don't Look Back / Hey Pretty Baby [1964]
Tear Drop 3175   Cold, Cold Heart / Don't Let the Stars Get in Your Eyes
Tear Drop 3190   Fever / Mr. Sandman
Tomi 100   Lovely Lady / Why Don't You Believe Me [1965]
Tomi 104   Slippin' and Slidin' / Love Is a Many Splendored Thing [1965]
Tomi 107   Hello Stranger / Let It Be Me [1965]
Tomi 110   My Girl / Get Out of My Life Woman [1965]
Tomi 111   Don't Go Please Stay / Pretty Woman [1965]
Tomi 113   Ain't No Big Thing / In Crowd [1965]
Tomi 122   Bring It Up / Love Is a Hurtin' Thing [1966]
Tomi 123   Knock on Wood / Show Me [1966]
Valmon 1-015   Cartucho Quemado / No Destruyas El Nido
Valmon 1-016   Confidential / The Dog
Valmon 1-021 Echale un Cinco Al Piano / Por Un Amor
Valmon 1-022   Someday / Let the Good Times Roll
White Whale 304 Why Don't You Write Me / Crazy Baby [1969] as David Coronado and the Latinaires
Torero xxx   Safari pt.1 / pt. 2
as La Familia Inc
Buena Suerte 50302   Do You Love Me / Exigency [1975]

LP: Follow The Leader [Buena Suerta 1003]
  Little Joe and the Latinaires Addios Margarita Linda [Buena Suerte 1004]
  Arriba! [Buena Suerte] 1968
  Peace and Good Will [Buena Suerte 1007] 1968
  Mas Arriba! [Buena Suerte 1011] 1969
  Que Bruti [Buena Suerte 1017] 1969
  La Familia Little Joe and Johnny Hernandez [Buena Suerte 1023] 1970
  Las Viejas De Little Joe y la Familia Buena Suerte [1030]1972
  Para La Gente [Buena Suerte 1038]
  Little Joe y la Familia Total [Buena Suerte 1041]
  La Familia de Little Joe Nos Otros [Buena Suerte 1048]
  Por Un Amor [El Zarape 1002] 1965
  On Tour: Prisonero de Tus Brazos [El Zarape 1003] 1965
  Amor Bonito [El Zarape 1008] 1966
  Best of…. [El Zarape 1012]
  Little Joe, Johnny and the Latinaires [El Zarape 1016]
  Freddy and Joe [El Zarape 1084]
  Incomparable [Ivan 1001]
  Chicano's Can Too [Good Luck 0001]
  Don't Let the Stars Get in Your Eyes [Latin Sol 4002]
  Little Joe y la Familia La Voz de Aztlan [LRC 007] 1977
  Unbeatable [Tomi 1002]

Little Jr. Jesse and the Tear Drops plus the Tears
San Antonio, TX
Jesse Vallado (vocals), Bobby Bustos (organ), Jesse Jimenez (drums), Jesse De La Garza (bass, Paul Aleman (guitar), Larry Filippone (sax), Isidore Arias (sax), Richard Telez (trumpet), Armenel Tellez (trombone)
Dynamic 101   Give Your Love to Me / It Keeps Raining [1966]
Dynamic 110   Ain't No Big Thing / If You Don't Love Me [1966]
Metro-Dome 1001   Cry Baby / Little Playgirl [1967]
Metro-Dome 1002   Giving Up on Love / Kansas City [1967]

Metro-Dome 1003   Funky Stuff / Give Him Up [1967]
LP: El Gigante Chaparrito [Discos Vallado 101] 1970
see: Zapata

Little Lawrence and the Suspenders
Fort Worth, TX
Lawrence Lueras (guitar, accordion, keyboards), Fernando Lueras (bajo sexto), Guadalupe Lueras (drums), Rudy Valdez (accordion), Anselmo "Chico" Martinez (bass), Roscoe Young (vocals)
Franco105   Don't Mess Around / Babee [1963]
Gabe 101   Highway 81 / Six Flags over Texas [1967]
Gabe 1029   Senaida Engrata
Mex-Melody 153   La Hilacha / Que Te Vayas

Little Manny with the Ricky Aguirre Band
Oakland, CA
Velltone 110   Chuke Baby / La Carta

Little Ray (Jimenez)
Los Angeles, CA
Ray Jimenez (vocals), Joe Urzua (barritone sax), Tony Garcia (sax), "Bones" (trumpet, French horn), Clarence Playa (guitar, vocals), Tony Escalante (guitar), John Pride (keyboards), Mike "Bozo" Rodriguez (bass), Marshall Tavarez (bass)
Atco 6455   I (Who Have Nothing) / I Been Trying [1965]
Donna 1404   I (Who Have Nothing) / I Been Trying [1965]
Dore 590   My Rainbow / There Is Something on Your Mind [1961]
Faro 617   Karen / Come Swim with Me [1964]
Mustang 5   It's Good Enough for Me [1965]
Warner Bros 5351   Come Baby Dance / You Can't Hurt Me [1963]
as Little Ray and the Midniters
Impact 30   Loretta / My Girl [1962]
as Little Ray and the Premiers
Impact 26   Shake, Shout and Soul / Soul Stomp [1962]
as Ray Jimenez
Columbia 44287   I'll Keep On Loving You / Leave Her Alone

Little Ricky
Picture 10002   Asking Your Forgiveness / How You Doing

Little Russell and the Pharaohs see Big Man & the Pharaohs

Living Us
Big Springs, TX
Nomad 1704   Steal Away / Understand

Lord August and the Visions of Light
San Antonio, TX
Augie Meyers, Publio Casillas, Harvey Kagen
V.O.L. 132   Found Me a New Love / Gigilo [1967]

Los Blue Lites
Rosenburg, TX
Jesna 028   Color My World / Cuatro Caminos

Los Blues
San Antonio, TX
Randy Garibay, Cleto Escobedo, Frank Rodarte, Jim Waller, Richard Garza, Louie Leos, Jimmy McFarland
United Artist 50801   God Help Me / Ain't That Lovin You [1969]
United Artist 50968   Life Is Just a Bowl of Cherry Bombs / The Squirrel [1969]
LP: Los Blues [United Artist] 1969
see: Pharaohs, Dell-Kings, Charlie and the Jives, Randy Garibay

Los Cuatro de Rudy
Corpus Christi, TX
Beca 110   The Wild One

Los Diamantes
Horoscopo 5004   Baby Giving Good Loving / Triunfal

Los Elegantes
Tucson, AZ
Copper State1068   La Bamba / Lonely Street

Los Keys
San Antonio, TX
Scotchman 101   Mister T.C.B. / pt. 2

Los Muchachos with Big Lu Valeny
Houston, TX
Lupe Valenzuela (vocals), Paul Arendondo Jr. (organ), Robert Navarro Jr. (sax), Vincent Rodriguez (sax), Arnold Garza (guitar), Alfred Mireles (drums), Larry Alvarado (bass), Earnest Flores (trumpet)
Good Luck 010   Baby's Gone Away / Domino
Lp: Frijolitos Pinto [teardrop 2011]
   La Barriga de Big Lou [Buena Suerte 126]
   Un Amigo Borracho [Buena Suerte 1031]

Los Premiers
Los Lunas, NM
Johnny Torres, Ricky Romero, Johnny Zamora, Clem Romero, LeRoy Torres, Chris Garcia
Tamray 1002 Premiers Rock / Mi Carrito

Los Rondels see: Rondels
Laredo, TX

Los Santos
San Antonio, TX
Cardenal 106   We Belong Together / Disha Inefable (Spanish)

Los Stardusters (Sunglows)
San Antonio, TX
Tear Drop 3106   Forever / All Night Worker [1964]
Tear Drop 3113   We're Just Lonely / El Papalote [1964]
Tear Drop 3156   Mama Didn't Know / Dream of Our Future Tonight [1964]
Tear Drop 3262   It Must Be the Girl / Peanuts
LP: All Night Worker [Tear Drop 2019]
see: Sunglows, Ricky Vee and the Stardusters

Los Statics de Richmond, Texas
Richmond, TX
Gilbert Flores
Jesna 018   To Love, to Love / Te Fueste Corazon

Los Two Tones
San Antonio, TX
Eddie Aleman, Blas Bustamante, Juan Aguilar
AAA 106   Fuiste Tu (Till There Was You) / Te Vas (You're Gone)

Vic Love and the Lovells
San Antonio, TX
Vic Love (vocals), Tony Jimenez (guitar), Lupe Sanchez (bass), Charlie Crystal (keyboards), Jimmy Montez (drums), Raymond Gutierrez (trumpet), Norbert Hernandez (trumpet), David Mireles (sax), Richard Carillo (sax)
Latin Soul 105   Make a Celebration / No More Loneliness [1970]
Tear Drop 3246   Tell Me the Truth / You're a Friend of Mine [1969]
see: Lovells, Sequence

Lovells
San Antonio, TX
Ernest Camarillo (vocals), Tony Jimenez
Pan-Am 118   Cariño Pasado / Llorando por Ti
Pan-Am 4003   Pledging My Love / El Sandiyero (Watermelon Man) [1967]
see: Vic Love and the Lovells, Sequence

Lyrics
San Antonio, TX
Dimas Garza, Carl Henderson, Abel Martinez, Alex Pato, Pache de la Vega (guitar), Raul Velasquez (piano), Joe Dominguez (bass), Raul Garcia (drums)
Coral 62322 Oh Please Love Me / The Girl I Love [1959]
Harlem 101   Oh Please Love Me / The Girl I Love [1958]
Harlem 104   The Beating of My Heart / I Want to Know [1959]
Wildcat 28   Oh Please Love Me / The Girl I Love [1959]
see: Dimas Garza, Royal Jesters

M.A.R.O.
Odessa, TX
Butter Sound 81277   Just Cause You're Gone / Mil Copas

George Macias and the Original Royal Bops
San Antonio, TX
R-B xxx   So Alone / Dreaming

Machismo
San Antonio, TX
Matias Muñoz (vocals), Arturo Aldrete (bass), Jesse Martinez (guitar), Jose Jimenez (drums), Gilbert Perez (trumpet), Joey Perez (sax), Ben Serrato (sax), Fred Salas (keys), Steve Silva (keyboards), David Mares (congas)
GCP 1069   Everybody's Getting So Funky / Call Me [1977]
LP: Faces South [GCP 135] 1977
     Machismo con Matias [GCP 117]
     Enamorado [GCP 130]

Macondo
Los Angeles, CA
Max Uballez (vocals, rhythm guitar), Bobby Hernandez (lead guitar, vocals), Fred Ramirez (keyboards, vibes), Ron Chretin (bass), Frank Martinez (drums), Lee Pastore (percussion), Eddie Caicedo (timbales, percussion)
LP: Macondo [Atlantic 7234] 1972
see: Romancers

Majestic Knights
Deming, NM
Johnny Garcia (vocals)
Santa 7865   Queen of Fools / Jerk Like Me [1965]

Majestics
La Puente, CA
David Robles, Ruben Robles, Arthur Robles with the Romancers band
Linda 121   Girl of My Dreams / (I Love Her So Much) It Hurts Me [1965]
see: David and Ruben, Little D and the Bel-Aires

Majestics
Phoenix, AZ
Big Al, Little Al, Art Bojorquez (bass), Jerry Cruz (vocals), Joe Saenz (drums), Benny Dimas (guitar)
Lady 36741   Turn Back the Hands of Time / Y Volvere [1979]
as the Majestic Five
Majestic 28741   Whenever I'm with You / Pajarillo Barranqueño

Mando and the Chili Peppers
San Antonio, TX
Armando Almandarez, Juventino Garcia Elizondo, Jesse "Chucho" Perales, Abel Garcia, Rudolph Martinez
Golden Crest 105   Don't Say Goodnight / South of the Border [1957]
LP: On the Road with Rock 'n Roll [Golden Crest 3023] 1957

Maria Elena (Guerrero) and the Sunglows
San Antonio, TX
Sunglow 124   Sick and Tired / Just a Game [1964]
see: Sunglows

Mark and the Escorts
Los Angeles, CA
Mark Guerrrero, Trini Basulto, Robert Warren, Richard Rosas, Ernie Hernandez, Ricky Almaraz
GNP Crescendo 350   Get Your Baby / Tuff Stuff [1965]
GNP Crescendo 358   Dance With Me / Silly Putty [1965]

Mar-Kels
San Antonio, TX
Amos Pacheco (trumpet), Tony Soto (sax), Robert Leal (bass), Paul Longoria (lead guitar), Able Martinez (drums), Richard Padilla (vocals), Benny Rodriquez (trumpet)
Gunzo 640305   Something's Got a Hold on Me / I Love You [1964]

Andy Martinez and Indigo
Albuquerque, NM
Le Mans 1025   You Control My Soul / Dile

Freddy Martinez
Corpus Christi, TX
Geno 12346   Hey Little Girl / Breaking Hearts Is Wrong
Ideal 2345   Walking the Dog
Acorn 102   Will You Love Me Tomorrow / Today

Marty y Los Chicano '5'
Discos S&R 10187   Chicano Soul Pt. 1
LP: Chicano Soul [Discos S&R 836]

Mike "Keys" Martinez
San Antonio, TX
Great 702   Here I Stand / Sugar Baby

Robert "Boo Boo" Martinez and his combo
Corpus Christi, TX
Geno 12345   Scramble / Arrived the Drunker Borracho
Geno 12347   Henry's Memories / Cielito Lindo

Oscar Martinez
Corpus Christi, TX
Pepe Cavasos (vocals, guitar), Oscar Martinez (trumpet), Domingo Garcia (bass), Raul Ornelas (drums), Rudy Alvarado (sax), David Reyes (tenor), Victor Martinez (trumpet), Jose Morris (trumpet), George Rodriguez (trumpet), Gilbert Itza (tenor)
Disco Grande 1041   Oscar's Special
Ideal 1724   El Diablo / El Mascatabasco
Impala 107   Let's Pretend / Corpus Christi Rock [1962]
Impala 116   Darling I'm in Love with You / Gigolo [1962]
Impala 118   El Mala Vida / Consejo [1962]
Impala 124   You Went Away / Funny Feeling [1962]
Impala 12432   Makes No Difference / La Bamba [1963]
El Zarape 115   Mi Nueva Vida / Mas Que Nunca
El Zarape 123   Me Quieres O-No Me Quieres?/ Tortillas de Manteca
El Zarape 136   El Camisa Negra / Contigo con Ellas
Sombrero 239   Te He de Querer / Corazon Donde Estas
LP: El Tejano Enamorado [Corona]
   Mardi Gras Tejano [El Zarape 1017] 1968

Mar-Vells
San Antonio, TX
Harlem 108   Tonight / The Wobble Trot [1959]

Matadors
Mexicali, CA
Jimmy Meza
Chartmaker 404   Let Me Dream / Wobble, Wobble [1966]
Forbes 230   Let Me Dream / Wobble, Wobble [1967]

Ray Medina and the New Latin Breed
Los Angeles, CA
Prod Memo Mata (also produced Sly, Slick and Wicked) & Earl Chavez
Mares 006   Head's Head / Dr. Felix

Memories
EL Monte, CA
Old Sound 809   Itty Bitty Girl / Darling It's Wonderful [1962]
see: Doug and Freddy

Mexican Revolution de Ruben Ramos
Austin, TX
Ruben Ramos (vocals), Leonard Davila (vocals, trombone), Mike Saldivar (guitar), Roy Ramos (bass), Robert Moreno (organ), Sergio Salas (drums), Manny Guerra (percussion), trumpets: Albert Amesquita, Edward Vasquez, Richard Leal
El Zarape 315   Revolution
El Zarape 316   Na Na Na Hey Hey / El Toque y Toque
El Zarape 408   Listen Here / Te Sigo Queriendo
LP: The Mexican Revolution [El Zarape 1035] 1971
   Return of the Mexican Revolution [El Zarape 1048] 1972
   Ratos Felices [El Zarape 1058] 1972
   La Revolucion Mexicana [El Zarape 1075] 1972
   Eres la Mas Bonita [G.C.P. 100]
   Quiro una Cita [G.C.P. 116]

Midniters, Thee
Los Angeles, CA
Willie Garcia (vocals), Larry Rendon (sax), Romeo Prado (trombone), George Dominguez (lead guitar), George Salazar or Danny Lamont (drums), Roy Marquez (guitar), Benny Lopez replaced by Jimmy Espinosa (bass), Ronnie Figueroa (keyboards)
Al Anaya (vocals) on La Raza 711
Chattahoochee 666   Land of 1000 Dances / Ball O Twine [1965]

Chattahoochee 674 Sad Girl / Heat Wave [1965]
Chattahoochee 684 Whittier Blvd / Evil Love [1965]
Chattahoochee 693 I Need Someone / Empty Heart [1965]
Chattahoochee 694 That's All / It's Not Unusual [1965]
Chattahoochee 695 Brother Where Are You / Heat Wave [1965]
Chattahoochee 706 Are You Angry / I Found A Peanut [1966]
La Raza 711 Chicano Power / Never Gonna Give You Up [1968]
Whittier 200 Come Back Baby / Sad Girl [1966]
Whittier 203 Giving Up on Love / Are You Angry [1966]
Whittier 500 Love Special Delivery / Don't Go Away [1966]
Whittier 501 It'll Never Be Over for Me / Thee Midnite Feeling [66]
Whittier 503 Dragon Fly / The Big Ranch [1966]
Whittier 504 Never Knew I Had It So Bad / The Walking Song [1967]
Whittier 505 Never Knew I Had It So Bad / Everybody Needs Somebody [1967]
Whittier 507 Looking Out a Window / Jump Jive and Harmonize [1967]
Whittier 508 Chile Con Soul / Tu Despedida [1967]
Whittier 509 Dreaming Casually / Breakfast in the Grass [1967]
Whittier 511 Your Gonna Make Me Cry / Making Ends Meet [1968]
Whittier 512 Ballad of Cesar Chavez / [1968]
Whittier 513 Chicano Power / Never Gonna Give You Up [1968]
LP: Thee Midniters [Chattahoochee 1001] 1964
Thee Midniters [Whittier 1001] 1964
Love Special Delivery [Whittier 5,000] 1966
Unlimited [Whittier 5,001] 1966
Giants [Whittier 5,002] 1967
see: Willie G, Thee Impalas, Little Ray

Mike and the Belairs
San Antonio, TX
Mike Villa, Mando Lucio, Alfred Pinkney, Charles Virgil
Cobra 666 She's Mine / Buscando (searchin') [1963]
Holiday 3001 Everyone Knows / Tiffany Twist

Mike and the Del-Rays
San Antonio, TX
Mike Gonzales
Jox 018 You Talk Too Much / Restless [1963]

Mike and the Hi-Fi's
San Antonio, TX
Mike Martinez (vocals), Roy Cantú (bass), Luis Cantú (guitar), Henry Hernandez (drums), Abel Hernandez, Joe Gonzáles (sax), Robert Gonzáles (sax)
Middle C 101 Day and Night / Boogie Woogie Twist
Middle C xxx Mr. Nobody / Twistin' Keys

Mike and Leo with the Del-Rays
Albuquerque, NM
Hurricane 7008 Take Me Back / Vuela-Ya (con los Del-Rays)

Mixtures
Oxnard, CA
Del Franklin, Johnny Wells, Jesse Porras, Leroy Soto, Eddie De Robles, Steve Mendoza, Dan Pollock
Linda 104 Rainbow Stomp / part II
Linda 106 Jawbone / It's Gonna Work Out Fine
Linda 108 Olive Oyl / Canadian Sunset
Linda 109 Poochum / Tiki
Linda 113 Chinese Checkers /
Linda 115 The Last Minute / Sen Sa-Shun
as Phil and Del
Linda 105 My Girl / Don't Play with Love
as Phil and Harv
Rampart 611 Darling (Please Bring Your Love) / Friendship
LP: Stompin' at the Rainbow [Linda 3301] 1962

Mondie and the Mystic Ones
Pecos, Texas
Mystic 1001 Sabor A Mi / Yo No Se Matar

Monsanto
San Antonio, TX
Joe Martinez
Lp: Monsanto: In the Mood [Canoch 5001]

Roy Montelongo
Austin, TX
Bego 019   Sera La Ultima Ves / Corazoncito Tirano
Tear Drop 3149   Man of Action / No Letter Today
Tear Drop 3179   Piedad (Mercy Mercy)
Texas 011   I Make a Fool of Myself / El Aeroplanito
Valmon 074   We'll Make It / Porque Dios Mio
Valmon xxx   Just Because (w/Augustine Ramirez)
LP: Brindo por Ti [Tear Drop 2009]
　　A Dios Chiquita [Tear Drop 2013]

Chris Montez
Hawthorne, CA
Guaranteed 217   They Say / I Lost My Baby [1960]
Monogram 500   All You Had to Do Was Tell Me
Monogram 505   Let's Dance / You're the One [1962]
Monogram 507   Some Kinda Fun / Tell Me (It's Not Over) [1962]
A&M 598   Love Is Here to Stay
A&M 780   Call Me / Go Head On [1966]
A&M 796   The More I See You [1966]
A&M 810   There Will Never Be Another You [1966]
A&M 822   Time After Time / Keep Talkin'
A&M 839   Because of You [1967]
A&M 855   Dindi (Jin-Jee) / Foolin' Around [1967]
as Chris and Kathy (Young)
Monogram 517   All You Had to Do Was Tell Me / You're the One [1963]
Monogram 520   It Takes Two / Shoot That Curl [1963]
LP: The More I See You [A&M 115] 1966
　　Foolin' Around [A&M 128] 1967
　　Time after Time [A&M 4120]
　　Let's Dance [Monogram]

Julio Moreno and the Centennials
Austin, TX
Julio Moreno, Joe Rodriguez, Roy
Valmon 072   Lee Frog / A La Ru Ru Nino
Valmon 086   Dreaming / Junito a Mi

Mystics
Chicago, Ill
Teako 370   That's the Kind of Love / I Really Love You

Dave Newman (David Nuñez)
Albuquerque, NM
Look 5011   Make Up Your Mind / Can't Take No for an Answer [1968]
see: Chekkers

Night Dreamers
El Paso, TX
Sonny Powell (lead)
Frog Death 66/1   Mr Pitiful / I Can't Help It [1966]
Frog Death 67/1   Wisdom of a Fool / I Take What I Want [1967]

David Nuñez see: David Newman, Thee Chekkers
Albuquerque, NM

Frank Nuñez and the Imperials
Austin, TX
Frank Nuñez (trumpet), James Castrita (sax), Ben Garcia (sax), Ben Marines (bass), Julio Moreno (organ), Charlie Alvarez (guitar), Sergio Salas (drums), Joe Castillo (vocals), Ray Torres (vocals), Felipe Alvarez (vocals)
Estrella 13   Can't Turn You Loose / Fallastes Corazon
Fiesta xx   Las Noches Las Hago Dias / Las Piriswiris
LP: Las Morenitas [Capri 1003]

Oaxaca
Mariposa 131   Stop Your Crying / Sancho

Frank Olvera
Los Angeles, CA
NRM 903   Huggies Bunnies / Something Like Mr. C
Lolla 104   Huggies Bunnies / Something Like Mr. C

One G Plus Three
Los Angeles, CA
Rudy Salas (guitar), Manuel Mosqueda (drums), Max Garduno (percussion), Randy Thomas (keyboards)
Gordo 705   Poquito Soul / Summertime [1970]
Paramount 0054   Poquito Soul / Summertime [1970]

Joe Ortega
Do-Go 1   20-20 Vision / Take a Little Look

Cruz Ortiz and the Flames see: Sherman Evans

Pagents
Los Angeles, CA
Roy Marquez (guitar), Joe Urzua (baritone sax)
I.K.E. 631   Enchanted Surf / Big Daddy [1963]
ERA 3119   Enchanted Surf / Big Daddy [1963]
ERA 3124   Glenda / Shake [1964]
ERA 3134   Pa-Cha / Sad and Lonely [1964]

Parlay Brothers
Los Angeles, CA
George Aguilar, Mickey Gonzales
Valjay 2725   My Girl (Please Be True) / Do You Really Want to Dance

Peanuts
Texas
Sergio Garcia
Pic 1 110   We're Just Lonely

Pendletons
Black Jack 108   One More Kiss / Pancho Loco [1959]

Perez Brothers with the Gents
Canoga Park, CA
Louie "Donsi" Perez (vocals, bass), Ralph "Gordy" Perez (vocals, drums), Danny Rosales (keyboards), Gil Rocha (vibes), Sal Barragan (sax), Phil Barragan (trumpet), Gil Luna (trumpet), Dick Lowe (trumpet), Walter Takate (trumpet)
Ofies 200   Dream a Little Dream / Truly, Truly Yours [1960]
Wolfies 103   Dream a Little Dream / Truly, Truly Yours [1961]

Dario Perez
Alice, TX
vocals: Tommy Carrera
Nopal 101   Do You Love Me / Sylvia

David Perez
San Antonio, TX
Del-West 117   When a Man Loves a Woman / La Bamba

Neto Perez and the Originals *canta: Little Ricky*
Houston, TX
Capri 142   La Ingrata / La Rosa de Oro [1973]
Capri 153   TCB or TYA / For Once in My Life [1973]
Capri 161   Oily / Callejon Sin Salida [1973]
as Neto Perez and the Young Originals
Buena Suerte 970   Mi Charchina / Poquito Fe
Lp: In Memory of Neto Perez [Capri 1029] 1973
      Perdoname [Buena Suerte 1009]

Personalities
Falcon 1349   Scratching the Dog / I'm Convinced

Pharaohs
San Antonio, TX
Randy Garibay, Duke Anthony, Joe Perez, Oscar Cavasos, Richard Garza
Wild Cat xxx   Dream Girl / Baby Doll [1960]
Pegaso 550   The End / Merry Widow [1960]
see: Al Epp and the Pharaohs, Charlie and the Jives, Randy Garibay

Playboys
San Antonio, TX
Floyd Coleman (vocals), Carlitos Pierro, Robert Reyes (bass), Ernie Saldana (keyboards) Hector Molina, Robert Suarez, Robert Lopez, Henry Garcia (drums), Roger Sanchez (trumpet)
Satin 111   Dame Licencia / Nomas Por Quererte [1966]
Satin 113   All I Do Is Cry / Little Playgirl [1967]
Satin 115   Falling in Love with You / Let Them Talk [1967]

G. Potillo with Mike and the Latin Notes
Lee 1   Just Because / Since I Met You Baby

Preludes featuring: Gabriel Lopez
El Paso, Texas
D.J. 101   How Does It Feel / Baby Make My Dreams Come True

Premiers
San Gabriel, CA
Lawrence Perez (guitar), Frank Zuniga (bass), George Delgado (rhythm guitar), John Perez (drums), Joe Whiteman jr. (sax) replaced by Phil Ruiz
Faro 615   Farmer John / Duffy's Blues [1964]
Faro 616   Get Your Baby / Little Ways [1964]
Faro 624   Get on This Plane / Come On and Dream
Faro 627   Ring around My Rosie / inst. version
Warner Bros 5464   Blues for Arlene / Annie Oakley [1964]
Warner Bros 5488   Little Irene / So Fine [1965]
LP: Farmer John [Warner Bros. 1565] 1964
   Farmer John [Rampart] 1964

Noé Pro and the Semitones (Blue Valiants)
Corpus Christi, TX
Mercury 72341 Yesterday's Dream / Come Along My Baby (Dance with Me) [1964]
Pharaoh 118   I Know (You Don't Love Me Anymore) / Reina de Mi Vida [1962]
as Noé Pro and the Semitones
Falcon 1656   Yo Te Daria Mas / Llora (cry)
Falcon 1675   Cuando Estoy Contigo / No
Pharaoh 124   I Love My Darling / I Know What's Going On [1962]
Norco 110   If You Would See Me Tomorrow / I'm Gonna Leave This Town
ARV 5056   Buenas Noches Mi Amor (Goodnight My Love) / Estaba Todo Escrito [1973]

Prophets
Norco 100   Til the Day I Die / Mr. Go-Go

P.T. and the Portables w/ Mike and the Royal Notes
Dallas, TX
Siesta 1002   Smile Now Cry Later

Publio and the Valiants
San Antonio, TX
Publio Casillas (guitar), Morgan Leeth (bass, vocals), Jerry Savoy (sax, keys), Ruben Ramirez (percussion), Augie Meyers (keyboards), Charlie Walters (harmonica), Linda Casillas (vocals)

Menard 6252   Image of Love / Out of Town [1963]
Menard 6253   Teenage Heaven / Dragstrip [1963]
see: Lord August and the Visions Of Light

? and the Mysterians
Saqinaw, MI
Rudy "?" Martinez (vocals), Bobby Balderama (guitar), Frank Rodriguez (organ), Eddie Serrato (drums), Frank Lugo (bass), Robert Martinez, Larry Borjas
Cameo 428   96 Tears / Midnight Hour [1966]
Cameo 441   I Need Somebody / "8" Teen
Cameo 467   Can't Get Enough of You, Baby / Smokes [1967]
Cameo 479   Girl (You Captivate Me) / Got To [1967]
Pa-Go-Go 102   96 Tears / Midnight Hour [1966]
LP: 96 Tears [Cameo 2004] 1966

Eddie Quinterros
Daly City, CA
Brent 7009   Come Dance with Me / Vivian [1960]
Brent 7012   Looking for My Baby / [1960]
Brent 7014   Linda Lou / [1960]
Del-Fi 4156   Pretty Baby, I Love You [1961]
Ed-Dar 102   Come on Little Girl / Waited for You [1962]
M&K 102   Come on Little Girl / Waited for You [1961]

Rachel and the Originals
National City, CA
Rachel Legerretta, David Ponce
Nite Star 010   I'll Always Remember / The Sound [1962]
see: Rosie and the Originals

Augustine Ramirez
Corpus Christi, TX
Valmon 143   Just Because / El Aquila Negra
LP: Paloma Dejame Ir [El Zarape 1029]
   Y Su Orqusta [El Zarape 1066]
   Te Quiero Cariñito [El Zarape 1076] 1973
   Es Tierra Chicana [El Zarape 1085]

Fred Ramirez
Warner Bros 7081   Hold on I'm Comin' / There Is a Mountain

Joe Ramirez
Gyro100   Couldn't Keep from Crying / Run You Down

Alfonso Ramos Orquesta *canta: Ruben Ramos*
Austin, TX
Rosina 116   Acabame De Matar / La Tijera
Rosina 118   Como Fue / La Veintiunica
Rosina 121   Comprende Cariño / Mujer de la Calle
Rosina 135   Seis Años / Me Regalo con Tigo
Tomi 101   Try Me / Rainbow Riot [1965]
Valmon 146   Dancing in the Streets / Pledging My Love

Paul Ramos
San Antonio, TX
Harlem 1005   Fence Walk

Ruben Ramos
Austin, TX
Capri 130   Slip Away / You Can Make It If You Try
LP: Yo No Se [El Zarape 1091]
see: **Mexican Revolution de Ruben Ramos**

Doc Rand and the Purple Blues
Albuquerque, NM
Doc Rand (vocals), Ray Cruz (guitar), Gene Romero (Bass), Max Perlata (sax), Pete Cockroft (trumpet), Randy Castillo (drums)
Lance 105   I Want You (Yea, I Do) / I Need a Woman
Lance 119   Hold On (I'm Coming) / Something You Got [1967]
Landra 020   I Need a Woman

Ray and the Bel-Aires
ARV 5008   The Blame Is on You / I Wish I Could [1967]

Ray and the Blue Notes
ARV 5002   She Doesn't Love Me / Thank You for the Memories [1967]

Ray and the Blue Satins
Falcon 1630 Regalame Esta Noche / Que Se Me Acaba la Vida

Ray and the Dreamers
Austin, TX
Raymond Torres (vocals)
Dreamy 48   Oh I Need You / Love at First Sight
Valmon 1-184   I'll Never Smile Again / Compro Amores

Donald Ray and the El Paso Chessmen
El Paso, TX
Coronado 147   Can't You See That I Love You / Cry Like a Baby [1968]
As Donald Ray and his Revue
Aslon 1   Strut Your Stuff / Leave It to Your Heart

Redbone
Los Angeles, CA
Lolly Vegas, Pat Vegas, Butch Rillera, Tony Bellamy
Epic 10670   Maggie / New Blue Sermonette [1970]
Epic 10749   The Witch Queen of New Orleans / Chant 13th Hour [1973]
Epic 1830   Wovoka / Sweet Lady of Love [1973]
Epic 11035   Come and Get Your Love / Day to Day Life [1974]
Epic 2664   One More Time / Clouds in My Sunshine [1974]
LP: Potlatch [Epic 30109] 1970
    Already Here [Epic 31958]
    Wovoka [Epic 32462] 1973
    Una Vez Mas [Epic 80429]
    Message from a Drum [Epic] 1971
see: **Pat and Lolly Vegas**

Al Reed and the Bluenotes
San Antonio, TX
Albert Gonzáles aka Al Reed
TNT140   Darling of Mine / I Love Her So (Sonny Ace) [1958]

Wayne Reed and the Reno-Bops
San Antonio, TX
Red Top   When I Think of You / Going Home

Rene and Ray
Hawthorne, CA
Pablo Venezuela, Ray Quiñones with the Velveteens
Donna 1360   Queen of My Heart / Do What You Feel [1962]
Donna 1368   Too Late / I Can't Let You Go [1962]
see: Velveteens, Terri and Johnnie, Rosie and Ron, Spider Ray & the Velveteens

Rene and Rene
Mission, TX
Rene Ornelas, Rene Guerrera
ARV xxxx   Hiding in the Shadows / Enchilada Jose
Cobra 212   No Soy El Unico / Crei [1965]
East Bend 209   Really Hurtin' This Guy / El Mexicano
East Bend 213   Put Me in Jail / El Bandito
East Bend 409   Love Is for the Two of Us / Lloraras
Epic 10443   Our Day Will Come / Muchachita [1969]
Falcon 626   LLorar / Day Tripper
Falcon 1774   Lo Mucho Que Te Quiero / Mornin' [1968]
Jox 017   Angelito / Write Me Soon [1964]
Jox 025   Pretty Flowers Fade Away / Yo Te Lo Due [1964]
Jox 031   Peanuts / Little Vagabond 1964]
Jox 032   I'm Not the Only One / Chantilly Lace (w/ Dreamliners) [1965]
Jox 041   Little Peanuts / Vagabond

Revells
San Antonio, TX
Joe "Jama" Perales (vocals, bass), Fred Lozano (vocals, guitar), John Gutierrez (guitar), Henry Medrano (drums)
Prism 101   I Want to Know / You Turn Your Back on Me [1964]
see: Royal Jesters, Joe Jama, Casino Royale, Eptones

Revolution, The
M&Ms 1001   The Siesta Is Over / Part 2

Little Bobby Rey and the Masked Phantom Band
Los Angeles, CA
Original Sound 008   Corrido De Auld Lang Syne / Rockin' J Bells [1960]
Original Sound 011   Night Beat / Night Theme [1960]
Indigo 103   I'm Gonna Sit Right Down and Write Myself a Letter / Such a Fool [1960]

Tony Rey with the Sunglows
San Antonio, TX
King Bee 102   Something on Your Mind / Play It Cool [1963]
see: Sunglows

Simon Reyes
San Antonio, TX
Rival 1202 I'm a Hog (for You)/Just Like Touching Your Hand

Rhythm Heirs
El Paso, TX
Virgie Gallegos
Yucca 105   Cradle Rock / Strange World [1959]

Rhythm Kings
Delano, CA

Rick and Mann featuring the Sonics see: Dimas Garza

Ricky and the Keys
San Antonio, TX
Ricky Aguary (piano, vocals)
Savoy 1529   Come on Liza / Can't You See [1959]
See: Ricky Aguary

Chuck Rio see: Danny Flores

Paul Rios and the Rivieras
Dallas, TX
Paul Rios, Gilbert Solano, Alfonso Villanueva, Ramiro Amaya, Gabino Villanueva, Johnny Contreras, Pete Contreras, Preston Rodriguez, Joe Palma, Clyde AlvarezIvan 103   She's My Woman, She's My Girl / You Don't Know Like I Know [67]
LP: El Tracalero [El Zarape 1030]

George Rivas
San Antonio, TX
Rivas 1004   On the Outside Looking In / Sherry

Robert and Rey with the Romancers Band
Watts, CA
Music 2473 I Found a New Love / Please Forgive Me [1962]

Robert and the Eternals
San Antonio, TX
AAA 108   I'm in Love / I'll Try to Forgive You

Rockin' Aces
Santa Fe, NM
Hurricane 6976   Your King Of Fools / Cathy [1966]
Lance 121A   If You Only Knew / If You're Ever Gonna Love Me [1967]

Henry Roe
Dallas, TX
Henry Rodriguez
Tomi 105   Tu Da Do / Hot Tamales

Romancers
Los Angeles, CA
early group included: Max Uballez (guitar, vocals), Richard Provincio & Andy Tesso (guitar), Manuel "Magoo" Rodriguez or Chris Pascual (bass, vocals), David Brill or Manuel Mosqueda (drums), Joe Whiteman, Armando Mora, Bobby Marty, or David Bajorquez (sax)
Linda Records: Max Uballez (guitar, vocals), Bobby Hernandez (guitar, vocals), Manuel "Magoo" Rodriguez (bass, vocals), Ralph Ventura (sax, trumpet), Manuel Mosqueda (drums, vocals), Cesar Valverde (sax), Johnny Diaz (guitar, background vocals) Linda #120 only
Del-Fi 4225   Slauson Shuffle / All Aboard [1963]
Linda 117   Don't Let Her Go / I Did the Wrong Thing [1964]
Linda 119   My Heart Cries / Tell Her I Love Her [1965]
Linda 120   Do You Cry / Love's the Thing [1965]
Linda 124   She Gives Me Love / Take My Heart [1966]
Linda 125   She Took My Oldsmobile / That's Why I Love You [66]
as the Smoke Rings
Dot 16975   Love's the Thing / She Gives Me Love [1966]
Prospect 101   Love's the Thing / She Gives Me Love [1966]
as Maximillian
Magic Circle 4226 You'd Better / Butter Ball [1962]
as Max Uballes
Donna 1377   Rock Little Darling / Shirley [1962]
LP: Do The Slauson [Del-Fi 1245] 1963
   Do The Swim [Selma 1501] 1963
see: Macondo

Ron and Don
Tex-Mex 101   My Best Girlfriend / I'll Never Know until I Try

Ron and the Embracers
Los Angeles, CA
Spectrum 2   You Came into My Heart / Latin Blood

Rondels with Carlos Landin
Laredo, TX
Carlos Landin, Ricco
Capri 150   Gettin' the Corners / Hey Jude [1969]
Capri 151   La Raya / La Medallita [1969]
Capri 168   Ay Mama / Ojitos Pajaritos [1969]
Capri 173   Love Bones / Let It Be Me [1970]
Capri 228   Una Pura y Dos con Sal / La Huerfanita
Frontera 107   YaYa / Lo Mucho Que Te Quiero
Impacto 103   La-La Te Amo (La La Means I Love You) / Eres Casado
Impacto 108 La Ultima Cancion / Desde Las Sombras (I Can Remember)
LP: Rondels [Impacto]
   Rondels: Tierrita de Panteon [Capri]
   Rondels: Eres Casado [Bego 1072]

Ronnie and the Pomona Casuals
Pomona, CA
Ronnie Duran (lead guitar), Charles Lett (vocals), Jimmie Duran (tenor sax), Robert Foley (baritone sax), Robert Arroyo (organ), Ryan O'Brien Jr (bass)
Donna 1400   Casual Blues / Swingin' at the Rainbow [1964]
Donna 1402   I Wanna Do the Jerk / Sloopy [1964]

Mustang 3005   Please, Please, Please / We're Gonna Do the Freddie [1965]
LP: Everybody Jerk [Donna 2112] 1964

Ronnie and the Premiers
San Diego, CA
Highland 1014 Sharon / Cha Cha [1961]

Rosie and the Originals
National City, CA
Highland recording: Rosalie Hamlin (vocals), Tony Gomez (bass), Dave Ponci (guitar), Noah Tafolla (guitar), Alfred Barrett (sax), Carl Von Goodat (drums)
Highland 1011   Angel Baby / Give Me Love [1961]
Highland 1025   Angel from Above / Why Did You Leave Me [1961]
Highland 1032   Lonely Blue Nights / We'll Have a Chance [1961]
Globe 401   My One and Only Love / Kinda Makes You Wonder [62]
Wax World 3265   You're No Good / You Don't Understand [1973]
as Rosie
Brunswick 55205   Lonely Blue Nights / We'll Have a Chance [1961]
Brunswick 55213   My Darling Forever / The Time Is Near [1961]
LP:Lonely Blue Nights [Brunswick 54102] 1962

Rosie and Ron with the Velveteens
Ontario / Pomona / Hawthorne, CA
Lucy Duran, Ralph Valdez with the Velveteens: Johnny Valenzuela Jr (piano, sax, trumpet), Danny Espinosa (sax), Poly Rodriguez (guitar), Joe Valenzuela (bass), Danny Valenzuela (drums)
Donna 1338   So Dearly / Bring Me Happiness [1962]
see: Triangles, Terri & the Velveteens, Rene and Ray, Spider Ray & the Velveteens

Roy and the Dew Drops
Phoenix, AZ
Wind Hit 100   The One Who's Hurtin' Is You / I'm Gonna Hurt You [1967]

Roy and the Romans
Dallas, TX
Tomi 114   Mr. Pitiful / Security [1965]
Tomi 120   Se Que Te Vas a Casar / Yo Tienia Dos Corazones [1965]

Royal Checkmates
Los Angeles, CA
Faro 626   Get Out of My Life Woman / Cried All I'm Gonna Cry [1967]

Royal Chessmen
El Monte, CA
David Luna (vocals), Joe Luna (drums), Gilbert Zabala (lead guitar), John Albert Zabala (rhythm guitar), Raul Dovalina (bass), Ray Juarez
Custom Fidelity 742   Beggin' You / You Must Believe Me [1966]

Royal Five
San Antonio, TX
Jox 1128   My Baby Just Cares for Me
Satin 142   Monkey Time / Song for My Father

Royal Jesters
San Antonio, TX
Oscar Lawson, Henry Hernandez, Louie Ecalante
Vocalist also included: Joe Jama, Dimas Garza, Jack Martinez, David Mares, Ralph Cortez musicians: Drums: Manuel "Bones" Aragon, Keyboards: Lavine Reyes, Bobby Fraga, Frank Vadez, Bass: Danny Escobedo, Guitar: Ignacio De La Vega, Gilbert Velasquez, Trombone: Alex Martinez, Paul Rivera, Trumpet: Vic Alvarado, Anthony Martinez, Sax: Joe Posada, Danny Perez, Alex Hernandez

Bell 105   She's Coming Home / Every Little Step of the Way
Bell 964   That Girl / Lady Sunshine [1971]
Clown 104   I Know, I Know / Happily Ever After [1966]
Clown 10   Not the Right Time / So Much in Love [1966]
Clown 107   Girl I Can't Forget / Private Number [1967]
Clown xxx   Aquel Que Parandea / Adoro
Cobra 126   Poco a Poco / Emocion Pasajera [1962]
Cobra 210   Compañera / Amaneci en Tus Brazos [1963]
Cobra 222   Love Me / Let's Kiss and Make Up [1963]
Cobra 223   El Desesperado / Amor de Alma [1963]
Cobra 611025   Is That Good Enough for You / Ask Me to Move a Mountain [61]
Cobra 7777   I Want to Be Loved / I Never Will Forget [1962]
G.C. 128   Yo Soy Chicano / Perdon [1973]
G.C.P.1050   Latin Rhapsody / Tues Dulces Labios
G.C.P.5005   I Just Fell for You / Misty Eyed Loretta [1971]
G.C.P. xxx   Chicanita / Yo Tengo Amor [1974]
Harlem 105   My Angel of Love / Those Dreamy Eyes [1959]
Jester 102   Wisdom of a Fool / What Love Has Joined Together [1964]
Jester 103   My Love My Love / Use Your Head [1965]
Jester 104   We Go Together / I Want You Around [1965]
Jester 106   Let There Be You / I Really Don't Want to Know [1965]
Jester 107   De Nadie Me Quiero / Sirvame Otra Copa [1965]
Jester 108   I'm So Sorry / Take Me for a Little While [1965]
Jox 029   Please Say You Want Me To / What'cha Gonna Do About It[1965]
Jox 036   Wishing Ring / Perdon [1965]
Jox 046   Look for a Star / Muchachita [1966]
Optimum 101   I've Got Soul / My Kind of Woman [1969]
Optimum 104   That Girl / Lady Sunshine [1970]
Optimum 105   Back to You / Theme for a Lonely Girl [1970]
Optimum 106   Sing a Song For Peace / Manning Ave [1970]
Optimum 107   Wishing It Was Yesterday, as Joe Jama
Optimum 102   Sleep Late My Lady Friend / My Life [1969]
Optimum 103   Phases of Time / Down, Down, Down [1970]
LP: We Go Together [Jester 1000] 1965
   Yo Soy Chicano [GCP 109] 1971
   Their Second Album [GCP 112]
   Royal Jesters: The Band [GCP 118] 1975
   Chévere [Optimum 001]

Royal Knights
San Antonio, TX
Gilbert Sanchez (vocals), Albert Arguello (vocals), Johnny Esparza (guitar), Gilbert Rodriguez (bass), Alex Uribe (trumpet), Noé Lozano (drums), Jerry Cortez (drums), Alex (Keyboards), Al Hernandez (Trumpet/Coronet), Martin (trumpet), Martin Lechuga-drums (died in Vietnam) Daniel Medina, Trumpet (died in Vietnam)
Tear Drop 3151   I Need You / I Can't Please You [1966]
Tear Drop 3160   Que Linda Eres / Busco un Amor

Royal Lancers
Waco, TX
Danny Torres, Bill Garcia
TRC 2076   Hey Little Girl What Is Your Name / Soul '68 [1968]

Royal Spades
San Antonio, TX
Spade 101   Love Between Us / Soulful Sax

Rudy and the Cruisers
San Jose, CA
Lolita 1300   Car Show / Crusin' Baby [1981]

Rudy and the Reno-Bops
San Antonio, TX
Rudy T. Gonzales, Manuel "Red" Gonzales, Fernando Aguilar
AAA 103   Rudy's Monkey / Together Again [1963]
El Zarape 240   Eso Merece un Trago / Fallaste Corazon
Red Top 504   Morning Glory / The Stomp
Renner xxx   El Twist
Ru-Tee Hit 102   Talk about Soul / The Fire Is Gone [1968]
Ru-Tee Hit501   Sentimento / La Divina Garza
Sunglow 113   All I Could Do Was Cry / Have Faith [1963]
Tear Drop 3038   Rudy's Monkey / Together Again [1963]
Tear Drop 3050   Do the Jerk Like Me / Once a Day [1963]
Tear Drop 3057   All I Could Do Was Cry / Have Faith [1964]
Tear Drop 3063   It Was Just an Illusion / The Phillie [1964]
Tear Drop 3064   Goodbye Heartaches / Adios Dolores [1964]
Tear Drop 3097   In the Palm of Your Hand / The Tables Have Turned
Tear Drop 3109   La Bamba / Those Long Lonely Nights

Tear Drop 3138 Cuando Vuelvas a Mi / La Tierra Donde Naci
Tear Drop 3285 Together Again / Rosas Son Rosas [1964]
Tear Drop xxxx Tell Me What You Gonna Do [1965]
Tear Drop 3335 Pledging My Love / Jalisco [1975]
VOK 72 Never Let Me Go / Walk through This World with Me
as Wayne Reed and the Reno Bops
Red Top xxx Going Home / When I Think About You
**LP: Un Ratito el Tejano Enamorado [Tear Drop 2005]
    Dejame Sonar [Tear Drop 2010] 1964**

Rudy and the Soul-Setters
Albuquerque, NM
Lance 124 I Dig Girls / Ain't too Proud to Beg [1967]

Runabouts, Thee
Los Angeles, CA
Bobby Torres (vocals), Ron Lemos (guitar), Dean Lemos (bass), B.B. Rico (Farfisa keyboard), Jack D'Amour (drums), Gilbert Priest (trumpet), Ernie Salas (saxophone)
MOD 913 Sacred Love / Skyjack [1968]
MOD 913 Viva Chicano / Skyjack [1968]
Rampart LP 3305 By the Time I Get to Texas (never released as a single)

Doug Sahm
San Antonio, TX
With the Pharaohs: Dough Sahm (tenor sax), Bobby Jett (baritone sax), Johnny Nebauer (piano), Bobby Lynn (drums)
Pharaohs: Randy Garibay, Duke Anthony, Richard Garza, Joe Perez, Oscar Cavasos
With the Markays: Rocky Morales (tenor sax), Bobby Jett (2nd tenor), Doug Sahm (guitar). Umberto Reyes (guitar), Clifford Sten (piano), James Kelly (bass), Eddie Valdez (drums)
With the Dell-Kings: Frank Rodarte (tenor sax), Cleto Escobedo (alto sax), Doug Sahm (piano), Randy Garibay (guitar), Wayne Reed (bass), Richard Garza(drums)
Renner 212 Makes No Difference / Big Hat [1963]
Renner 226 Just Because / Two Hearts in Love [1963]
Renner 232 Cry / Little Angel [1964]
Renner 240 Lucky Me / [1964]
Renner 247 Mr. Kool / [1965]

Doug Sahm with the Dell-Kings
Harlem 113 Slow Down / More and More [1960]
Harlem 116 Just a Moment / Sapphire [1961]
Jox 116 Just a Moment / Sapphire [1961]
with the Markays
Harlem 107 Why, Why, Why / If You Ever Need Me [1960]
Harlem 114 Baby Tell Me [1960]
Swingin'625 Why, Why, Why / If You Ever Need Me [1960]
with the Pharaohs
Warrior 507 Crazy Daisy / If You Ever Need Me [1959]

Saints and Sinners
Dallas, TX
Capri 257 Cayuco / Cien Millas [1973]

Freddy Sal
Austin, TX
Freddy Salas (also as Freddy Salas and the Dominos)
Laura 101 Please Don't Leave
Jox 033 Watermelon Man / Pt. 2
Jox 034 Someday / All These Things
as Fred Salas
Sound Tex xxx This Guy's in Love with You / San Antonio I Love You
Valmon 001 Que Debo Acer / Cartas Marcadas

Joel Salas and the Corvairs
Austin, TX
El Zarape 279 Tough Talk / Al Ver Que Te Vas
with Shorty and the Corvettes
El Zarape 151 El Desgastado / Querida Polka
Tomi 103 Long Tall Shorty / Nuevo Laredo

Salas Brothers with the Jaguars
Los Angeles, CA
Rudy Salas, Steve Salas
Faro 614 Darling (Please Bring Your Love) / Leaving You [1964]
Faro 619 One Like Mine / Donde Esta Santa Claus? [1965]
Faro 625 Return of Farmer John / Love Is Strange [1965]
see: Tierra, El Chicano, Six Pak

Oscar Saldana and His Orchestra
Los Angeles
R&B 1302   Mambo Hop / Bop Hop [1954]

Saliens
Albuquerque, NM
Delta 2209   Top Cat / Sticky

Sam the Sham and the Pharaohs
Dallas, TX / Memphis, TN
Sam Samudio
Tupelo 2982   Betty and Dupree / Manchild [1963]
Dingo 001   Haunted House / How Does A Cheating Woman Feel [1964]
MGM K13322   Wooly Bully / Memphis Beat [1965]
MGM K13397   Ring Dang Do / Don't Try It [1965]
MGM K13452   Red Hot / A Long Long Way [1966]
MGM K13506   Lil' Red Riding Hood / Love Me Like Before [1966]
MGM K13581   The Hair on My Chinny Chin Chin / The Out Crowd [1966]
MGM K13649   How Do You Catch a Girl / The Love You Left Behind [1967]
XL 906   Wooly Bully / Memphis Beat [1964]
see: **Big Man and the Pharaohs**

Sammy and the Sunlites Orchestra
Odessa, TX
Elena 110   Sunlite Soul / Nada Contigo

Mike Sanchez and the Rock-A-Tones
Linn, TX
Mayté 24   The Things You Are / Wicked

Sancho Bros.
El Paso, TX
Sancho 0001   Funky Cha, Cha / Yoy Soy Nada
Sancho 0002   Red Wine / Live and Love
Sancho Bros 1   Cachita / La Ley del Norte

Danny Sandoval
Southern California
Cashmere 1641   Hardly See My Way / Angel City Jam [1963]

Satin Kings
San Antonio, TX
Otis Santiñanas (lead vocals), Robert Reyes (guitar)
Satin 101   Matilda / Put Another Nickle in the Piano [1963]
Satin 106   Echale un Cinco Al Piano / Mil Veces

Satin Souls
San Antonio, TX
1963-Joe Flores (bass), Roger Sanchez (sax), Madison Mitchell (vocals), Emilio Moran (sax), Joe Martinez (guitar), Henry Garcia (drums)
1965-Madison Mitchell (vocals), Manuel Escobedo (bass), Ray Gonzales (drums), Joe Martinez (guitar), Joe Rodela (trumpet), Chris Hernandez (trumpet), Lowell Thompson (sax)
Satin 137   I'd Rather Go Blind / Gimmie Some Lovin' [1966]
ZAZ 183   Columpio / Se Acaba el Mundo

Danny Segovia and the Sessions
San Antonio, TX
Cobra 1114   Mojo / Grand Time and Gay Nights [1965]
Cobra 253   My Angel Diane / Hey Babe [1965]
as Danny Segovia and the Reno-Bops
Renco 3001   With This Ring / Tell Her [1965]
Renco 3003   For Your Love / So Many Girls [1965]

Sequence, The
San Antonio, TX
Robert Kuwamura (lead), Martin Mauricio (first tenor), Vic Love (second tenor), Reynaldo Sanchez (baritone)
Pegaso 552   Night Owl / My, My, My [1961]
see: Vic Love and the Lovells

Sevilles see: Jaguars

Shadows see: Carlos Brothers

Sheltons
Albuquerque, NM
Steve Lucero (lead vocals), George "Bud" Lucero (lead guitar), Bob Elks (rhythm guitar), Toby Romero (drums)
Bar-Bare 1265   I Who Have Nothing / Find It [1967]
Dot 17174   Find It / The Cat [1967]
Lance 104   Find It / Yesterday's Laughter [1967]
Lance 117   I Who Have Nothing / Knock on Wood [1967]
Souled Out 101   The Cat / That's All

Shorty and the Corvettes
Austin, TX
El Zarape 171   Muy Despacito / Gritenme Piedras de Campo [1965]
Valmon 1-032   Un Ratito / Amor de Todos
Valmon 1-032   Corazon / Mañana y Despues
Valmon 1-051   Tres Balas / Otra Vez
Valmon 1-056   Cielito Lindo / El Vagabundo
Valmon 1-073   Hot Cha / La Adelita
with Joel Salas
El Zarape 151   El Desgastado / Querida Polka
Tomi 103   Long Tall Shoty / Nuevo Laredo

Shorty and the Enchanting Souls
Los Angeles, CA
Faro 629   Tears of No Return / Chew, Chew, Chew [1967]

Jimmy Sierra y Su Orquesta
San Antonio, TX
vocals: Rudy G. Vasquez
Sierra 101   Just Because / Negra Cosentida

Silver Rockets
Ideal 2152   Tarzan

Sisters
Los Angeles, CA
Rosella, Ersi, Mary Arvizu
Del-Fi 4300   Gee Baby Gee / All Grown Up [1965]
Del-Fi 4302   Poo Pa Doo / Happy New Year Baby [1965]

Del-Fi 306   Sentimental Reasons / [1965]
see: El Chicano

605 South
Los Angeles, CA
Bob Hernandez
EastLA 1001   Nah, Nah Baby / E.L.A.

Six Pak
Los Angeles, CA
Rudy Salas, Steve Salas, George Salazar
Gordo 701   Tombstone Shadow / Vuela Vuela Palomita
Gordo 704   Weep No More / Bring 'Em Home
see: Tierra, Jaguars, Salas Bros

Skytones
Dallas, TX
Charlie Benavides, Charlie Rios
Gallito 103   Unchain My Heart / She's Gone
Jox 027   Pretend / You're So Fine
Jox 028   Lucille / You're So Fine

Slauson Brothers
Los Angeles, CA
George Ochoa, Johnny Ochoa
Gee Kay 1003   Rosalie / Power Glide (Impalas)
Kay Gee 102   Baby Come Back / Two O'Clock Blues

The Sneakers
Albuquerque, NM
Sidro Garcia
Delta 1868   You Belong to Me / Mary Lou

Sol
San Antonio, TX
Joe Gallardo
GCP 1   Marantha [1975]
LP: Sol [GCP 120] 1975

Sole Inspiration
San Antonio, TX
Juan Gonzales
Soulsville U.S.A. 1003   Life / Hold On

Sonics
Austin, TX
Curtis Dean, Hernando Montoya
Valmon 188   Find Myself Another Girl / Arriendo Semos

Soulsations
Phoenix, AZ
Sandy Flores (drums), Tony Flores
Out Of Sight 671   Soul Skate / A Woman 73

Soulsetters with Freddi and Henchi
Phoenix, AZ
Onacrest group: Tony Neibles (vocals), Bobby "Soul" Frajo (sax), Jimmy Frajo (trumpet), Ruben Fierro (sax), Frankie Felix (Bass), Paul Hendrix (guitar), Sookie Charles (keyboards), Sandy Flores (drums)
with Freddi & Henchi: Fred Gowdy (vocals), Marvin "Henchi" Graves (vocals), Larry Wilkins (guitar), Jesse Escoto (bass), Epifanio Guerrero (drums), Chuy Castro, Arnold Andrews
as the Soulsetters
Onacrest 503   Out O' Sight / Cecil the Unwanted French Fry [1965]
as Freddi & Henchi and the Soulsetters
Bell 951   Um Um Um Um Um Um / Come Down
DJM 1002   Cartoon People / Try to Get to Know Me [1975]
MoSoul 102   Biscuits and Buttermilk / I'm Just a Nobody [1967]
Pathway 107   Things Are Changing / Clancy, He's a Real Good Cop [1968]
Reprise 1175   Funky to the Bone / I Want to Dance Dance Dance [1973]
Reprise 1207   Moonlightin' / Mr. Funky [1974]
The Record Co. 102   Funky to the Bone / I Want to Dance Dance Dance [1972]
Tower 479   Popcorn Baby / Folsom Prison
LP: Dance [The Record Company 1001] 1972

Sounds
San Antonio, TX
Manuel Ortiz (vocals), George Ortiz (vocals), Mario Moran (guitar), Ruben Ramirez (drums), Frank Valdez (piano)
Sunglow 126   You Could Never Be Mine / Little Joe [1967]
Sunglow 129   To Each His Own / Brown Eyed Soul Man [1967]

Spider and the Playboys
San Antonio, TX
Spider (vocals), Robert Reyes (bass), Henry Garcia (drums)
AAA 101   Come Back to Me / Yo Te Perdono (Ramon Ruiz) [1965]
AAA 104   My Heart Remembers / Tell Me Darling [1965]

Spider Ray and the Velveteens
Pomona, CA
Ray Quiñones Velveteens: Johnny Valenzuela Jr (piano, sax, trumpet), Danny Espinosa (sax), Poly Rodriguez (guitar), Joe Valenzuela (bass), Danny Valenzuela (drums),
Boss 102   Maria / While We Dance [1962]
see: Terri and Johnnie, Terri & the Velveteens, Rene and Ray

Staffs
San Antonio, TX
David Ceballos (guitar), Ruben Ceballos (keybord), Jesse Salinas (bass), Raul Altamirano (vocals), Emilio Reyna (drums)
Pa-Go-Go 118   Another Love / Just Can't Go to Sleep

Stand Free
El Paso, TX

Mike Martinez, Joe Martinez
Freedom 2105   I Really Care/ Shepa

Stardusters
Houston, TX
Jesse Casas (vocals), Jesse Villanueva (drums), Oscar Villanueva (guitar), Ray Villanueva (sax), Alfred Luna (keyboards), Frank Ardela (bass), Joe Moreno (alto), Joe Gonzales (trumpet)

Pic-1 109   It Must Be the Girl / Big Paper Heart [1964]
Tear Drop 3113   We're Just Lonely / El Papolote
see: Jesse Casas and the Crystals, Little Jesse and the Rockin' Vees

Starlets
San Antonio, TX
Willie Martinez
Middle C 100 Guitar Twist

Starlights
Houston, TX
Bobby Russell, Carlos Ureste, Frank Partida, Pete Falcon, Mario Ureste, Marcelino Rodriguez, Tony Tostado, Alberto Calderon, Joe Gutierrez
Tear Drop 3099   Boot Leg / My Special Angel [1965]
LP: Triste Payaso- Presentando a Bobby Russell [Tear Drop 2105]

Sting Reys
Denver, CO
CrazyTown101   When You Wish Upon A Star / You're Looking Good [64]
CrazyTown102   Let Them Talk / Alli Alli Auksun Free [1964]

Story Tellers
San Gabriel, CA
Alvin Sanchez, Ruben Ochoa, Nick Delgado, Ray Baez
Zenith 101   You Played Me a Fool / Hey Baby [1959]
Stack 500   You Played Me a Fool / Hey Baby [1959]

Sueños
Sacramento, CA
Richard "Flea" Martinez (drums), Jose "Pepe" Ochoa (vocals, percussion), Jaime Zuniga (vocals, percussion), Bernave Torres (sax, flute), Rudy Alcantar (trumpet), Frank Lizarraga (bass, vocals), Rudy Marrones (percussion, vocals), Polo Martinez (guitar, bass), Roy Santos (guitar), Andre Macias (keyboards)
Luna 318   Baby, I Love You / Y Que [1982]
Luna 359   Oh, Little Girl / People Get with It [1983]

Sunglows
San Antonio, TX
1965 line-up: Manny Guerra (drums), Greg Ramirez (bass), Henry Nuñez (guitar), Andrew Ortiz (organ), Jaime Martinez (trumpet), Tommy Luna (tenor sax), Richard Cordova (baritone sax), Martin Linan (alto sax)
vocalist: Sunny Ozuna, Joe Bravo, Bobby Mack, Freddy Salas, Maria Elena
Harlem 109   So Long Darling / Bobby Sox and Stockings [1959]
Harlem 110   From Now On / When I Think of You [1959]
Kool 1006   Just A Moment / Up Town [1959]
Lynn 511   Just A Moment / Up Town [1960]
Okeh 7143   Golly Gee / Touring [1962]
Sunglow 101   Pa Todo el Año / Llevas Mi Nombre [1962]
Sunglow 102   Sylvia / Caminos Chuecos [1962]
Sunglow 103   Dream / The Lasso [1962]
Sunglow 104   Golly Gee / Touring [1962]
Sunglow 105   Once in a While / Ho Ho, Ha Ha [1962]
Sunglow 106   El Reloj / Laguna de Pesares [1962]
Sunglow 106   Won't You Tell Me / Lasso Twist [1962]
Sunglow 107   Peanuts / Fallaste Corazon [1963]
Sunglow 107   Love Me (All My Love Belongs to You) / Happy Hippo [63]
Sunglow 107   Popcorn / All Night Worker [1963]
Sunglow 109   Close Your Eyes / Ooh Poo Pah Doo [1963]
Sunglow 110   Talk to Me / Pony Time [1963]
Sunglow 111   It Won't Be Me / Rags to Riches [1963]
Sunglow 112   The Dog / You Can Make It If You Try [1963]
Sunglow 115   Til the End Of Time / La Bamba [1963]
Sunglow 116   Guess Who / Just As I Thought [1963]
Sunglow 117   Honey Child / Love Me [1964]
Sunglow 118   Popcorn / The Circus [1964]
Sunglow 119   Baby I Apologize / Cut Across, Shorty [1964]
Sunglow 120   Latin Trumpet / Oh, Heart [1965]
Sunglow 122   Fly Me to the Moon / La Macarena [1965]
Sunglow 123   You're the One / If You Don't Love Me [1965]
Sunglow 125   Again / Roly Poly [1966]
Sunglow 3014   Talk to Me / Every Week, Every Month, Every Year [1963]
as Maria Elena and the Sunglows

Sunglow 124   Just a Game / Sick and Tired [1965]
as Joe Bravo and the Sunglows
Sunglow 127   It's Okay / Ninety-Nine Plus One [1966]
Sunglow 130   Does He Remind You of Me / Think It Over [1966]
Sunglow 159   Te Regaña Tu Señora / Si No Te Vas
Sunglow 172   Please Call Me Baby / Tres Flores [1967]
as Ricky Vee and the Sunglows
Sunglow 1002   How to Make a Little Girl Cry / Linda Lou [1964]
LP: The Original Peanuts [Siesta 101] 1965
    Sunny Ozuna and the Sunglows [Sunglow 101] 1960
    Los Fabulous Sunglows [Sunglow 102] 1965
    The Original Peanuts [Sunglow 103] 1965
    Sus Ultimos Exitos [Sunglow 104] 1965
    Los Fabulosos Sunglows [Sunglow 110] 1966
    Los Fabulosos Sunglows [Sunglow 112]
    Los Fabulosos Sunglows [Sunglow 125]
see: Rudy Guerra, Freddy Sal, Maria Elena, Sunny and the Sunliners, Joe Bravo, Sounds

Sunliners Band
San Antonio, TX
Henry Parilla (keyboards), Rudy Palacios (guitar), Chente Montes (bass), Armando Alba (drums), George Morin (trumpet), Rudy Guerra (baritone), Jay Johnson (trombone).
Key-Loc' 1013   Soul Power / Maria Bonita [1968]
Key-Loc' 1015   Chinches Bravas / Mala Cabeza
see: Sunny and the Sunliners, Sunglows, Latin Breed, Little Henry Lee

Sunlites
Ennis, TX
Paul Rodriguez (sax), Ramon Fira (sax), Richard Fira (sax), Johnny Valdez (guitar), Samuel Gonzáles (bass), Aby Rodriguez (keyboards), Benny Fira (vocals), Eddie Martinez (vocals), Jesus "Crazy Chuy" Hernandez (drums)
Segogovia 111   When a Man Loves a Woman / Con Cualuiero [1968]

Sunny and the Sunliners
San Antonio, TX
1963 line-up: Sunny Ozuna (vocals), Jesse Villanueva (drums), Tony Tostado (bass), Oscar Villanueva (guitar), Ray Villanueva (sax), Gilbert Fernandez (sax), Alfred Luna (organ)
Live In Hollywood line-up: Sunny Ozuna (vocals), Henry Parilla (keyboards), Rudy Palacios (guitar), Armando Alba (drums), George Morin (trumpet), Rudy Guerra (baritone), Jay Johnson (trombone)
Key-Loc' 1001   Dia Tras Dia / Lagrimas del Alma [1966]
Key-Loc' 1002   Smile Now Cry Later / Hopeless Case [1966]
Key-Loc' 1004   Put Me in Jail / Baby, I Apologize [1966]
Key-Loc' 1005   The One Who's Hurting Is You / I'm a Practical Guy [66]
Key-Loc' 1007   Give Me Time / The Thing [1966]
Key-Loc' 1009   Dile a Dios / Bonita [1966]
Key-Loc' 1010   I Want to Come Home for Christmas / part II [1966]
Key-Loc' 1012   Runaway / Give Me Time [1966]
Key-Loc' 1018   Reach Out (I'll Be There) / I Can Remember
Key-Loc' 1025   Norma de la Guadalajara / Banana Juice [1968]
Key-Loc' 1026   Should I Take You Home / If I Could See You Now [1968]
Key-Loc' 1030   En Esta Calle Fue / Los Amores de la Guera [1968]
Key-Loc' 1031   Get Ready / I Want Somebody [1968]
Key-Loc' 1038   When My Baby Cries / Saving My Love for You [1969]
Key-Loc' 1041   El Milagro / Solo De Dios [1969]
Key-Loc' 1044   I'm No Stranger / When It Rains [1969]
Key-Loc' 1051   Love Is for Fools / Happiness Is You [1969]
Key-Loc' 1054   Cariñito / Tormento [1969]
Key-Loc' 1055   I Was Born a Free Man / Sunshine Girl [1969]
Key-Loc' 1056   Lover to a Friend / Love's Illusion [1969]
Key-Loc' 1057   Token of Love / Hey! Little Dance Girl [1969]
Key-Loc' 1059   Get Down / We Can Make It Together [1969]
Key-Loc' 1065   Los Enamorados / No Voy a la Luna
Key-Loc' 1077   Greater, Greater, Greater / I Love My Friend
Latin Soul 102   Sitting in the Park/ Come Back Baby [1970]
London 135   I'm No Stranger / When It Rains [1969]

RPR 102   My Dream / Hip Huggin' Mini [1969]
RPR 105   Should I Take You Home / If I Could See You Now [1969]
Tear Drop 2006   La Cuidades
Tear Drop 3014   Talk to Me / Pony Time [1963]
Tear Drop 3016   Cariño Nuevo / Sufriendo Y Piensando [1963]
Tear Drop 3022   Rags to Riches / Not Even Judgment Day [1963]
Tear Drop 3025   Cuando el Destino / Emocion Pasajera [1964]
Tear Drop 3027   No One Else Will Do / Out of Sight Out of Mind [1964]
Tear Drop 3035   It's Too Late / You Gave Me True Love [1964]
Tear Drop 3037   Tu Nueva Vida / Dime Como Le Aces [1964]
Tear Drop 3040   You Send Me / His Greatest Creation [1964]
Tear Drop 3045   Something's Got a Hold On Me / I'm Not a Fool Anymore [1964]
Tear Drop 3056   Hey Little Dancing Girl / Token of Love [1965]
Tear Drop 3067   Hitch Hike / That Night in San Antonio [1965]
Tear Drop 3071   Too Young / The Very Thought of You [1965]
Tear Drop 3072   Padre Del Padre / Aquanta Corazon [1965]
Tear Drop 3081   Trick Bag / Cheatin' Traces [1966]
Tear Drop 3094   Short, Short, Shorty / Fly Me to the Moon [1966]
Tear Drop 3111   Que Sera Mi China / Por Se Me Olvidas
Tear Drop 3123   No One Else Will Do / Cheatin' Traces [1966]
Tear Drop 3183   Talk That Trash / Wonderful Girl
LP: Smile Now Cry Later [KL 3001] 1966
   No Te Chifles [KL 3002] 1966
   Live in Hollywood [KL 3003] 1966
   Canta Sunny   [KL 3004] 1966
   Little Brown Eyed Soul [KL 3005]
   This Is My Band [KL 3006]
   The Versatile Sunny &…[KL 3007]
   Adelante [KL 3008]
   Sky High [KL 3009]
   The Missing Link [KL 3010]
   El Monito de Chocolate [KL 3012]
   Exitos Supremos [Latin Soul 4000]
   Talk to Me   [Tear Drop 2000] 1963
   Las Vegas Welcomes….[Tear Drop 2001]1966
   Cariño Nuevo [Tear Drop 2002]
   Ciudades [Tear Drop 2006]
   Tear Drop Presents….[Tear Drop 2008]
   The Missing Link [Tear Drop 2010]
   From the Past [Tear Drop 2018]
   Sunny Y Los Sunliners [Tear Drop 2040]
   Yesterday…. and Sunny [Tear Drop 2054]
see: the Sunliners Band, Sunglows, Latin Breed, Little Henry Lee

Sweet Rain
ARV 5041   Fire and Rain / And Suddenly

Teen Kings
Sanderson, TX
Royal xxx   To Be in Love / Hep Cat

Terri and Johnny
Pomona, CA
Terri Bonilla (vocals), Johnny Valenzuela (piano, sax, trumpet), Danny Espinosa (sax), Poly Rodriguez (guitar), Joe Valenzuela (bass), Danny Valenzuela (drums)
Donna 1365   I Miss You So / Your Tender Lips [1962]
see: **Velveteens, Rosie and Ron, Rene and Ray, Terri and the Velveteens**

Terri and the Velveteens
Pomona, CA
Terri Bonilla (vocals), Johnny Valenzuela (piano, sax, trumpet), Danny Espinosa (sax), Poly Rodriguez (guitar), Joe Valenzuela (bass), Danny Valenzuela (drums)
Kerwood 711   Bells of Love / You've Broken My Heart [1960]
Arc 6534   I'm Waiting / La Flor [1960]
see: **Velveteens, Rosie and Ron, Rene and Ray, Terri and Johnny**

Those Fabulous Jokers
Phoenix, AZ
Tony Neibles (vocals), Bobby "Soul" Frajo (sax), Jimmy Frajo (trumpet), Ruben Fierro (sax), Frankie Felix (bass), Paul Hendrix (guitar), Sookie Charles (keyboards), Sandy Flores (drums)
Madley 102   The No, No / Frankie's Jerk [1964]
see: **Soulsetters, Soulsations**

Three Dudes
San Antonio, TX
Satin 130   Sad Little Boy / I'm Beggin' You [1967]

Tierra
Los Angeles, CA
1973- Rudy Salas (guitar, vocals), Steve Salas (bass, vocals), David Torres (keyboards), Rudy Villa (sax), Kenny Roman (drums), Conrad Lozano (bass)
1980-Rudy Salas (guitar, vocals), Steve Salas (vocals, trombone, timbales), Joey Guerra (keyboards), Bobby Navarette (sax), Andre Baeza (Percussion), Steve Falomir (bass), Phil Madayag (drums)
ASI 005   Sonya / Body Heat [1983]
ASI 201   Tierra / Together [1980]
Boardwalk 5702   Together / Zoot Suit Boogie [1980]
Boardwalk 7-11-129 La, La Means I Love You / Summer Daze [1981]
Boardwalk 11-52-7   Hidden Tears / Baila Gente Baila [1982]
Boardwalk 70073   Memories / Time to Dance [1981]
Boardwalk   Are We in Love / It's Too Late [1982]
MCA41067   Gonna Find Her / Tierra [1979]
20th Cen-Fox 2023   Tierra / Together [1973]
20th Cen-Fox 2064   La Feria / We Belong Together [1973]
20th Cen-Fox 2083   Gema
Satellite12011   Hollywood / inst [1986]
Salsoul 3137   My Lady / My Lady [1981]
Susie Q 100   Mind Games / You're in Love [1986]
Tody 2126   Memories
LP: Tierra [20th Century 412] 1973
   City Nights [Boardwalk 36995] 1980
      Together Again [Boardwalk 33244] 1981
      Bad City Boys [Boardwalk 53255] 1982
see: Salas Brothers, Tocayo, One G Plus Three, El Chicano

Tiny Morrie w/ Al Hurricane and the Night Rockers
Albuquerque, NM
Amador Lorenzo Sanchez
Challenge 9210   Maria Christina / The Choo Choo
Challenge 9136   My Lonely Heart / Bumbity Bump
Dot 16847   Lonely Letters / Bernadine [1966]

Hurricane 2   Everybody Rock / After I Had Gone
Hurricane 1716   La Bamba / Twistin' Boy [1963]
Hurricane 6985   Look at the Rain / The Other Side of Love [1967]
Hurricane 6992   Wasted Days and Wasted Nights / I Want You [1967]
Hurricane 6994   Lonely Woman [1967]
Hurricane 7007   Another Lonely Letter [1967]
Hurricane 7094   Those Lonely, Lonely Nights / Mi Primer Amor
Hurricane xxx   Don't Take Advantage [1963]
LP: Lonely Letters [Hurricane 10003] 1967
   Canta Canciones Tristes Y Alegres [Hurricane 0007] 1968

Tito and the Silhouettes
San Antonio, TX
Tito (vocals) Chente Montes (bass), Vic Montes (guitar), Johnny Garcia (sax), Isidro (drums), Tommy Luna (sax), Rocky Gonzales (sax)
Rival 03   Baby Doll / Sight Seeing [1959]

Tocayo
Los Angeles, CA
Rudy Salas (guitar), Randy Thomas (organ), Manuel Mosqueda (drums), Max Garduno (percussion)
Gordo 201   Con Safos / same [1972]

Albert Torres and the Starfire Band
San Jose, CA
Starfire 089-1   Somebody Please ? Maria's (Richard Bermea)

Tortilla Pete
Imperial 5501   Corrido Rock / part 2 [1958]

Triangles
Ontario/Pomona, CA
Ruben Pando, Lucy Duran, Frankie Gonzalez
Fifo 107   My Oh My / Really I Do [1961]

Two Tons of Love (Dos Chicanos Mas)
Los Angeles, CA
Bobby Reyes, Linda Lopez
Gordo 706   Brown and Beautiful / It's a Bad Situation in a Beautiful Place [69]
Kapp 2095   Brown and Beautiful / It's a Bad Situation in a Beautiful Place [69

Unknown 4, Thee
Los Angeles, CA
R.P.C.   Sad Girl / Hold It

V.I.P.'s (El Chicano)
San Gabriel, CA
Clarence Playa, Bobby Espinosa,
Guitarsville 2123 Don't Turn Around / It [1969]
Valasquez Brothers
Galactic 1001   I Still Love You / It's You

Jim Valdez and the Blues Evolution
Cheyenne, Wyoming
Macshar 56737   Daddy's Home / I Want You So Bad

Ritchie Valens (Richard Valenzuela)
Pacoima, CA
Ritchie Valens (vocals, guitar), Irving Ashby (rhythm guitar), Carol Kaye (rhythm guitar), Buddy Clark (bass), Earl Palmer (drums)
Del-Fi 4106   Come On, Let's Go / Framed [1958]
Del-Fi 4110   Donna / La Bamba [1958]
Del-Fi 4114   That's My Little Susie / In a Turkish Town [1959]
Del-Fi 4117   Little Girl / We Belong Together [1959]
Del-Fi 4128   Stay Beside Me / Big Baby Blues [1960]
Del-Fi 4133   Cry, Cry, Cry / Paddiwack Song [1960]
as Arvee Allen
Del-Fi 4111   Fast Freight / Big Baby Blues [1958]

Valentines
San Antonio, TX
King Bee 103   This Is My Story / More Peanuts [1963]

Valiants see: Ray C. and His Valiants

Vandels featuring Martin Duran
Albuquerque, NM
Souled Out 130   All in My Mind / Soulin'
Lance 117   Try Me / Booga-Louie [1967]
Lynn's 1728   Try Me / Booga-Louie [1967]

Vaqueros
Los Angeles, CA
Sal Murillo
Vaquero 101   Vaquero Beat / Oh, So Tenderly
see: Blendells

Chelo Vasquez
San Antonio, TX
G.C. 1017   The Preacher / Contestacion a Que Tal Si Te Vas

Ray Vasquez and the Dreamers
Austin, TX
LP: Exitos de Ray Vasquez and the Dreamers [Capri 1002]

Raymond Vasquez Jr. Y Su Orquesta
Austin, TX
Valmon 1-023   Jam Session / El Reloj

Rickey Vee and the Stardusters
San Antonio, TX
Rickey Villanueva
Jet Stream 723   'Taint No Big Thing / Pretty Girls [1966]
Sunglow 1002   How to Make a Little Girl Cry / Linda Lou
see: Sunglows
LP: Stardusters "All Night Worker" LP

George Vela
San Antonio, TX
G.V.   Let's Rock and Roll

Pat & Lolly Vegas
Los Angeles, CA
Pat Vasquez, Lolly Vasquez

Apogee 101   Don't You Remember / Robot Walk [1964]
Mercury 72509   Let's Get It On / Walk On [1965]
Reprise 20199   Boom, Boom, Boom / Two Figures [1963]
LP: Pat & Lolly Vegas at the Haunted House

Velveteens
Pomona, CA
Johnny Valenzuela Jr (piano, sax, trumpet), Danny Espinosa (sax), Poly Rodriguez (guitar), Joe Valenzuela (bass), Danny Valenzuela (drums)
Emmy 1005   Dog Patch Creeper / Johnny's Jump [1959]
See: Mary Lou Zuetta, Terri & the Velveteens, Rene & Ray, Rosie & Ron

Village Callers
Los Angeles, CA
Angela Bell (vocals), Ernie Hernandez (guitar), Johnny Gonzales (keyboards), Joe Espinosa (bass), Manuel Fernandez (drums), Adolfo "Fuzzy" Martinez (sax), Charles Masten (congas)
Bell 624   Evil Ways / When You're Gone [1968]
Rampart 659   Evil Ways / When You're Gone [1968]
Rampart 660   Hector / I'm Leaving [1969]
Rampart 663   Hector part II / Mississippi Delta [1969]
LP: Village Callers "Live" Rampart 3304

Rey Villar and the Royal Flush
Anderson, IN
Ebolic WHA 0140 Heaven Is My Whitness / Feeling

Volumes
San Antonio, TX
Garu107   I'm Gonna Miss You / I've Never Been So in Love

Volunteers
San Antonio, TX
AAA 1003   Baby, Baby, Baby Love / Seeing You Again

Leroy Williams with Felipe and His Sensationals
Odessa, TX
Elena 103   Linda Lou / I Want to Thank You

Willie and the Dots
San Antonio, TX

Guillermo Flores
Jox 005   So Much on My Mind / Let's Crackle

Gene Willis and the Aggregation
El Paso, TX
Coronado 139   We Got It / Shing-A-Ling's the Thing

Yaqui
Los Angeles, CA
Rudy Regalado, Ronnie Reyes, Larry Cronin, George Ochoa, Art Sanchez, Eddie Serrano, Ray Rodriguez
LP: Yaqui [Playboy 127] 1973
see: Thee Impalas, Slauson Brothers

Yolanda and the Charmanes
Los Angeles, CA
Yolanda Lea
Smash1777   There Ought to Be a Law / Hootchy Cootchy Girl [62]

Yolanda and the Naturals
Corona,CA
Yolanda Campos
Kimley 923   My Memories of You / Jambone [1962]

Zapata
San Antonio, TX
Jesse Vallado
Metro-Dome 1003   Make It All Go / A Certain Kind [1969]
Metro-Dome 1004   Do Your Thing / part II [1969]

Zapata
Los Angeles, CA
Original Sound 107   Viva La Raza / Una Ves Mas

Refino Zapata y Los Tejaniotos
Jesse Zapata (vocals)
Kool 1019   Sound Barrier / Give Me a Chance
Tejanito 1002   Baby, I Go Crazy / Pajarito

Zeke and His Ambassadors
Tucson, AZ
Zeke "Sonny" Herrera
Santa Cruz 10,001   Por Tu Culpa / Rincon Nortenio [1965]
Santa Cruz 10,005   La Mira / Se Me Acabra La Vida [1966]
Santa Cruz 10,007   I Miss You So / I'll Never Let You Go [1966]

Mary Lou Zuetta and the Velveteens
Pomona, CA
Mary Unzuetta (vocals), Freddy Unzuetta (piano), Johnny Valenzuela Jr (sax, trumpet), Danny Espinosa (sax), Poly Rodriguez (guitar), Joe Rodriguez (bass), Danny Valenzuela (drums)
Emmy 1007   Oh Baby / Come Back [1960]
see: the Velveteens, Terri & the Velveteens, Rene & Ray, Rosie & Ron

www.ingramcontent.com/pod-product-compliance
Lightning Source LLC
Chambersburg PA
CBHW080838230426
43665CB00021B/2874